The Open University

MU123

Discovering mathematics

BOOK D

Units 11–14

This publication forms part of an Open University module. Details of this and other Open University modules can be obtained from the Student Registration and Enquiry Service, The Open University, PO Box 197, Milton Keynes MK7 6BJ, United Kingdom (tel. +44 (0)845 300 60 90; email general-enquiries@open.ac.uk).

Alternatively, you may visit the Open University website at www.open.ac.uk where you can learn more about the wide range of modules and packs offered at all levels by The Open University.

To purchase a selection of Open University materials visit www.ouw.co.uk, or contact Open University Worldwide, Walton Hall, Milton Keynes MK7 6AA, United Kingdom for a brochure (tel. +44 (0)1908 858779; fax +44 (0)1908 858787; email ouw-customer-services@open.ac.uk).

The Open University, Walton Hall, Milton Keynes MK7 6AA.

First published 2010. Second edition 2014.

Edited, designed and typeset by The Open University, using the Open University TEX System.

Printed in the United Kingdom by Henry Ling Limited, at the Dorset Press, Dorchester DT1 1HD

ISBN 978 1 7800 7866 3

2.1

Contents

Contents

UNIT 11

Statistical pictures

Introduction

In Unit 4, you looked at a variety of statistical summary values that can be used to describe a dataset. Some of these measure location – that is, where the data are centred – these include the mean and median. Others – the range, interquartile range and standard deviation – give an overview of how widely the data are spread.

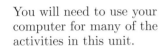

You will need to use your computer for many of the activities in this unit.

In this unit you will look at a second important set of tools for providing an overview of the data in a dataset. This time, rather than carrying out calculations, you will be focusing on producing and analysing pictures of the data, in the form of statistical graphs and charts, to help to reveal significant features.

Unit 4 also provided you with a number of small datasets. You will be using some of these again, but this time to see how they may be interpreted pictorially.

Another of the big statistical ideas in Unit 4 was the statistical investigation cycle, as shown in Figure 1. You saw that it was useful, in any investigation, to break your thinking down into clear steps, defined by the acronym PCAI (*pose* a question, *collect* the data, *analyse* the data, *interpret* the results).

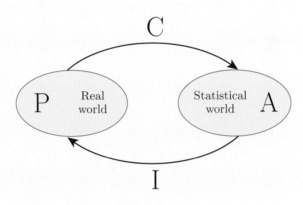

Figure 1   The PCAI statistical investigation cycle described in Unit 4

You will be making use of the PCAI cycle in this unit also, particularly in the final section, where you are asked to apply some of the skills and ways of working of the statistician to investigate a controversial question: Does extra-sensory perception (ESP) exist?

1 Dotplots and boxplots

In Unit 4 you were asked to investigate the responses of 30 Open University students who were asked to attach a number to how they interpreted the words 'possible' and 'probable', on a scale from 0 to 100 where 0 means impossible and 100 means certain. Any conclusions that you were able to draw were based on summaries of location and spread – in other words, on a purely numerical analysis of the data.

Figure 2   A picture can be worth a thousand words

However, it is sometimes said that a picture is worth a thousand words. In this section you will revisit the 'Possible' and 'Probable' data, but now in pictures. You will return to using the computer resource Dataplotter, which can display either one or two datasets in the form of any of four different types of statistical plot: *dotplots*, *boxplots*, *histograms* or *scatterplots*. (You used Dataplotter in Unit 4 to create dotplots and in Unit 6 to draw scatterplots.)

This first section describes two of these graphical tools: dotplots and boxplots. You will see how these plots are constructed and how they can be used to interpret data. Histograms are introduced in Section 2.

1.1   Dotplots

Dotplots were introduced in Unit 4 as a pictorial way of displaying values in datasets. They are based on the simple principle that each value in a dataset can be represented by a dot positioned above a horizontal axis so that you can see, at a glance, the location and spread of the values.

Activity 1   *Using Dataplotter to draw a dotplot*

Dataplotter

More details on how to use Dataplotter are given in Subsection 2.4 of the MU123 Guide.

Open Dataplotter. There may still be data from previous activities in one or both of the two data columns on the left. If so, click the 'New' button under each column. Then click the 'Dotplot' tab, if it is not already selected.

(a) Position the cursor in cell 1 of the left-hand data column, click, and enter the numbers 1, 2, 5, 8, 15, pressing Enter after each entry (including the last). Watch what happens in the graphing area as each number is entered. Notice that the horizontal axis automatically rescales to accommodate each new number.

(b) Spend a few moments making sure that you understand what the ten summary values on the right of the software display mean. For example, the final summary value, labelled 'n', tells you how many data values there are in the dataset.

(c) Based on your work in Unit 4, explain in your own words the meaning of the summary values median and standard deviation.

The dataset that you have created in this activity will not be needed again, so you may wish to delete it. To do this, click the 'Delete dataset' button at the bottom of the column.

In the next activity, you are asked to compare the dotplots for the 'Possible' and 'Probable' datasets. The dotplots provide a useful overview of the data, allowing you to see where each value is positioned in relation to the others. Values that are repeated are stacked up in vertical lines, which makes it easy to see at a glance how many students gave a particular value.

Activity 2   *Comparing dotplots*

Dataplotter

(a) In Dataplotter, click on the drop-down menu for the left-hand column and select the dataset '# Possible'. Click on the 'Dotplot' tab if it is not already selected.

How many students gave the value 30?

(b) Now click on the drop-down menu for the right-hand column and select the dataset '# Probable'. You should now see the two dotplots corresponding to the '# Possible' and '# Probable' datasets, one below the other. Based on these plots, identify two basic differences between these datasets.

1.2 Boxplots

As you have seen, a dotplot is a simple but powerful form of graphical representation, where every value in a dataset is represented by a dot above a horizontal axis. However, it is not always sensible to include every single value in a picture representing a dataset, particularly if the dataset is large. Instead, a graphical representation showing a selection of some key values from the dataset can be used.

The boxplot was invented by the American statistician John Tukey (1915–2000). Tukey was also partly responsible for the word 'software', referring to computer programs as opposed to the machines that they run on (the hardware).

A **boxplot** is a popular way of depicting data, based on showing the locations of the following five key summary values of a dataset:

> minimum value (Min),
> lower quartile (Q1),
> median (also known as Q2),
> upper quartile (Q3),
> maximum value (Max).

You should already be familiar with these five summary values from Unit 4, but the next paragraph gives a brief reminder of what they are and how to find them.

For a given dataset, first sort the data into ascending order. Look at the beginning and end of the sorted dataset for the minimum and maximum data values. To find the median, look at the middle of the sorted dataset. If there is an odd number of data values, the median is the middle data value. If there is an even number of data values, the median is the mean of the two middle data values. To find the lower and upper quartiles, look at the data values that are, respectively, one-quarter and three-quarters of the way through the data. The lower quartile is the median of the lower half of the dataset, and the upper quartile is the median of the upper half of the dataset (with the middle data value in the dataset thrown out if the number of data values in the dataset is odd).

For example, here is the 'Possible' dataset, in ascending order, with the positions of these five summary values marked.

```
 1  1  1  1  5  10  10  20  20  30  30  30  30  30  30  35  40  50  50  50  50  50  50  50  50  60  70  80  85  90  98
 ↑                   ↑                        ↑                             ↑                          ↑
Min                 Q1                     Median                          Q3                         Max
```

The summary values for this dataset are

$$\text{Min} = 1, \quad \text{Q1} = 20, \quad \text{Median} = 32.5, \quad \text{Q3} = 50, \quad \text{Max} = 98.$$

The median is $(30 + 35)/2 = 32.5$.

For large datasets, you may prefer to use Dataplotter to calculate the summary values.

In this module, you can either draw boxplots by hand or you can use Dataplotter.

Drawing boxplots by hand

The steps below explain how to draw a boxplot by hand. It is best to use squared paper or graph paper.

Boxplots can be drawn either horizontally or vertically, but in this module we will draw them horizontally.

Step 1   Draw a horizontal axis and mark a scale that covers values from the minimum data value to the maximum data value. Add an axis label, including units if appropriate. Also add a suitable title, and the source of the data.

Figure 3 shows this step for the 'Possible' dataset. Since the data values are just numbers, no units are given in this case.

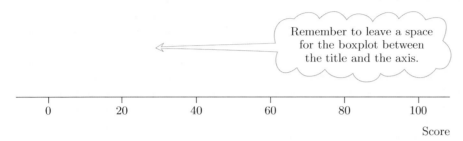

Figure 3 The labelled axis, title and source for the 'Possible' dataset

Step 2 Mark the locations of the minimum, lower quartile, median, upper quartile and maximum, as five vertical lines above the axis. Usually shorter vertical lines are used for the minimum and maximum than for the other three values.

Figure 4 shows this step for the 'Possible' dataset.

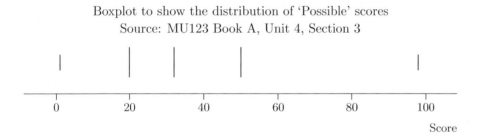

Figure 4 The locations of the five key summary values for the 'Possible' dataset

Step 3 Draw a box around the lower and upper quartiles (to include the median) and draw two lines (called **whiskers**) between the box and the minimum and maximum values. (These features are included simply to make the picture clearer.) Finally, write the five key summary values on the boxplot, so that it is clear at a glance what these values are.

Figure 5 shows this step for the 'Possible' dataset.

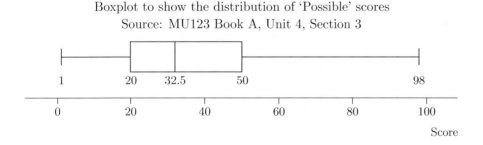

Figure 5 The completed boxplot for the 'Possible' dataset

Figure 6   An entrant from the World Beard and Moustache Championships 2007 held in Brighton, England

The range and interquartile range of a dataset were introduced in Unit 4.

Notice the characteristic appearance of a boxplot, which is a central box with horizontal lines to either side that look rather like a pair of waxed whiskers, such as those in Figure 6. In fact, an alternative name for a boxplot is a *box-and-whiskers diagram*. The box is drawn between the quartiles; the whiskers reach out to the extremes of the dataset.

The method for drawing a boxplot is summarised below.

> ### How to draw a boxplot
>
> **Step 1**   Draw the axis, mark the scale and add an axis label, including units if appropriate. Add a title and the source of the data.
>
> **Step 2**   Mark the five key summary values Min, Q1, Median, Q3, and Max with vertical lines.
>
> **Step 3**   Add the box and whiskers and label the vertical lines with the five key summary values.

It is worth spending a few moments thinking about the information that can be gleaned from a boxplot. For example, as shown in Figure 7, the length of the entire boxplot represents the *range* of the dataset – the difference between the minimum and maximum values. The length of the box component represents the *interquartile range* (IQR) – the difference between the lower and upper quartiles.

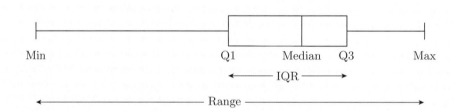

Figure 7   The range and interquartile range as seen on a boxplot

The main features to take note of in a boxplot are the five vertical lines that mark the locations of the five key summary values (Min, Q1, Median, Q3 and Max). Everything else (the box and the two horizontal whiskers) is included to identify which summary value is which.

A special feature of boxplots is that they enable you, quickly and easily, to make remarks about, say, 'the upper quarter' of the data, or 'the middle 50%' of the data, and so on. So a boxplot provides a simple and useful summary of some of the key features of a dataset.

Drawing boxplots on Dataplotter

The boxplots produced by Dataplotter are the same as the hand-drawn ones described above, except that the five key summary values are listed in the right-hand column rather than being displayed on the boxplot itself.

Activity 3 illustrates how two datasets can be compared by using Dataplotter to draw their boxplots one below the other, using the same axis.

Dataplotter

Activity 3 *Using Dataplotter to draw boxplots*

In Dataplotter, select the '# Possible' and '# Probable' datasets, if they are not already loaded. Then select the 'Boxplot' tab to display the boxplots, one above the other.

(a) As you did with the dotplot in Activity 1, spend a few moments relating the boxplots to the summary values given. For example, confirm that the five key positions on the 'Possible' boxplot match up with the five key summary values Min, Q1, Median, Q3 and Max.

(b) Based on the second boxplot on your screen, write down the following values for the '# Probable' dataset:

(i) the median

(ii) the upper quartile

(iii) the lower quartile.

(c) Which of the following statements are correct?

(i) All the 'Probable' data are greater than the upper quartile of the 'Possible' data.

(ii) The interquartile range of the 'Probable' data is greater than that of the 'Possible' data.

(iii) The bottom half of the 'Possible' data is more widely spread than the bottom half of the 'Probable' data.

(d) Comment on the differences between the two boxplots, with particular reference to the five key summary values. How can these differences be interpreted?

As with other statistical charts, if you wish to use a Dataplotter boxplot to present results from a statistical investigation or as part of an assignment question, then remember to include a title and the source of the data. Figure 8 shows a title and source written above a boxplot, but you can also write these below the chart, or anywhere that seems appropriate. For a boxplot, you should also include the list of summary values, as shown in Figure 8.

There are instructions for producing a screenshot of Dataplotter or Graphplotter in Subsection 2.4 of the MU123 Guide.

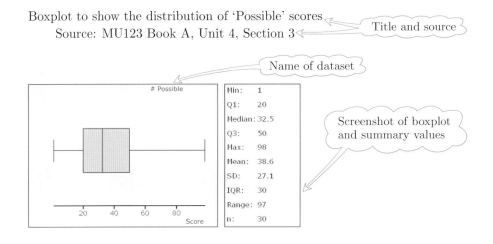

Figure 8 Presenting a Dataplotter chart

Shapes of boxplots

In the activity below, you are asked to type some simple numbers into one of the data columns in Dataplotter, to find out more about what the shape of a boxplot can reveal about the data that it represents.

 Dataplotter

---

Activity 4 *Investigating the shapes of boxplots*

Use Dataplotter, with the 'Boxplot' tab selected.

(a) Click each of the two buttons marked 'New' to open a new, blank dataset in each of the two columns. Then enter the following numbers into the left-hand column: 1, 2, 3, 4, 5, 6, 7.

As the numbers in this dataset are symmetrically spaced, you may not be surprised that the corresponding boxplot is also symmetrical.

Again, try to match up the key features of the boxplot with the five corresponding summary values listed on the right of the screen.

(b) Now change the 7 to 20 (by selecting the seventh cell and overtyping with 20 followed by Enter), and observe the effect on the shape of the boxplot. Check the new scale carefully. Have any of the five key summary values (Min, Q1, Median, Q3, Max) changed? Can you explain why some values have not changed?

(c) Has the mean changed? If so, can you explain why?

An important feature of the five key summary values depicted in a boxplot is that, provided that the dataset contains six or more values, making either of the two extreme values (the minimum or maximum) more extreme will have no effect on the other four summary values.

Activity 5 *Matching datasets and boxplots*

(a) Look at these two datasets (both ordered from smallest to largest).

Dataset 1	0	6	7	8	9	10	11	12	13	19
Dataset 2	0	1	2	3	9	10	16	17	18	19

Try to match each dataset to its corresponding boxplot below.

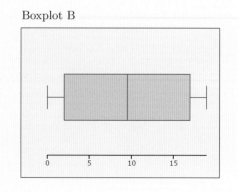

Boxplot A   Boxplot B

(b) Now look at these two datasets and try to match each one to its corresponding boxplot below.

| **Dataset 3** | 0 | 1 | 2 | 3 | 9 | 10 | 11 | 12 | 13 | 19 |
| **Dataset 4** | 0 | 6 | 7 | 8 | 9 | 10 | 16 | 17 | 18 | 19 |

Boxplot C

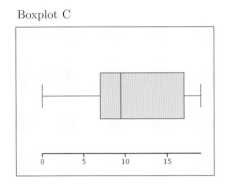

Boxplot D

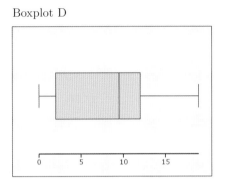

There are several general features of the shape of a boxplot that are worth thinking through. Each of the four sections of a boxplot – the two parts of the box and the two whiskers – represents approximately the *same number* of data values – a quarter of the total number. For example, the left-hand whisker represents all the data values lying between the minimum value and the lower quartile, and the left-hand part of the box represents all the data values lying between the lower quartile and the median. So if one of these four sections of a boxplot is comparatively long, then the data in the corresponding quarter of the dataset are comparatively spread out – in other words, the data values are less densely packed together.

For example, Boxplot C in Activity 5 has a long left whisker and a short right whisker. This reflects the fact that the data in the bottom quarter of Dataset 4 are more spread out than those in the top quarter. Similarly, the left part of the box in Boxplot D is longer than the right part, which reflects the fact that the data in the second quarter of Dataset 3 are more spread out than those in the third quarter.

So a boxplot provides a useful picture of how the data are spread.

In the boxplot in Figure 9(a), the left whisker is longer than the right whisker, and the section of the box to the left of the median is longer than the section of the box to the right of the median. This indicates that the smaller values in the dataset are more spread out than the larger values. In cases like this, the dataset and the boxplot are said to be **left-skewed**. The boxplot in Figure 9(b) indicates that the larger values in the dataset are more spread out than the smaller values. A dataset like this, and its boxplot, are said to be **right-skewed**.

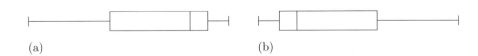

(a)   (b)

Figure 9   (a) A left-skewed boxplot (b) A right-skewed boxplot

If all four regions of a boxplot are approximately equal in length, then the data tend to be fairly uniformly spread between the minimum and maximum values. However, an interesting phenomenon about data drawn

Measurements like those listed in the paragraph here often concentrate in the middle in a characteristic way, which is described by a famous mathematical function called the *normal distribution* or *Gaussian distribution*. The second name refers to the great mathematician Karl Friedrich Gauss, who was mentioned in Units 3, 7 and 9.

 Dataplotter

from the natural world (for example, people's heights, weights of robin eggs, midday temperatures at a particular location in June, lengths of human gestations, and so on) is that they tend not to be uniformly spread. Instead there is, typically, a concentration of values in the middle, with values spread more sparsely at the extremes. As you'll see from the next activity, this means that such data tend to produce boxplots with whiskers that are longer than either of the two parts of the box.

Activity 6   *Using a boxplot to investigate the spread of data*

Use Dataplotter, with the 'Boxplot' tab selected.

Select the dataset '# Weight baby' (not the scatterplot version '# SP Weight baby' that you used in Unit 6) from the left-hand drop-down list. This dataset contains the weights, in kg, of 32 babies, which were listed in a table in Unit 4.

If there are any data in the right-hand column, then remove them to avoid distractions. You can do this by clicking 'New' to open a new, blank dataset. Alternatively, if you created the data in the right-hand column but no longer want them, then you can click 'Clear' to remove them from the dataset.

(a) Look at the boxplot that represents the baby weights. Which are longer, the whiskers or the two parts of the box?

(b) What does this tell you about how the data are spread?

The data in some other types of datasets also tend to be spread in a similar way to the data from nature discussed above – bunched in the middle and more sparse elsewhere. For example, when a quantity is measured there is a small difference between the true value of the quantity and the measurement – this is known as a *measurement error*, and it can be either positive or negative, depending on whether the measurement is larger or smaller than the true value. It is important to consider measurement errors in subjects like physics. Measurement errors tend to bunch around zero, with very high and very low errors less common, so boxplots of measurement errors tend to have narrow boxes and long whiskers.

To summarise this subsection, the following box presents three key facts to remember when studying the shape of a boxplot.

Characteristics of boxplots

- A boxplot is composed of four sections (two whiskers at either end and two sections within the central box), each of which contains approximately the same number of data values.

- Where a particular section of a boxplot is narrow, this indicates a dense concentration of the data, whereas a wide section indicates where the data are more sparsely spread.

- A boxplot with a narrow box and long whiskers indicates that the data are concentrated in the middle and more widely spread at the extremes. This is typical of data drawn from nature.

1.3   Investigating poverty levels

According to Help the Aged's report *Spotlight on Older People in the UK*, which was published in January 2009, one in five older people lives 'in poverty'.

Clearly most people have a general sense of what it means to be in poverty, but when it comes to serious debate about the issue, such labels need to be tied down more quantitatively, to ensure that everyone is referring to the same phenomenon. There are several different definitions of poverty, used by different institutions. The World Bank defines poverty in *absolute* terms as living on less than $1.25 per day (at the time of writing). However, this is not a suitable definition for richer countries such as those in the European Union, where a *relative* figure is used.

Absolute and *relative* comparisons were explained in Unit 1.

Read the extract below, which includes a commonly-used definition of the term *poverty* in the UK and other European countries.

> The widely accepted definition of poverty is having an income which is less than 60% of the national average (excluding the wealthiest members of society). On this measure, the proportion of the UK population defined as in poverty is roughly one in five. And this roughly one in five figure has remained stubbornly high through both Conservative and Labour governments.
>
> Julian Knight, 'The changing face of poverty', BBC News, 26 July 2005

A more precise formulation of the definition of poverty referred to in the extract is that a person is in poverty if they live in a household with an income that is less than 60% of the national median household income. The amount of money that is 60% of the national median household income is referred to as the *poverty threshold*.

Sometimes adjustments are made to this definition of poverty to make it appropriate for households of different sizes, for example. But, to keep things simple, we will work with this basic definition, and we will look at households each containing just one person, who is an earner.

You may be wondering why the one-in-five figure mentioned in the extract does remain so 'stubbornly high', even as earnings change over time. In the next activity boxplots are used to illustrate the changes in earnings as different types of pay rises are applied, and you are asked to investigate the effect of these pay rises on the number of people in poverty.

Activity 7   *Investigating different types of pay rise*

 Dataplotter

Use Dataplotter, with the 'Boxplot' tab selected.

In the left-hand data column select the dataset '# Earnings 1', which consists of the hypothetical weekly earnings of 13 people, each of whom is the only person in his or her household. These are shown below.

Hypothetical weekly earnings of 13 people (£)

160, 190, 220, 240, 290, 350, 400, 480, 510, 530, 590, 600, 800.

The corresponding boxplot should look like this.

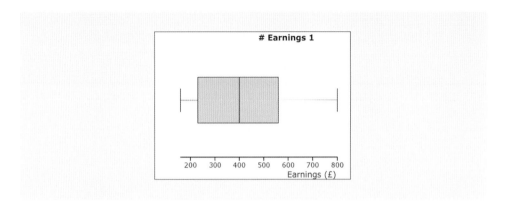

Now consider the poverty threshold in the microworld of just these 13 earners. Suppose that it is defined to be 60% of the median earnings, as discussed above.

(a) Calculate the amount of money that is the poverty threshold.

Hence calculate the number of people and the percentage of people in poverty.

(b) Now let's increase everyone's wages by 25%.

Revised weekly earnings of the 13 people (£)
200, 237.5, 275, 300, 362.5, 437.5, 500, 600, 637.5, 662.5, 737.5, 750, 1000.

In the right-hand data column, open the dataset '# Earnings 2', which contains the revised earnings of these 13 people, based on an across-the-board percentage increase of 25%.

The corresponding boxplot is shown below.

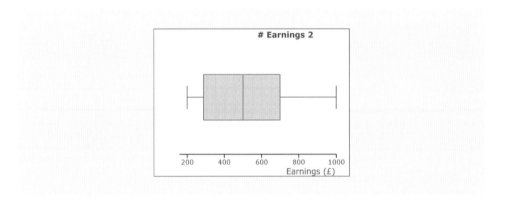

Based on these revised earnings, calculate the new poverty threshold.

How has this pay rise affected the number and percentage of people in poverty?

(c) Now, rather than increasing everyone's earnings by the same percentage, let's give everyone a fixed pay rise of £100.

Revised weekly earnings of the 13 people (£)
260, 290, 320, 340, 390, 450, 500, 580, 610, 630, 690, 700, 900.

Again in the right-hand data column, open the dataset '# Earnings 3', which contains the revised earnings of these 13 people, based on an across-the-board £100 increase.

The new boxplot is shown below.

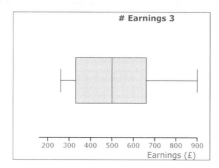

Earnings 3

Earnings (£)

Based on these revised earnings, calculate the new poverty threshold.

How has this pay rise affected the number and percentage of people in poverty?

To understand the reasons behind the results obtained in Activity 7, consider a group of earners (of any size), with each earner the only person in his or her household. Suppose that the median of the earners' weekly wages, in £, is m, and suppose, as in Activity 7, that the poverty threshold is based just on this group of earners. Then the poverty threshold, in £, is $0.6m$.

Now suppose that everyone is given a 25% pay rise. Then everyone's wage is 1.25 times what it was before, so the new median wage is also 1.25 times what it was before. That is, the new median wage, in £, is

$1.25m$

and hence the new poverty threshold, in £, is

$0.6 \times 1.25m,$

which is the same as

$1.25 \times 0.6m.$

This is 1.25 times the old poverty threshold. So the poverty threshold has risen by 25%. As everyone's wage has also risen by 25%, no one has moved over the poverty threshold.

Now suppose, instead, that everyone is given a pay rise of £100. Then the new median wage is also £100 more than it was before, so the new poverty threshold, in pounds, is

$0.6 \times (m + 100).$

Multiplying out the brackets gives

$0.6m + 60.$

This is the old poverty threshold, plus 60. So the poverty threshold has risen by £60. But everyone's wage has risen by £100, so anyone whose wage was £40 or less below the poverty threshold, before the wage rise, has now moved over the poverty threshold and is no longer in poverty.

Activity 7 raises some important questions about wage increases and their effect on income inequalities. A particular question of interest is: How can wage increases be organised so as to reduce the number of people in poverty?

A fixed percentage increase means that, in absolute terms, the high wage earners get a bigger rise than the lower earners, thereby stretching the boxplot wider. This means that absolute inequalities widen. Relative inequalities are maintained, and there is no change in the number of people whose earnings lie below the poverty threshold.

With a wage increase of a fixed amount, however, a different picture emerges. Here, the boxplot is not stretched but simply moved to the right by the amount of the rise (in the case of Activity 7, by £100). So in absolute terms, the amounts of the inequalities are maintained (in Activity 7 the highest earner earns £640 more than the lowest earner both before and after the rise). However, in relative terms, such an arrangement is much better for the lowest earners, as for them a £100 rise represents a larger percentage increase than is the case for the most well-off. This type of pay rise is one way to reduce the number of people below the poverty threshold.

In general, if poverty is measured in the way discussed in this subsection, then the way to achieve a reduction in the number of people below the poverty threshold is to increase the household incomes of the low-income households by a greater percentage than those of the middle-income households. This can be achieved in various ways, such as by awarding greater percentage wage increases to low earners than to middle earners, increasing the number of earners in low-income households, reducing the amount of tax that low earners pay or increasing the benefits paid to low-income households.

In this section, you have seen how to use dotplots and boxplots to illustrate datasets, and how to interpret these plots. Dotplots are useful for small datasets, as they give a quick impression of all the data values. Boxplots tend to be more useful for large datasets, as they summarise data by displaying key summary values, although the detail of the individual data values is lost.

2 Histograms and bar charts

2.1 Histograms

In the last section you saw how to use dotplots and boxplots to provide pictorial representations of datasets.

A third way to represent a dataset pictorially is to use a *histogram*. For example, consider the dataset below, which consists of the weights in kilograms of 32 women at the start of their pregnancies. It is part of the backache dataset that was given in Unit 4.

54.5 59.1 73.2 41.4 55.5 70.5 76.4 70 52.3 83.2 64.5 49.5
70 52.3 68.2 47.3 66.8 70 56.4 53.6 59.1 44.5 55.9 57.3 69.5
73.2 62.7 73.6 70 56.7 58.2 68.2

This dataset can be represented by the chart in Figure 10. The chart shows that there are two data values in the interval 40–45, two data values in the interval 45–50, four data values in the interval 50–55, and so on.

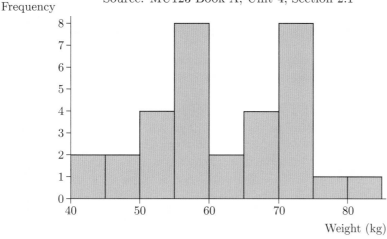

Histogram to show the distribution of the weights
of 32 women at the start of their pregancies
Source: MU123 Book A, Unit 4, Section 2.1

Figure 10   A histogram representing the dataset of women's weights

Charts like this are called **histograms**. In general, if you want to draw a histogram to illustrate a dataset, then the first step is to choose a sequence of contiguous intervals that together cover all the values in the dataset. The intervals are usually chosen to have equal widths, and, if this is the case, then for each interval you just draw a rectangle whose height is proportional to the number of data values that lie in that interval, in the way shown in Figure 10. These rectangles are called *bars* or sometimes *columns*.

Contiguous means 'touching'.

A data value that lies on the boundary between two intervals is usually included in the bar to the *right* of the boundary. There is no obvious reason for this choice – it is just the usual convention. So, for example, in the histogram in Figure 10, the bar covering the interval 70–75 represents values that are *at least* 70 but *less than* 75, and the three values of 70 kg in the dataset are represented in this bar. In general, each interval includes the left boundary value but not the right boundary value.

The left boundary value of the *first* interval is called the *start value* of the histogram. For example, the start value of the histogram in Figure 10 is 40.

The vertical scale of the histogram in Figure 10 indicates the frequencies with which the data values in the different intervals occur, but other types of vertical scale can be used, provided that the heights of the bars are proportional to the frequencies of the data values in the intervals. For example, the vertical scale in Figure 10 could instead have indicated the *percentages* of the women in the survey whose weights fell into the various intervals. In that case, it would have gone from 0% to 25% (because the highest bars, indicating frequencies of 8, each correspond to 25% of the 32 women).

A histogram whose vertical scale shows frequencies (rather than percentages, for example) is sometimes called a frequency diagram. In general, a *frequency diagram* is any diagram that shows the frequencies of particular items, values or groups of values.

The shape of a histogram indicates the distribution of the data values in the dataset that it represents. For example, in the histogram in Figure 10, the heights of the bars are fairly similar, apart from two peaks at around 55 kg and 70 kg. A histogram can show more detail than a boxplot about the distribution of the data values in a dataset. As you have seen, a boxplot just shows five summary values.

You learned about the distinction between discrete and continuous data in Unit 4.

Histograms are usually used to represent *continuous* data, such as measurements. However, if the data values in a dataset are discrete but take a large number of different values, then they are often treated as continuous and can be represented by a histogram. For example, you could draw a histogram of examination scores, which may take any whole-number value from 0 to 100.

2.2   Bar charts

If the data values in a dataset are discrete and take only a small number of values, then it is usual to represent them not by a histogram, but by a similar-looking type of statistical chart called a **bar chart**. When a dataset is depicted by a bar chart, each bar corresponds to a *single* possible data value, rather than an interval of possible data values. The bars in a bar chart are drawn with gaps between them to reflect this fact.

For example, the bar chart in Figure 11 shows the frequencies with which the six scores 1, 2, 3, 4, 5, 6 cropped up as a result of 30 rolls of a die.

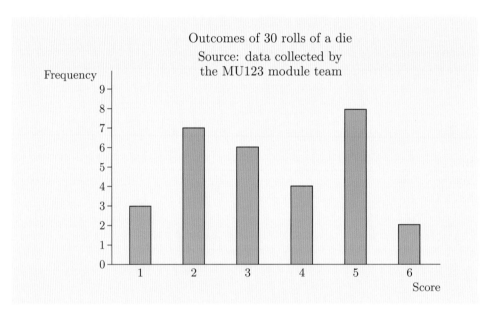

Figure 11   A bar chart

The data values represented by a bar chart do not have to be numbers – they can be 'categories', such as colours, countries, and so on. Data of this type are called **categorical data**. For example, Figure 12 shows the various types of housing accommodation used in England in a particular year (2007–08). The length of each bar corresponds to the percentage of all accommodation that was of that particular type. Because the categories are non-overlapping and cover *all* accommodation in England, the percentages add to 100.

The bars in a bar chart can be drawn either vertically or horizontally, as you can see from Figures 11 and 12. In contrast, the bars in a histogram are nearly always drawn vertically.

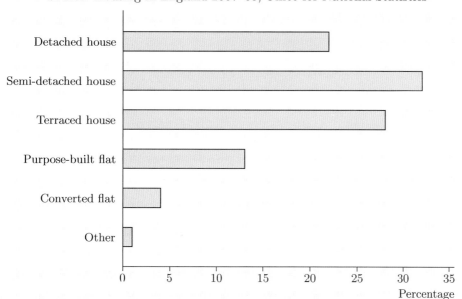

Type of accommodation of households in England, 2007–08
Source: Housing in England 2007–08, Office for National Statistics

Figure 12 A bar chart representing categorical data

2.3 Exploring histograms

In this subsection you will use Dataplotter to explore histograms. The histograms drawn by Dataplotter have equal interval widths, and they have frequency of occurrence on the vertical axis.

In the next activity you will use Dataplotter to explore different histograms for the dataset consisting of the weights of 32 women at the start of their pregnancies that was given on page 20. One possible histogram is given in Figure 10 on page 21, but you can produce different histograms by changing the start value and/or interval width.

Activity 8 *Exploring histograms with Dataplotter*

 Dataplotter

Use Dataplotter, with the 'Histogram' tab selected.

(a) Select the dataset '# Weight start' (not '# SP Weight start') in the first data column. Remove any data in the second column – you can do this by clicking 'New' to create a new, blank dataset.

Locate the 'Start value', 'Interval' and 'Auto' boxes just below the histogram. When 'Auto' is ticked, as it is by default, the software chooses a start value and an interval width for the histogram automatically. Click in the box to switch 'Auto' off, then set 'Start value' to 40 and 'Interval' (which means interval width) to 5.

You should see the same histogram as in Figure 10 on page 21. How many data values are there in the interval 65–70?

(b) The histogram has two peaks at around 55 and 70. Now try increasing the interval width from 5 to 10 and note where the peaks occur.

Then reduce the interval width to 2 and observe the effect.

Finally, reduce the interval width to 1 and observe the histogram again.

In general, what effect do you find that the interval width has on the shape of the histogram?

In Activity 8, you saw that a small interval width results in a 'spiky' histogram that displays lots of detailed features in the distribution of the data but may fail to give a good picture of its overall shape. On the other hand, a large interval width results in a 'lumpy' histogram that displays the large-scale structure in the distribution of the data, but at the expense of the detail. A good choice of interval width is usually a compromise between these two extremes.

The 'Auto' setting gives reasonable choices for the start value and interval width and these are often adequate. However, in order to create a histogram exactly as you want it to appear, you may need to choose these values yourself.

Sometimes you may need different interval widths in different parts of the horizontal axis in order to produce a good overall picture. This happens when there are many data values in some parts but few in others. In cases like these, different interval widths can be used, but then the number of data values in an interval is represented not by the height of the corresponding bar, but by its *area*.

For example, suppose that a statistical investigation has been carried out to find the weekly earnings of a large group of people, and the results are illustrated by the histogram in Figure 13. Notice that the intervals on the left are narrow and widen as you go to the right, where earnings are higher. The reason for drawing the histogram like this is that the narrow intervals for the lower earnings show the shape of the distribution well, but there are relatively few people with the higher earnings and so it makes sense to have wider intervals here, to avoid spikiness. The size of each column must now be judged on the basis of the key alongside the chart, which indicates the size of the area corresponding to 500 people.

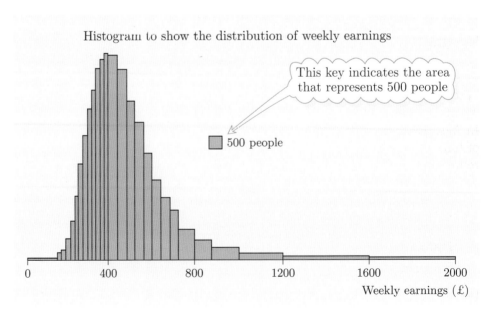

Figure 13 A histogram with unequal interval widths

Histograms with unequal interval widths are relatively uncommon, and all the histograms in the remainder of the module have equal interval widths. As mentioned earlier, Dataplotter can plot only histograms with equal interval widths.

There is another thing worth noticing about the histogram in Figure 13: it is asymmetric, with its right tail longer than its left tail. This indicates that the dataset is right-skewed, and the histogram itself is also described as being right-skewed. Similarly, a histogram whose left tail is longer than its right tail indicates that the dataset is left-skewed, and is itself said to be left-skewed.

In the next activity, you are asked to use histograms to compare the data in two datasets.

Dataplotter

Activity 9   Using histograms to compare datasets

Use Dataplotter, with the 'Histogram' tab selected.

(a) Make sure that '# Weight start' dataset is still in the first data column, and select the '# Weight end' dataset in the second column.

Make sure that the start value and interval width for the first histogram are set to 40 and 5, respectively. Uncheck the 'Auto' box for the second histogram, and set its start value and interval width to the same values.

What does the 'Weight end' histogram tell you about the distribution of the weights of the women at the end of their pregnancies?

(b) Compare the shape and position of the 'Weight end' histogram with those of the 'Weight start' histogram. How do you account for the differences between them?

(c) Now select the 'Boxplot' tab, and describe what the boxplots show. Which of these two types of chart do you think is easier to use if you want to compare the two datasets?

In the next activity you are asked to match up some small datasets with histograms that represent them.

Activity 10   Matching datasets and histograms

In Activity 5 you were asked to match up each of four datasets consisting of ten integer values with their corresponding boxplots. These datasets are reproduced below.

Dataset 1	0	6	7	8	9	10	11	12	13	19
Dataset 2	0	1	2	3	9	10	16	17	18	19
Dataset 3	0	1	2	3	9	10	11	12	13	19
Dataset 4	0	6	7	8	9	10	16	17	18	19

(a) The figure overleaf shows Dataplotter histograms representing these four datasets. Without using Dataplotter, work out which histogram corresponds to which dataset. All four histograms have been set to have an interval width of 5.

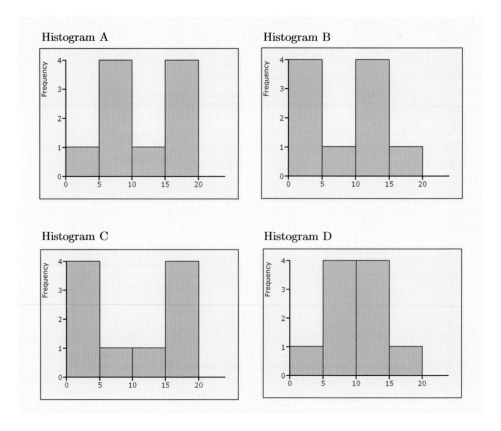

(b) Now compare the histograms in part (a) with the boxplots of the same datasets in Activity 5 on pages 14–15. How are the shapes of the boxplots reflected in the shapes of the histograms?

Histograms and boxplots both provide useful pictures of data. They each have their advantages and disadvantages.

Boxplots give a quick overall impression of how the data in a dataset are distributed, and important statistical summary values for the data can be read directly off them. They are also good for comparing datasets.

Histograms provide more detailed information about how the data in a dataset are distributed. They are not as good as boxplots for making comparisons, and there's the problem of what interval width to select.

In this section you have looked at histograms and bar charts. You saw that histograms are suitable for use with continuous data, whereas bar charts are used to depict discrete data (which can be either categorical data or numerical data). For bar charts, the convention is to include gaps between the bars, whereas in a histogram the bars touch. With the exception of the illustrative example in Figure 13, all the histograms presented in this module are constructed using equal intervals.

For more information about pie charts, see Maths Help, Module 5, Subsection 2.3.

There are other types of statistical charts that are not covered in this module, such as *pie charts*.

The next section introduces a new topic, *randomness*, and explores the natural variation that you might expect a sample of random numbers to exhibit.

3 Random numbers

In this section you will use bar charts to explore features in random numbers that arise from chance alone. The aim is to help you to develop a better understanding of features and variations that occur naturally in random data, which will be a useful benchmark against which to compare data arising from a statistical investigation. This is something that you will get an opportunity to do in Section 4, where you will use this approach to test whether or not it can be demonstrated that someone possesses extra-sensory perception (ESP). The key issue underlying all investigations of this nature is to analyse and interpret the observed features in data, and conclude that either:

- yes, there is a real effect here, or
- no, these features could simply be random fluctuations.

3.1 Clusters

When medical case histories are collected together, it is often possible to see a bigger picture about issues such as which categories of patients are becoming ill with what illnesses, and where these illnesses are occurring. In particular, cases of an illness sometimes cluster in certain geographical areas. A problem lies in interpreting such a cluster of ill health, particularly if it occurs close to an unpopular installation such as a phone mast or a nuclear power plant. The key questions here are:

- Is the cluster larger than you might expect?
- If it is, then is its size sufficiently large to lead you to believe that it is more than just a random fluctuation?

Activity 11   *Reading a news story critically*

Have a look at the news story below.

Nuclear link to child leukaemia 'cluster'?

The nuclear industry last night rejected claims of a cluster of children's cancer in North Wales. Radiation expert Chris Busby says the Menai Strait area has a 28-fold rate of child leukaemia compared to the UK average and blames the Sellafield nuclear reprocessing plant in Cumbria in an HTV programme tonight. Dr Busby, of Aberystwyth, who sits on government committees, said: 'There is a 28-fold excess of child leukaemia in Caernarfon over the period 2000–03, three cases, whereas only 0.1 should be expected in comparison with the national average.'

Hywel Trewyn, *Daily Post*, 10 February 2004

(a) What data have been used as evidence in the article?

(b) Can you suggest any problems with the way that the data have been interpreted?

A key question in any analysis of clusters of ill health in particular towns or regions is whether such a cluster is a direct result of some identifiable factor or factors, or whether it is simply a chance occurrence.

In order to make an informed comparison between a cluster of ill health and what you might reasonably expect to happen by chance alone, you need to have an understanding of just what sort of variations you are likely to get due to chance. In this section, therefore, you will be asked to consider just this – what sort of variations tend to crop up naturally through chance alone? Research suggests that many people have a rather poor sense of this, and typically underestimate the extent to which the outcomes of chance events tend to vary and cluster. As a result, they have a tendency to be more surprised and impressed by everyday coincidences and associations than they should be. This subtle but important point was understood nearly two thousand years ago by the Greek essayist Plutarch when he wrote:

> It is no great wonder if, in the long process of time, while Fortune takes her course hither and thither, numerous coincidences should spontaneously occur.

Plutarch (c. AD 46–AD 120)

The main purpose of this section, therefore, is to invite you to explore and develop your own understanding in this area of chance. You will be looking at simple experiments – in statistics these are often referred to as *trials* – and their corresponding outcomes. In general, a **trial** is associated with a number of possible outcomes, but only one of these outcomes can occur at a time. For example, a trial might be the tossing of a coin, while its corresponding outcomes are heads and tails.

You will be asked to use a module software tool to generate some random numbers, and check just how much variation and clustering appears to occur from chance alone. After you have worked through this section, you should be more aware of how variations can arise by chance and be less ready to jump to unjustified conclusions.

3.2 How random numbers vary

Imagine that you have ten identical balls, labelled 0 to 9. They are placed inside a bag and thoroughly mixed around. Now, without looking inside the bag, you pick a ball. Each ball should have an equal chance of being chosen – a condition that ensures that the selection is *at random*. The number of the ball chosen is written down, the ball is replaced, and you repeat this activity a further nineteen times.

This should result in a run of twenty randomly-chosen numbers from 0 to 9. Such lists of numbers are called lists of **random numbers**.

Activity 12   *Making up your own 'random' numbers*

Write down the sort of run of twenty numbers that you think might result from the exercise described above. Don't skip over this, as you are shortly going to be asked to analyse the run of numbers that you think up.

Any made-up run of 'random' numbers might look truly random. But how random is it really?

Here are twenty made-up 'random' numbers:

4 1 9 0 6 3 2 7 8 3 4 6 5 9 3 2 0 8 5 7

And here are twenty computer-generated random numbers (obtained by using the random command on a computer):

9 0 8 3 7 8 8 6 1 1 1 4 6 6 8 1 8 2 9 2

You might be wondering whether the random numbers produced by a computer's random command are truly random. Computer-generated random numbers are often referred to as **pseudo-random**, and there is no guarantee that the computer's random number generator is a perfect model for random selection. However, in practice, they do provide a good match with numbers selected randomly using dice, coins or spinners, or by drawing balls from a bag, in terms of the properties explored in the next few activities. It's not just computers that generate pseudo-random numbers – many calculators have a random number generator.

At first sight, the two runs of numbers above seem rather similar – each is merely a run of digits from 0 to 9 with no special pattern. However, as you will see, the person who made up the twenty numbers actually imposed a greater degree of orderliness than was produced by the computer.

Children in playgrounds use various rhymes to pick people out 'randomly' for games, such as 'One potato, two potato, three potato, four; five potato, six potato, seven potato more'. Of course, these choices aren't really random. If you use the 'One potato...' rhyme, for example, you will always finish on the fourteenth person. (If there are fewer than 14 to choose from, you go round the circle however many times it takes.) But without thinking carefully, it's hard for a child reciting the rhyme to work out in advance who is going to be picked – so the choice is effectively random.

Activity 13   Checking for number pairs

Look at the two runs of numbers above and check whether any pairs of consecutive numbers are the same.

Typically, you find that a person making up a run of 'random' numbers tends to avoid having two consecutive numbers the same, whereas the computer may not.

Activity 14   Checking your own run of numbers for number pairs

Now check your own made-up run for pairs of consecutive numbers that are the same. Have you tried to avoid repetitions (consciously or subconsciously)?

Here is another check on orderliness.

Activity 15   Finding the frequencies of the numbers

For each of the two runs of numbers above, count the frequency of occurrence of each number.

Activity 15 shows that the computer-generated random numbers showed greater variation in the frequency counts than the made-up numbers.

Activity 16   *Finding the frequencies in your own run of numbers*

Now check the frequencies of the numbers in your own made-up run. Did each of your numbers come out with roughly the same frequency, or did the frequencies fluctuate widely, as for the computer-generated run of numbers?

When people make up their own 'random' numbers, they tend to produce numbers with much narrower variations in frequency than is found in random numbers generated by a computer or calculator. This contrast between made-up and computer-generated random numbers is even more evident when the frequencies are displayed in bar charts. Figures 14 and 15 show the bar charts for the two runs of numbers on page 29. The numbers 0 to 9 are shown along the horizontal axis, and the heights of the bars indicate the frequencies with which the numbers occur.

Note the gaps between the bars, which are a feature of bar charts.

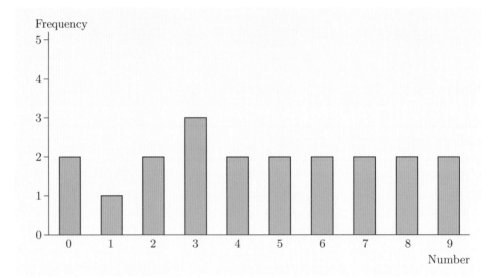

Figure 14   A bar chart showing the frequencies for the made-up run

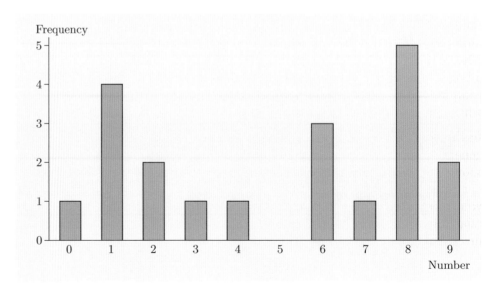

Figure 15   A bar chart showing the frequencies for the computer run

The point of the activities that you have done so far in this subsection was to indicate that random events may produce outcomes that fluctuate more widely than most people expect. However, it is difficult to show this convincingly on the basis of a single run of twenty computer-generated numbers. You really need to generate more than one run of random numbers from your computer if you are to develop a good sense of the disorderliness of random events.

Note that one important characteristic of a run of random numbers is that the selection of each new random number does not depend in any way on which numbers were selected previously in the run. You can see that this is true when the numbers are generated by choosing balls numbered 0 to 9 from a bag, in the way described earlier. We say that each new selection is **independent** of the previous selections.

At this point, it is useful to distinguish between uniform and non-uniform random numbers.

The random numbers that you have been thinking about in this subsection are *equally-likely* random numbers. For example, if you generate the random numbers by choosing balls from a bag in the way described, then you are just as likely to choose any of the balls as any of the others, so the random numbers generated are all equally likely. Equally-likely random numbers are also known as **uniform random numbers**.

Now imagine that there are eleven balls in the bag, the same ten as before, together with an extra ball labelled 0, making two balls labelled 0 altogether. Now when you generate a run of random numbers by choosing balls out of the bag, you are twice as likely to generate a 0 as you are to generate any of the other numbers. So the random numbers produced in this way are not equally likely; that is, they are *non-uniform*. Similarly, rolling a die whose faces are labelled 1, 1, 2, 2, 3, 4, for example, will produce non-uniform random numbers.

All of the random numbers generated in this unit are uniform random numbers.

Investigating variation in random numbers

In the rest of this subsection you will have the opportunity to use a module computer resource called 'At random' to generate some runs of random numbers for yourself. The process of generating a run of random numbers in this way will be referred to as a **simulation**, since it simulates what might happen if, for example, you were to pick numbered balls out of a bag in the way described earlier. Simulations involving computer-generated random numbers are often used in statistics, to show what might happen in a real situation that involves randomness.

In the next activity, you are asked to use the 'At random' software to generate sixty random numbers between 0 and 9. Remember that even though the numbers are equally likely to occur, they will almost certainly not crop up equally often in practice. The objective of this activity is for you to get a sense of how much natural variation there is, particularly with relatively small runs of numbers such as the runs of sixty numbers investigated here, and to describe this variation.

The dice used in casinos are known as *precision dice*. They are carefully manufactured to ensure that the different numbers come up equally often. To ensure that they are perfectly balanced, the spots are completely filled with material of the same density as the rest of the cube, and often the plastic material is translucent, so that weights cannot be hidden inside!

At random

Activity 17   *Investigating variation in a run of random numbers*

Open the 'At random' software.

(a) Check that the settings at the bottom of the right-hand panel are as follows.

> Generate values between: 0 and 9
>
> Number of values (per run): 60
>
> Number of runs: 1

Then click 'Go' to run the simulation. The software generates 60 random numbers and draws a bar chart showing the frequencies.

(b) Write a few sentences describing the variation in the frequencies of the numbers.

As you saw in the comment on Activity 17, for the particular simulation shown there, the most frequent number occurred six times as often as the least frequent number. You might be wondering just how typical this degree of variation is. For example, if you calculate the ratio of maximum frequency to minimum frequency, based on your own results in Activity 17, is it as large as 6?

In the next activity, you are asked to run the simulation several more times to investigate the variation in the frequencies of the numbers. In particular, you are asked to look at the ratio of maximum frequency to minimum frequency in each run, which is calculated automatically by the 'At random' software.

 At random

Activity 18   *Investigating variation in more runs of random numbers*

(a) Look again at the results of the simulation that you carried out in Activity 17. (If you no longer have the results, then carry out another simulation, with the same settings.)

If the minimum frequency is 0, then the ratio cannot be calculated and a dash is displayed in the table. If this happens, then just continue with part (b), or carry out another simulation, if you wish.

In the table in the left-hand panel, in the column headed 'Max/Min', you will find the ratio of maximum frequency to minimum frequency. What is its value for your simulation?

(b) Now set 'Number of runs' to 10 (keeping the other settings the same as in Activity 17), and click 'Go'. The software generates 10 runs of random numbers. The maximum frequency, minimum frequency and ratio of maximum frequency to minimum frequency for each of the 10 runs are displayed in the left-hand panel. The bar chart displays the results of all 10 runs put together.

Write a few sentences describing your findings, and indicate what they suggest in terms of gaining an insight into the variability of random numbers.

The main point to emerge from your investigation in this subsection can be summarised as follows.

Suppose that you have a fairly small run of random numbers, such as a run of sixty random numbers. Then even if all the possible numbers are equally likely to occur, the degree of variation in frequency between the numbers is likely to be quite large, and probably larger than most people expect.

However, what happens if you look at larger runs of random numbers? This is the topic of the next subsection.

3.3   Larger runs of random numbers

So far, you have been looking at fairly small runs of random numbers (with no more than 60 numbers). What happens when the number of random numbers in a run is greatly increased? For example, would there be as much disorderliness if the number of random numbers were increased to, say, 300 or 10 000 or even 100 000? Fortunately, these are questions that are easily investigated using the 'At random' software.

Activity 19   *Increasing the number of random numbers*

At random

Return to the 'At random' software.

(a) Choose the following settings.

> Generate values between: 0 and 9
>
> Number of values (per run): 300
>
> Number of runs: 1

Run the simulation several times (by clicking 'Go' each time) and compare the overall shape of each bar chart, and each ratio of maximum frequency to minimum frequency, with the typical shapes and ratios that you got when the number of values was 60.

(b) Repeat part (a) with the number of values increased to 10 000. Compare the shape of each bar chart, and each ratio of maximum frequency to minimum frequency, with what you saw previously.

(c) The maximum number of values per run that the software will accept is 10 000, but you can see the shape of the bar chart that results from a run of 100 000 values by leaving the number of values per run at 10 000 and increasing the number of runs to 10. The corresponding ratio of maximum frequency to minimum frequency is then given in the bottom row of the table.

Make this change to the settings, then run the simulation several times and compare the shape of each bar chart, and each ratio of maximum frequency to minimum frequency, with what you saw for fewer random numbers.

Activity 19 illustrates some important facts about the nature of random numbers in which all the possible numbers are equally likely to occur – that is, uniform random numbers. These facts are set out in the box below.

Uniform random numbers

- When a fairly small run of uniform random numbers is chosen, the degree of disorderliness in the numbers is often surprisingly high.

- With larger runs, the frequencies tend to settle down and become approximately equal.

3.4   Using random variation as a basis of comparison

This final subsection in this section explains why it is useful to have a good grasp of randomness and the effects that it can produce. For example, some medical conditions such as leukaemia or high blood pressure sometimes appear to occur in identifiable clusters in particular regions of the country. In recent years, there have been many newspaper scare stories about possible causes (mobile phone masts, nuclear power plants, electricity lines, and so on). But a crucial question here is whether such a cluster is caused by some external factor or whether it is simply one of the high frequencies that occur naturally with random events.

At random

Activity 20   *Cause or coincidence?*

Imagine that in a particular year there is a total of 60 known cases of a particular type of leukaemia, spread randomly over six similar towns, all with roughly the same population.

(a) If there are no differences in the circumstances of the towns, how many cases of the disease, *on average*, might each town expect to have in that year?

(b) Think of each town as labelled with a different number from 1 to 6. Use the 'At random' software to generate sixty random numbers between 1 and 6 inclusive, and note how many times each of the numbers occurs. Explain how the random numbers that you have generated simulate the possible distribution of the leukaemia cases.

(c) Suppose that in the actual distribution of cases, one of the towns is unlucky enough to account for 17 of the 60 cases, and this town happens to be closest to a nuclear installation.

Set the 'At random' software to carry out the simulation ten times (by setting the number of runs to 10), and look at the results. On the basis of these simulations, do you think that the citizens from this town have a cause for concern?

Running the simulations in Activity 20 will produce different results every time. A member of the module team ran the ten simulations (see Figure 16) and found that in one of them, one of the numbers had a frequency of 19.

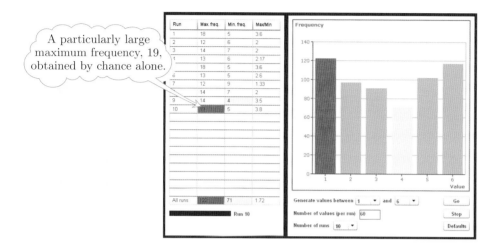

Figure 16 Ten simulations of the leukaemia scenario in Activity 20

So if you consider the frequencies of leukaemia cases in the six towns, then even a frequency as high as 19, which is well above the average value of 10, could arise by chance.

So is there a cause for concern for the town with a frequency of 17 cases of the disease? You might conclude that the cluster of cases experienced by this town is small enough to be just a chance occurrence. Although this may be the explanation, it would be sensible for the town authorities to monitor the number of cases carefully over subsequent years to check whether it continues to be higher than expected, in which case there would be a much greater cause for concern. They might also, particularly if the frequency continues to be high, seek scientific advice about whether the cluster of cases might be causally linked to the nuclear installation, or perhaps to some other factor.

So, in general, a cluster of ill health occurring in a particular region *may* imply a possible cause-and-effect explanation based on factors peculiar to that region. However, such a conclusion should be viewed with caution: it must be weighed against a possible alternative explanation that the cluster is just an extreme result due to random fluctuations.

In this section you have used the random number generating software 'At random' to explore variation in random numbers. The point of this exercise was to get a better sense of just how widely fluctuating this variation can be.

In statistics, knowing the extent of random fluctuations provides a useful benchmark against which to interpret experimental data – an idea that you will revisit in Section 4, where you will be asked to carry out an investigation on testing for extra-sensory perception (ESP).

4 Case study: a statistical investigation of the paranormal

In this final section, you are asked to take some of the statistical skills that you have learned in Unit 4 and in the first three sections of this unit, and apply them to an investigation that involves making a statistical judgement. The context is about how you might decide whether or not *extra-sensory perception* (ESP) exists.

Extra-sensory perception, if it exists, is the ability to acquire information by paranormal means – in other words, by a means that does not depend on any known physical sense or any deduction from previous experience.

As part of this investigation, you will be asked to carry out a short experiment to gather data. Bear in mind that the point of the case study is for you to gain insights about the statistical method of investigation. You can best do this by engaging with the experiment rather than simply reading about the statistical investigation in the abstract. Also, you will find that the experience of having collected, analysed and interpreted *your own data* will be helpful to refer to when you are working through some of the more complex ideas in the section.

You may possibly have an opinion about ESP already – you may strongly disbelieve in its existence, you may strongly believe in it, or you may be undecided. However, it is important to understand that the point of this section is not to prove or disprove the existence of ESP, but rather to demonstrate the general process of statistical decision making for questions where absolute proof is difficult to achieve.

A key role of the statistician when investigating some phenomenon is to abandon all personal opinions or prejudices and look only at the evidence. If a statistician is asked to investigate, say, whether a particular drug is effective or whether a certain factory poses health risks or whether ESP exists, then the methodology is always the same. The investigation should begin with the assumption that the phenomenon does not exist (that is, the drug isn't effective, the factory poses no health risks, ESP doesn't exist). This is the starting assumption of 'no difference', sometimes referred to as the **null hypothesis**. Bearing in mind the possibility that occasional fluke results will always happen randomly, the statistician must then examine the data and ask the question: How much evidence of difference would I need in order for me to abandon my null hypothesis and conclude that the phenomenon *does* exist?

You are asked to use this methodology to explore the question of the existence of ESP in a systematic manner, using the four-stage PCAI investigation cycle described in Unit 4, and summarised in the box below.

> ### The four stages of a statistical investigation
>
> Stage 1   **P**ose a question
> Stage 2   **C**ollect relevant data
> Stage 3   **A**nalyse the data
> Stage 4   **I**nterpret the results

4.1 Stage P: posing a question about ESP

The first stage in any statistical investigation is to clarify the question of interest. Often this involves maintaining a compromise between what you really want to know and what it is possible to find out with the statistical tools at hand. Here are some general issues that are an important backdrop to any investigation.

Starting an investigation

- Think carefully about the wording of the question of interest. Make sure that it is specific and unambiguous.

- Check that the question can be answered by undertaking a doable investigation. This requires anticipating the possible stages that will lie ahead – what data will you need and how will you collect them (the 'C' stage); how will you process the data (the 'A' stage); and is it likely that your choice of analytical tools will give you an answer to your question (the 'I' stage)?

In this section you are asked to work with the following question:

> Does a person whom I know have extra-sensory perception (ESP)?

This is a very open-ended question, and a great deal of work would be needed to investigate it thoroughly, so in this section you are asked to narrow it down and think about evidence of ESP in a particular context – namely, how good a person is at guessing numbers on cards that are hidden from him or her. A more specific version of the question above, to suit this context, is:

> Does a person whom I know show evidence of ESP when guessing hidden numbers on cards?

You will be asked to invite two friends or family members to be your *subjects*, and to test their card-guessing abilities using cards something like those shown in Figure 17. Playing cards would be suitable – for example, the Ace, 2, 3 and 4 of Spades.

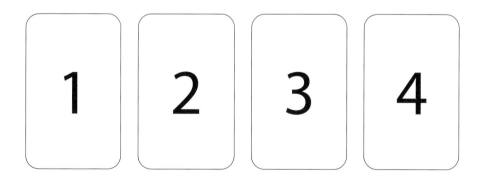

Figure 17 Cards numbered 1 to 4

As part of the investigation, you will explore what 'evidence of ESP' might mean, by considering computer simulations of results that might be obtained just by chance.

4.2   Stage C: collecting the card-guessing data

At the 'C' stage of any investigation, you need to collect relevant data. In the investigation here, an experiment must be designed to gather data to answer the question posed in the last subsection.

Here is the experiment that you will be asked to carry out later in this subsection.

Subject A

Card	Guess	Actual	
1	2	1	
2	4	4	✓
3	1	2	
4	3	4	
5	2	3	
6	1	1	✓
7	4	2	
8	3	4	
9	4	4	✓
10	2	4	
11	3	4	
12	3	4	
13	2	1	
14	1	1	✓
15	1	3	
16	3	3	✓
17	4	4	✓
18	2	1	
19	1	2	
20	3	1	

Score   6

Figure 18 An example of a completed table and Score box for the card-guessing experiment

Instructions for the card-guessing experiment

1. Identify two people who are willing to be tested to see how good they are at guessing numbers on cards. They can be reassured that you will require only five minutes of their time.

2. Prepare four cards, numbered 1, 2, 3 and 4, on one side, as shown in Figure 17 (or use playing cards).

3. Prepare a data collection sheet. You can either print out the sheet in the Unit 11 resources section of the module website, or draw up your own version. For each subject, you will need a table similar to the one shown (completed) in Figure 18, with three columns, headed 'Card', 'Guess' and 'Actual', and twenty rows. You will also need a 'Score' box for each subject, to record the number of correct guesses out of 20.

4. Test your first subject as follows. Shuffle the four cards thoroughly, choose one at random and, without looking at it yourself, lay it face down. The subject now says what they think the number is; write this in the first row of the column headed 'Guess'. Then look at the card and write down its number in the first row of the column headed 'Actual', without the subject seeing what you are writing. Put the chosen card back to rejoin the other three cards.

    Repeat this for twenty chosen cards, and then write the number of correct guesses in the Score box. The completed table and Score box should look something like those in Figure 18.

5. Repeat step 4 for your other subject.

Once you have completed the experiment, you will need to try to make a judgement from your subjects' scores as to whether they have shown evidence of possessing ESP.

An important issue in experimental design is how to ensure that a test is 'fair' – the experiment should test what you intend to test! A useful approach to thinking about this is to try to anticipate how a cheat might attempt to subvert any test that you devise, and then create 'laboratory conditions' to counteract such subversion. Activity 21 asks you to think about how the test in step 4 of the experiment above could be refined to make sure that it is fair.

Activity 21   *Checking whether the test is fair*

(a) What would count as cheating in the test described?

(b) How might you make it difficult for a subject to cheat?

In addition to minimising the possibility of cheating, your test must of course be open to the possibility that your subject has ESP. With some ESP experiments, it is possible that the circumstances of the actual test may affect the level of performance. For example, some people find tests stressful and they do not perform as well as they might have done. So it is important to provide a relaxed environment. Try to set aside a reasonable amount of time, and if possible ensure that you and your subjects will not be disturbed.

A common complaint of 'psychics' who fail to perform well when tested is that they have underachieved because of the 'sterile' atmosphere of the 'laboratory conditions'.

The next activity asks you to conduct the card-guessing experiment. If you find it impossible to do this (perhaps because you are unable to find suitable subjects who are willing and able to help), then you can instead carry out a different version of the experiment, which is available on the module computer resource 'By chance alone'. In this version, the numbers on the cards are computer generated, and *you*, rather than two different subjects, are tested on how good you are at guessing the numbers. The instructions for this version of the experiment are given in the activity.

Activity 22 *Conducting the experiment*

By chance alone

Either

Carry out the experiment with your two subjects as described on the opposite page. Keep a note of the two subjects' scores out of twenty, as you will need them in the rest of the section.

or

Carry out the 'self-test' version of the experiment, as follows.

(a) Open the 'By chance alone' software, make sure that the 'Card experiment' tab is selected, and click 'Self test'.

(b) The backs of twenty cards are shown on the left of the software display. Guess the number on the first card (1, 2, 3 or 4). Then, in the table headed 'Subject A', type your guess in the first cell of the 'Guess' column, and press 'Enter'. The first card turns over and its number is displayed in the first cell of the 'Actual' column. The cursor moves down, ready for you to guess the number on the second card.

(c) Enter your guesses for all twenty cards, and click 'OK' in the dialogue box that appears. The software displays the number of correct guesses in the Score box at the bottom of the table.

(d) Now the backs of a further twenty cards are shown. Enter your guesses for the numbers on these cards in the table headed 'Subject B', and click 'OK' in the dialogue box that appears.

(e) Make a note of the two scores out of 20 that are displayed in the Score boxes at the bottom of the tables, as you will need them in the rest of the section. If you plan to continue your study session, then leave the 'By chance alone' software open and unchanged, as you will be able to continue with it in the next activity. If you do not plan to continue, then just keep your note of the two scores.

(There are no comments on this activity.)

Whether you carried out the experiment on two subjects, or the alternative version in which you tested yourself, you should now have two scores out of 20, one for Subject A and the other for Subject B. You are now going to analyse these results to see just how well your subjects performed, by comparing their two scores with the scores that might be achieved by random guessing.

4.3   Stage A: analysing the card-guessing data

With the two scores for Subject A and Subject B in mind, you now need to think about how successful your two subjects really were. For example, suppose that one of them scored 7 out of 20. Is that a lot or a little, and by what criterion can you make that judgement?

As you saw in Section 3, the most useful way to judge results like these is by comparing them to the answer to the question: What sort of results would you expect to get by chance alone? Clearly if you simply guess the answers, then you are likely to get *some* right by chance. Evidence of possessing ESP would require a 'better-than-chance' performance.

As there are four cards in the test, a subject who guesses randomly has a one-in-four chance of guessing any particular card correctly. So he or she should get about 5 out of 20 guesses right, on average. But if you were to look at the scores out of 20 for a large group of subjects guessing randomly, would these scores tend to be bunched between, say, 4 and 6, or is the variation likely to be much wider – say between 1 and 9? It is important for you to know this if you are to identify a 'better than chance' performance by one of your subjects. To answer this question, some investigation is needed into scores that can be obtained by guessing randomly. This can be done by using simulations.

In this subsection you will use the module software 'By chance alone' to carry out suitable simulations. In each simulation, the software generates two lists of twenty random numbers from 1 to 4. One list of random numbers simulates the random guesses that are made, and the other list simulates the actual numbers on the cards. The software counts the number of 'correct guesses' to give a score out of 20. It can run the simulation many times, to give an indication of the variation in the scores.

In the next activity you will look at what happens if the simulation is run 100 times.

 By chance alone

Activity 23   *Simulating scores obtained by guessing*

Open the computer resource 'By chance alone', if it is not already open.

(a) If you have left this software open and unchanged since you carried out the previous activity, then click the 'Next' button at the bottom right of the software display, and go on to part (b).

Otherwise, make sure that the 'Card experiment' tab is selected, and click 'Enter scores'. You should then see the screen shown below.

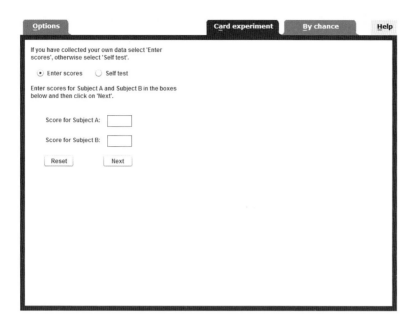

Enter the scores for Subjects A and B that you obtained in the previous activity. Then click the 'Next' button.

(b) You should now see a screen similar to the one below, but with the scores of your two subjects displayed at the top right and marked on the chart.

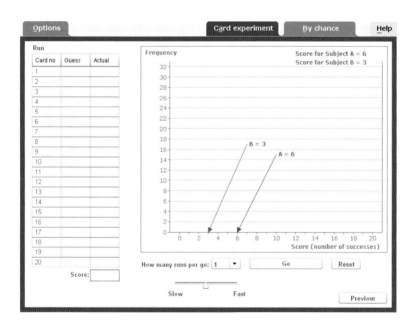

(c) Check that 'How many runs per go' (below the chart) is set to 1. Then click the 'Go' button. Several things will happen.

- Two lists of twenty random numbers are generated, one in the column headed 'Guess', to represent the twenty random guesses, and the other in the column headed 'Actual', to represent the actual numbers on the cards. All the 'correct guesses' are highlighted in red, and the total number of correct guesses is displayed in the Score box below the table.

- Once all twenty rows have been filled, a red dot appears on the chart, to represent the score. For example, if the score is 5, then the red dot appears above the point on the horizontal axis that represents 5, as shown in the screenshot below.

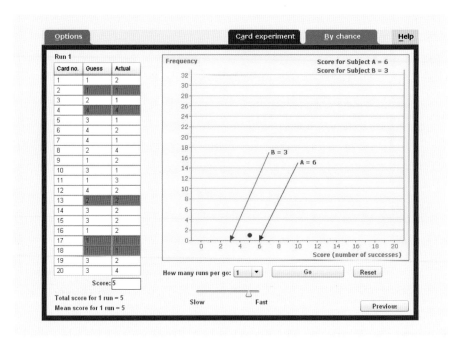

Run the simulation (by clicking 'Go') several times, in order to understand what is going on.

(d) Now change the number of runs per go to 10, click 'Go', and watch what happens. The simulation is run 10 times. The 'Run' number at the top left of the software display tells you which of the 10 simulations is currently being run. After each run, the score is plotted on the chart, so a dotplot of the scores is built up. The most recent score appears as a red dot.

> The dotplot displayed by the 'By chance alone' software has a vertical scale marked, so that the frequencies are easier to read off.

(e) Now run 50 simulations (by increasing the number of runs per go to 50 and clicking 'Go'), and finally run 100 simulations.

To speed things up, use the Slow–Fast slider near the bottom of the software display.

In the activity above you used the 'By chance alone' software to generate 100 scores typical of those that might be obtained simply by guessing the numbers on the cards. The dotplot of these scores gives you a sense not only of where the scores are centred – their location – but also of how they are spread.

For example, Figure 19 shows a dotplot of 100 scores obtained from the software. In this dotplot, the scores seem to be centred roughly at 5, as you would expect, but there are scores as low as 0 and as high as 11.

The set of scores in Figure 19 provides a useful, if rudimentary, benchmark against which to test your subjects' scores. For example, if one of your subjects scored 7 out of 20, say, then you would probably not consider this to be possible evidence of ESP, since this score seems to be well within the range of scores that are obtained simply by guessing. On the other hand, if your subject scored 9, say, then you might consider this to be of more significance, because, as you can see from the dotplot, only four of the 100 scores were as high as 9 or more (there were three scores of 9, no scores of 10, one score of 11 and no scores any higher than this).

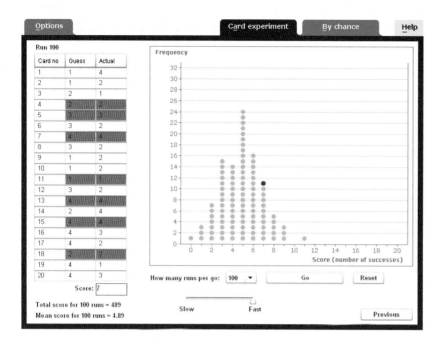

Figure 19   A screenshot of the 'By chance alone' software, showing typical scores for 100 runs of the card-guessing test if the subject simply guesses the numbers on the cards

So you now need to consider the question of how high a score has to be if you are to regard it as showing evidence of ESP. You would want the score to be high enough to ensure that there is only a very small chance of obtaining a score that high or higher simply by guessing the numbers on the cards.

Let's suppose that we want to regard a score as showing evidence of ESP if there is only a 5% chance, or less, of obtaining a score that high or higher by guessing. In other words, we will regard a score as showing evidence of ESP if it falls into the top 5% of scores that might be obtained by guessing. You might think that this percentage seems too high, but let's stick with it for the moment, to illustrate the ideas.

There are 100 scores in Figure 19, so the top 5% of scores are the top five scores. You cannot identify 'the top five scores' exactly, because they would have to be the score of 11, the three scores of 9 and one of the scores of 8 – but you can't say that one of the scores of 8 is higher than any of the other scores of 8.

However, you can say that a score of 9 or more is definitely in the top 5% of scores. So, if you are regarding a score as showing evidence of ESP if it falls into the top 5% of scores, and you are judging by Figure 19, then you would regard a score of 9 or more as showing evidence of ESP. You would not regard a score of 8 as showing evidence of ESP, because you cannot say that it falls into the top 5% of scores. All that you can say about a score of 8 is that it falls into the top 9 of the 100 scores – that is, into the top 9% of scores. Similarly, you would not regard any score smaller than 8 as showing evidence of ESP.

The top nine scores are the five scores of 8, the three scores of 9 and the score of 11.

If you think that a higher level of evidence is needed than the '5% criterion' described above, then you might instead use a '1% criterion': you would regard a score as showing evidence of ESP only if it falls into the top 1% of scores obtained by guessing. In this case, if you are judging by the dotplot in Figure 19, you would regard only scores of 11 or more as showing evidence of ESP. You might want to set a level of evidence even higher than this – we'll come back to the question of how high the level should be set later in the section.

A weakness of the analysis above is that the dotplot in Figure 19 is based on only 100 scores typical of those that might be obtained by guessing – really too few to provide a very robust test criterion. In the next activity, you are asked to use the 'By chance' tab of the 'By chance alone' software to generate many thousands of scores, which will provide a much better benchmark against which to judge your subjects' scores. The software displays the results as a bar chart rather than a dotplot.

 By chance alone

Activity 24   *Running many simulations*

Open the 'By chance alone' computer resource if it is not already open, and select the 'By chance' tab.

(a) Check that the three settings at the top left of the software display are set as follows:

Success probability: 0.25

Sample size n: 20

Number of runs: 100

The 'success probability' of 0.25 corresponds to the fact that one quarter of random guesses of a number on a card are expected to be correct, on average. This is because there are four possibilities for the numbers on the cards.

The 'sample size' of 20 corresponds to the fact that each simulation mimics a test in which the numbers on 20 cards are randomly guessed, so the scores obtained are scores out of 20.

The 'number of runs' refers, as before, to the number of times that the simulation is run. So, for example, setting 'number of runs' to 100 allows you to generate 100 scores typical of the scores that might be obtained by guessing.

(b) Check also that the box at the bottom left of the software display, labelled 'Cumulate data', is *not* ticked.

Now click 'Go'. The software generates 100 scores and displays the results as a bar chart.

Click 'Go' a few more times to get a feel for what is going on. What do you notice about the shapes of the bar charts?

(c) Set the number of runs to 100 000, and click 'Go'. The software generates 100 000 scores and displays the results as a bar chart.

Now click 'Go' a few more times. What do you notice about the shapes of the bar charts this time?

The very large number of scores that you can obtain from the 'By chance' tab of the 'By chance alone' software gives you a much better benchmark against which to judge the success, or otherwise, of your two subjects in the card-guessing test. Remember that the scores generated by the software simulate the kind of scores that you would expect to be obtained just by guessing. In the next activity you are asked to use a large number of scores to work out the minimum score that you would regard as showing evidence of ESP if you are using the '5% criterion', and similarly if you are using the '1% criterion'.

By chance alone

Activity 25 *Finding which scores satisfy the criteria*

Use the 'By chance alone' software, with the 'By chance' tab selected.

(a) Check that the three settings at the top left of the software display are set as follows:

> Success probability: 0.25
>
> Sample size n: 20
>
> Number of runs: 100 000

Also tick the box labelled 'Cumulate data' at the bottom left of the software display. The effect of this is that, each time you click 'Go', the new scores generated are put together with all the previous scores, to give you a larger and larger number of scores. The total number of scores represented in the bar chart is displayed on the left of the software display, labelled as 'Total number of runs'.

Click 'Go' repeatedly until the shape of the bar chart no longer seems to change.

(b) Now click 'Shade score' at the left of the software display, and change the number in the box after the words 'Shade score' from 5 to 8.

The effect of this is that the bars corresponding to scores of 8 or more are shaded, and the percentage of scores that are 8 or more is displayed above the 'Go' button, to three significant figures.

Click 'Go' a few more times – this will generate some more scores – to check whether the percentage of scores that are 8 or more seems to have settled down to a fairly consistent value. You should find that it settles down to 10.2% (to 1 d.p.).

(c) Use the 'Shade score' feature to complete the table below. Each time you change the number in the 'Shade score' box, click 'Go' a few more times to check that the percentage of scores seems to have settled down to a fairly consistent value. Round the percentages to one decimal place.

Score	Percentage of scores that are this high or higher (to 1 d.p.)
8	10.2%
9	
10	
11	
12	

(d) Suppose that you want to regard a score obtained by a subject in the card-guessing test as showing evidence of ESP only if it falls into the top 5% of scores that would be obtained by guessing. Use your answers to part (c) to determine the minimum score that would count as showing evidence of ESP.

(e) Suppose now that you want to regard a score obtained by a subject as showing evidence of ESP only if it falls into the top 1% of scores that would be obtained by guessing. Use your answers to part (c) to determine the minimum score that would count as showing evidence of ESP in this case.

The minimum score that falls into the top 5% of scores obtained by guessing is referred to as the 5% **critical value**, and any score greater than or equal to this value is said to lie in the 5% **critical region**. Similarly, the minimum score that falls into the top 1% of scores is referred to as the 1% critical value, and any score greater than or equal to this value is said to lie in the 1% critical region, and so on.

Before you can make a judgement about how your two subjects performed in the card-guessing test, you need to decide what level of evidence might be appropriate for regarding a score as showing evidence of ESP. Is either the 5% criterion or the 1% criterion good enough, for example?

The next activity should help you to think about this question.

Activity 26   *How many subjects might achieve a score in the critical region?*

(a) (i)   By using your answers to Activity 25, write down the 5% critical value for the card-guessing test. Hence, by looking at your answer to Activity 25(c), write down the percentage of subjects taking the card-guessing test that you would expect to achieve a score in the 5% critical region *purely by chance.*

    (ii)   Now consider all the subjects taking the card-guessing test in a given presentation of MU123. Work out an estimate for the number of these subjects that you would expect to achieve a score in the 5% critical region purely by chance. You can make the following (very approximate) assumptions.

- The number of students in a single presentation of the module is about 2000.

- The proportion of students who are able to find two subjects who agree to participate is about 90%.

(b) Repeat part (a) for the 1% critical value and region rather than the 5% critical value and region.

(c) Do you think that either the 5% criterion or the 1% criterion is strict enough for you to decide whether someone has shown evidence of ESP?

From what you saw in Activity 26, you would probably not consider either the 5% criterion or the 1% criterion to be a strict enough criterion for you to decide whether someone has shown evidence of ESP.

Instead, you would probably want to choose a criterion with a much smaller percentage. There is no correct answer for what the appropriate criterion should be: it is for the investigator to decide what seems appropriate.

For example, consider the '0.0001% criterion'. With this criterion, you would regard a score as showing evidence of ESP if it lies in the 0.0001% critical region. This means that the chance of obtaining a score that high or higher just by guessing is less than 0.0001%. If, say, 3600 subjects are tested in a given presentation of MU123, as estimated in Activity 26, then the number of these subjects that you would expect to obtain a score in the 0.0001% critical region purely by chance is less than

$$0.0001\% \text{ of } 3600 = 3600 \times \tfrac{0.0001}{100} = 0.0036.$$

So it seems very unlikely that any subject at all will achieve a score in the 0.0001% critical region purely by chance, and so you might be willing to accept a score in this region as evidence of ESP. As you can check by using the 'By chance alone' software if you wish, a score has to be 16 or more to lie in the 0.0001% critical region.

Activity 27   *Analysing your subjects' results*

Do either of your subjects' scores lie in the 0.0001% critical region? That is, are either of their scores greater than or equal to 16?

(There are no comments on this activity.)

The method that you have seen in this subsection for analysing subjects' scores – checking whether they are in the top so-many percent of results that might be obtained just by chance – is an important method in statistics. For example, the actual results in an investigation, such as a drug trial, might be regarded as showing evidence of a real effect if they are in the top 5% or top 1% (or some other percentage) of results that might be obtained just by chance. Much statistical decision making is based on methods of this kind.

4.4   Stage I: interpreting the ESP results

The final stage in the PCAI statistical investigation cycle is to interpret the results that have been obtained, in order to answer the question posed. In this investigation, the question was:

> Does a person whom I know show evidence of ESP when guessing hidden numbers on cards?

Towards the end of the last subsection you were asked to look at whether either of your subjects' results lies in the 0.0001% critical region – you saw that a score lies in this region if it is 16 or more. You may or may not have found that at least one of your subjects' scores lies in this region. But how should your results be interpreted?

If neither of your subjects achieved a score in the 0.0001% critical region – that is, if both of them scored 15 or less – then you might interpret their scores as 'insufficient to show evidence of ESP'. However, if a subject scored more than about 10, say, then you might point out that his or her score is quite high in comparison to the typical scores that are obtained by chance, and further investigation might be warranted.

What if one of your subjects achieved a score in the 0.0001% critical region – that is, what if he or she scored 16 or more? Although the chance of obtaining a score this high just by guessing is less than 0.0001%, it is still possible, of course, that a score this high *could* be obtained just by guessing. So, if one of your subjects achieved a score of 16 or more, then you might want to interpret their score as possible evidence of ESP, with the proviso that this conclusion is not a certainty.

In general, unlike the situation for much of pure mathematics, statistics offers no certainties. For this reason, decisions made on the basis of interpreting data sometimes turn out to be wrong.

Activity 28   *What if one of your subjects appeared to demonstrate ESP?*

Suppose that one of your subjects achieved a score of 16 or more on the card-guessing test. How might you proceed with regard to him or her?

The 'By chance alone' software uses a type of scientific notation to display very small numbers. For example, it would display the percentage

$$0.0000387\%$$

as

$$3.87\text{e-}5\%,$$

which means

$$(3.87 \times 10^{-5})\%.$$

Even an unlikely event can occur many times if you give it enough chances to happen. You might think that tossing 20 heads in a row with a coin would be an extremely unlikely event – and it is: the odds are about one in a million. But if all 60 million people in the UK tossed a coin 20 times, then you would expect about 60 of them (60 million divided by 1 million) to toss 20 heads in a row. Individually, these people are likely to feel that something spooky has happened, but if we look at the population as a whole, then we see that their results are no more than we would expect by chance.

Of course there are many ways to work with the card-guessing test, and to judge the results, other than those suggested in this section. For example, rather than looking for a score of 16 or more, say, on one test, you might ask each subject to take the test several times, and you might regard their scores as showing evidence of ESP if *each* of the scores is fairly high, though not necessarily as high as 16. You could decide, perhaps by using simulations, what you would want the minimum score on each test to be in order to ensure that the chance of achieving a score that high in each of several tests simply by guessing is very small.

The module software 'By chance alone' is not set up to carry out simulations for the approach described here.

Figure 20   James Randi

Parapsychology: science or pseudo-science?

Parapsychology remains a hugely controversial subject. Some parapsychology experiments have appeared to demonstrate evidence of ESP, but often these results can be explained by flaws in the experimental design or its execution, with fraud and collusion also sometimes coming into the frame.

An interesting player in the world of parapsychology is James Randi (Figure 20). Styling himself 'magician, sceptic and writer', Randi has spent decades challenging those who claim to possess paranormal powers to demonstrate objective proof of their abilities under scientific testing criteria. To date, the prize money offered for such proof by the James Randi Educational Foundation, which currently stands at $1 000 000, has not been won. In fact, no claimant has yet progressed past the preliminary test, which is set up on terms agreed in advance by both Randi and each claimant.

Critics of Randi argue that he has set himself up as judge and jury, and that a true prize would be controlled by an independent panel of neutral judges that would determine whether or not an applicant had truly demonstrated psychic powers.

Learning checklist

After studying this unit, you should be able to:

- appreciate how various statistical skills and techniques fit into the PCAI stages of a statistical investigation
- create a dotplot of a dataset (using Dataplotter), and understand what it reveals about the shape and location of the data values
- create a boxplot of a dataset (using Dataplotter), and interpret its shape and location
- create a histogram of a dataset (using Dataplotter), and interpret its shape and location
- relate the ideas of location and spread of a dataset (introduced in Unit 4) to pictorial representations of the data in the form of statistical charts
- understand some basic aspects of experimental design
- appreciate the degree of variation that might be expected when items are selected randomly
- appreciate an important idea in statistical decision making, namely, that a useful technique is to compare observed results with results that might be obtained by chance alone.

Solutions and comments on Activities

Activity 1

(a) The screenshot below shows the result of entering the numbers.

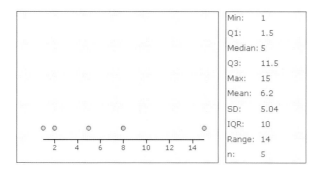

Min:	1
Q1:	1.5
Median:	5
Q3:	11.5
Max:	15
Mean:	6.2
SD:	5.04
IQR:	10
Range:	14
n:	5

(b) The summary values are: Min (the minimum value); Q1 (the lower quartile); Median; Q3 (the upper quartile); Max (the maximum value); Mean; SD (the standard deviation); IQR (the interquartile range); Range; and n (the number of values in the dataset).

(c) The median is a measure of location. If all the data values are sorted by size, from smallest to largest or vice versa, and there is an odd number of data values, then the median is the middle data value. If the number of data values is even, then there is no middle data value, and the median is the mean of the two middle data values in the sorted dataset.

The standard deviation is a measure of spread. Roughly speaking, it gives an idea of how far, on average, the data values are from the mean. It is calculated by finding the deviation (difference) of each data value from the mean of the dataset, squaring each of these deviations, finding the mean of the squared deviations and finally finding the square root of this mean.

Activity 2

(a) Six students gave the value 30.

(b) The two dotplots are shown below.

Dotplots to show the distributions of the 'Possible' and 'Probable' scores
Source: MU123 Book A, Unit 4, Section 3

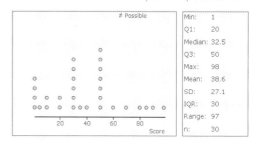

Min:	1
Q1:	20
Median:	32.5
Q3:	50
Max:	98
Mean:	38.6
SD:	27.1
IQR:	30
Range:	97
n:	30

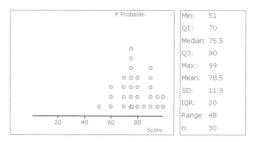

Min:	51
Q1:	70
Median:	75.5
Q3:	90
Max:	99
Mean:	78.5
SD:	11.9
IQR:	20
Range:	48
n:	30

It is clear from the fact that the 'Probable' data are further to the right than the 'Possible' data that the 'Probable' dataset contains generally larger values. Also, the 'Probable' data are more closely packed together – that is, the spread is narrower. These conclusions are in line with what you observed in Unit 4, where you made the comparisons based on numerical summaries of the data.

Activity 3

The two boxplots are shown below.

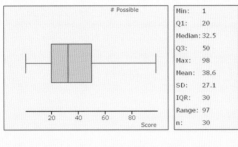

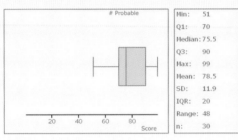

Boxplots to show the distributions of the 'Possible' and 'Probable' scores

Source: MU123 Book A, Unit 4, Section 3

(b) (i) The median is 75.5.

(ii) The upper quartile is 90.

(iii) The lower quartile is 70.

(c) (i) This statement is correct, because the minimum value of the 'Probable' dataset (which is 51) is greater than the upper quartile of the 'Possible' data (which is 50).

(ii) This statement is incorrect, because the interquartile range of the 'Probable' data is 20, which is *less* than the interquartile range of the 'Possible' data, which is 30.

(iii) This statement is correct, because for the 'Possible' data the difference between the minimum value and the median is $32.5 - 1 = 31.5$, whereas for the 'Probable' data it is $75.5 - 51 = 24.5$.

(d) All five key summary values for the 'Probable' dataset are higher than the corresponding values for the 'Possible' dataset; this indicates that the students gave higher numbers for the word 'Probable' overall. Both the length of the box and the length of the boxplot are narrower for the 'Probable' dataset than for the 'Possible' dataset; this indicates that the students were more consistent in the numbers that they gave for 'Probable' than for 'Possible'.

Activity 4

(a) The boxplot is shown below.

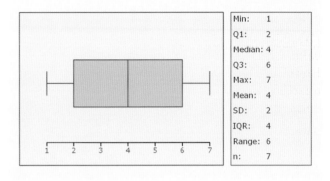

(b) When the 7 is changed to 20, the box part of the boxplot appears to shrink and move to the left.

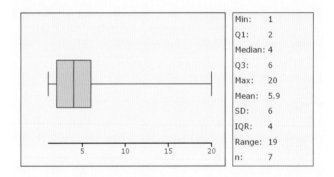

However, this is a misleading observation. In fact, the scale has automatically resized to accommodate the new higher maximum value, and the other four summary values are actually unchanged. They are unchanged because, in this case, the other summary values do not depend on the value of the maximum.

(c) The mean has increased from 4 to 5.9. This has happened because the mean is calculated *from every value in the dataset.*

Activity 5

(a) Each dataset has minimum value 0, maximum value 19 and median 9.5. However, Dataset 1 has lower quartile 7 and upper quartile 12, while Dataset 2 has lower quartile 2 and upper quartile 17, as shown below.

Dataset 1	0	6	7	8	9	10	11	12	13	19
			↑	↑		↑		↑		↑
			Min	Q1		Median		Q3		Max

Dataset 2	0	1	2	3	9	10	16	17	18	19
			↑	↑		↑		↑		↑
			Min	Q1		Median		Q3		Max

So Boxplot A represents Dataset 1 and Boxplot B represents Dataset 2.

(Another way that you might have matched up the datasets and boxplots is to observe that the values in the middle half, approximately, of Dataset 2 are more spread out than those in the middle half, approximately, of Dataset 1.)

(b) Each dataset in this part also has minimum value 0, maximum value 19 and median 9.5. However, Dataset 3 has lower quartile 2 and upper quartile 12, while Dataset 2 has lower quartile 7 and upper quartile 17, as shown below.

Dataset 3   0 1 2 3 9 10 11 12 13 19
            ↑   ↑   ↑   ↑   ↑
           Min Q1 Median Q3 Max

Dataset 4   0 6 7 8 9 10 16 17 18 19
            ↑   ↑   ↑   ↑   ↑
           Min Q1 Median Q3 Max

So Boxplot C represents Dataset 4 and Boxplot D represents Dataset 3.

The four correspondences are summarised below.

Dataset	1	2	3	4
Boxplot	A	B	D	C

Activity 6

The boxplot and its summary values are shown below.

Boxplot to show the distribution
of the baby weights
Source: MU123 Book A, Unit 4, Subsection 2.1

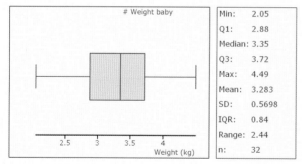

Min:	2.05
Q1:	2.88
Median:	3.35
Q3:	3.72
Max:	4.49
Mean:	3.283
SD:	0.5698
IQR:	0.84
Range:	2.44
n:	32

(a) As expected, the whiskers are longer than the two parts of the box.

(b) This indicates that the middle 50% of the weights are less spread out than the outer 50%. In other words, like most natural phenomena, the baby weights tend to bunch in the middle and are more sparse at the extremes.

Activity 7

(a) The median of the earnings is £400 (from Dataplotter), so the poverty threshold is 60% of £400, which is

$$0.6 \times £400 = £240.$$

(Notice that this is just greater than the value of the lower quartile, £230.)

Three people earn less than £240, so the number of people in poverty is 3.

The percentage of people in poverty is

$$\frac{3}{13} \times 100\% = 23\%$$

(to the nearest whole number).

(b) After the 25% pay rise across the board, the new median is £500, so the new poverty threshold is 60% of £500, which is

$$0.6 \times £500 = £300.$$

(Notice that this is still just greater than the new lower quartile value of £287.50.)

There are still three people earning less than the poverty threshold (those earning £200, £237.50 and £275), so the number of people in poverty is still 3.

Hence the percentage of people in poverty is also unchanged, at 23%.

So the 25% across-the-board rise has made no difference to the number of people in poverty.

(This is the principal reason why the proportion of people in poverty in the UK remained 'stubbornly' at one in five.)

(c) After the £100 pay rise across the board, the new median is again £500, so the new poverty threshold is 60% of £500, which is £300, as in part (b).

(Notice that this is now *less* than the new lower quartile value of £330.)

There are now only two people earning less than the poverty threshold (namely those earning £260 and £290); so the number of people in poverty is 2.

The percentage of people in poverty is

$$\frac{2}{13} \times 100\% = 15\%$$

(to the nearest whole number).

So the £100 across the board rise has had the effect of reducing the number of people in poverty.

Activity 8

(a) There are four data values in the interval 65–70.

(b) When the interval width is 10, there are two peaks, one at 50–60 and a smaller one at 70–80.

When the interval width is 2, there is a high peak at 70–72 and a smaller one at 52–60.

An interval width of 1 gives several peaks. The histogram is now considerably more 'spiky' than those with larger interval widths.

The interval width determines the number of intervals. A small interval width gives a large number of intervals and a spiky histogram.

Activity 9

The 'Weight end' histogram is shown below.

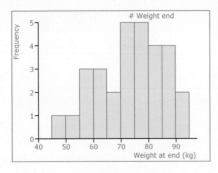

Histogram to show the distribution of the weights of 32 women at the end of their pregnancies
Source: MU123 Book A, Unit 4, Subsection 2.1

(a) In the '# Weight end' dataset, there are more high values than low values.

(Note also the change of scale – when just the 'Weight start' histogram was displayed, the scale on the horizontal axis extended up to 85 kg, but when both histograms are displayed, the scale on both horizontal axes extends up to 95 kg, to accommodate 'Weight end' data values up to 92.7 kg.)

(b) Comparing the two histograms shows that there has been an increase in weights during pregnancy. This is to be expected in healthy pregnancies!

(c) The values of the minimum, the lower quartile, the median, the upper quartile and the maximum are all higher for the 'Weight end' data than for the 'Weight start' data. This indicates that overall the weights increased during pregnancy. Also, both the range and the interquartile range are higher for the 'Weight end' data, indicating that there is more variation in the weights at the end of the pregnancies than in the weights at the start.

It is easier to use the boxplots to compare the datasets, as these charts are simpler and display five summary values. In contrast, the histograms give more details of the distributions.

Activity 10

(a) Histograms A and D each have only one data value in the interval from 0 to 5, so they match with Datasets 1 and 4. Histogram D has only one data value in the interval from 15 to 20, so it matches with Dataset 1, and so Histogram A matches with Dataset 4.

So Histograms B and C match with Datasets 2 and 3. Histogram B has only one data value in the interval from 15 to 20, so it matches with Dataset 3, and so Histogram C matches with Dataset 2.

(An alternative way to match up the datsets and histograms is to look at where the data are concentrated. For example, Histograms C and D are both symmetrical, with concentrations of data at the extremes for Histogram C and in the middle for Histogram D. These clues suggest that these histograms match with Datasets 2 and 1, respectively. Similarly, Histogram A shows a concentration of data in the top interval and Histogram B shows a concentration in the bottom interval, suggesting that these histograms match with Datasets 4 and 3, respectively.)

(b) The datasets match up with the histograms from this activity and the boxplots from Activity 5 as follows:

Dataset	1	2	3	4
Histogram	D	C	B	A
Boxplot	A	B	D	C

As you can see, the boxplots and histograms tell similar stories about the data. With boxplots, regions where the data are concentrated are represented by short whiskers and narrow box sections. On a histogram, these regions show up as having tall columns. For example, if the data values are concentrated in the middle, then the boxplot has a narrow central box and long whiskers (as in Boxplot A on page 14), while the corresponding histogram has tall columns in the middle (as in Histogram D).

General comparisons between histograms and boxplots are given in the main text.

Activity 11

(a) The article quotes the fact that there were three cases of child leukaemia in the Menai Strait area in the period 2000–03, and also uses data for the incidence of child leukaemia nationally in the UK, which gives an expected incidence of 0.1 cases in the Menai Strait area.

(It is not clear whether the article is referring to new cases over the period 2000–03, or all cases known during this period, including pre-existing ones.)

(b) By comparing the expected number of child leukaemia cases, which was close to 0.1, with the actual number of cases, which was 3, the article claimed a 28-fold increase over what was expected. Clearly it is impossible to have 0.1 of a case, so the '28-fold increase' is actually meaningless in this context. A related problem here is that the number of cases is really too small to enable any clear judgement to be made.

Activity 12

Here is a run of numbers that may be fairly typical of the sort of run that you might have written down.

Twenty made-up 'random' numbers:

4 1 9 0 6 3 2 7 8 3 4 6 5 9 3 2 0 8 5 7

Activity 13

Analysing the occurrences of pairs produces the following results.

There are no pairs of consecutive numbers the same in the made-up run.

As shown below, there are two pairs of consecutive numbers the same, and one triple of the same number, in the computer-generated run.

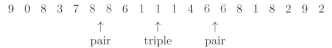

9 0 8 3 7 8 8 6 1 1 1 4 6 6 8 1 8 2 9 2

           ↑   ↑   ↑

       pair   triple   pair

Activity 14

If you did not avoid repetitions, well done for not imposing orderliness in this way!

Activity 15

A count of the numbers for each run produces the following results.

Number	Frequency in made-up run	Frequency in computer run
0	2	1
1	1	4
2	2	2
3	3	1
4	2	1
5	2	0
6	2	3
7	2	1
8	2	5
9	2	2

As can be seen from the table, the frequencies of the numbers generated by the computer vary from zero to five, but the frequencies of the made-up numbers vary only from one to three, with eight of the ten numbers having a frequency of two. So, in respect of their frequency of occurrence, the made-up numbers are much more orderly than the computer-generated numbers.

Activity 16

Again, if your frequencies varied quite widely, well done for not imposing orderliness in this way!

Activity 17

(a) The bar chart resulting from a simulation is shown below. (Yours will be different!)

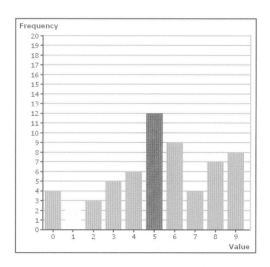

(b) There is considerable variation in the frequencies of the numbers depicted in the bar chart above. The number with the largest frequency is 5 (with a red bar), which occurred twelve times. The number with the smallest frequency is 1 (with a yellow bar), which occurred only twice. So the most frequent number occurred six times as often as the least frequent number.

Activity 18

(a) There is quite a wide variation in the possible ratios, as you'll see in part (b). So the ratio for your run might be substantially higher or lower than the value for the run shown in the solution to Activity 17, which was 6.

(b) The results of one set of ten runs are shown in the table below. (Your results are likely to be rather different.)

Run	Max. freq.	Min. freq.	Max/Min
1	11	3	3.67
2	11	3	3.67
3	11	4	2.75
4	8	3	2.67
5	9	4	2.25
6	13	1	13
7	8	3	2.67
8	11	1	11
9	10	2	5
10	9	3	3

In the ten runs whose results are shown in the table above, the maximum frequencies vary from 8 to 13 (the largest maximum frequency, 13, is marked in red). The minimum frequencies vary from 1 to 4 (the smallest minimum frequency, 1, is marked in yellow). The ratios of maximum frequency to minimum frequency vary from 2.25 to 13.

The results of the ten runs given in the table above seem to suggest that the run discussed in the solution to the previous activity (which had a maximum frequency of 12, a minimum frequency of 2, and hence a ratio of maximum frequency to minimum frequency of 6) is by no means atypical, and indeed runs with even greater variation in frequencies may occur.

Activity 19

(a)–(c) You should have observed that usually the more random numbers there are, the less variation there is in the heights of the bars, and the closer the ratio of maximum frequency to minimum frequency is to 1.

This illustrates that, as the number of random numbers is increased, the frequencies of the numbers tend to settle down and become approximately equal.

The bar charts below are fairly typical of what you will have observed for runs of 10 000 and 100 000 random numbers, respectively. In each case, the variation in the heights of the bars is small in comparison to the overall heights of the bars.

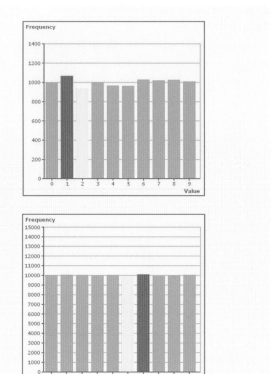

Activity 20

(a) On average, the number of cases that each town would expect to have in the year in question is

$$\frac{60}{6} = 10.$$

(b) To use the 'At random' software to generate 60 random numbers between 1 and 6, use the following settings:

Generate values between: 1 and 6

Number of values (per run): 60

Number of runs: 1

Each random number generated represents a case in one of the six towns. For example, an occurrence of the number 2 represents a case in Town 2. So the frequency of each number represents the number of cases in the corresponding town. There are sixty cases altogether, so sixty random numbers need to be generated.

(c) Comments on this part are given in the text.

Activity 21

(a) Cheating would be discovering the number on a card using sensory methods, that is, methods that don't require explanation in terms of ESP.

(b) Your suggestions might have included the following possibilities:

- If the cards look even slightly different from the back (perhaps a little smudged, or of marginally different sizes), then a subject might use that information. So you should ensure that the cards are exactly the same size, and their backs are identical and clean.

- A mirror in the room would obviously not be a good idea! But reflection from the table might also afford a possibility of cheating if it is glass topped. So you should make sure that there are no reflections that could give away the numbers on the cards.

- If you shuffle the cards in the sight of the subject, then someone who really wanted to cheat might be able to track the position of a particular card. So you may consider shuffling the cards behind a screen.

- Your own face may unintentionally give away some information, if you know what the card is at the time that the subject guesses. So you should ask the subject to make their guess before you look at the card yourself.

Activity 23

The screenshot below shows typical results for 100 runs of the simulation. Your dotplot is likely to be different.

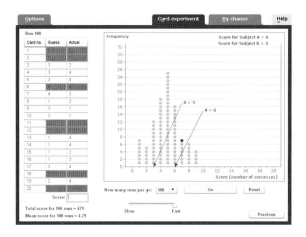

Activity 24

(a)–(b) What you are seeing is a series of repeats of the 100 simulations that you carried out in Activity 23, with each set of 100 scores represented by a bar chart rather than a dotplot. You will notice a fair amount of variation in the shape of the bar charts from one set of 100 scores to another. This is due to the fact that the number of scores is small (just 100), and random variation is strongly evident in the results. Typically, you should find that the scores range from around 1 to 11, with a concentration of scores at around 5.

(c) You should find that with 100 000 scores the amount of variation in the shape of the bar charts is much reduced. Also, typically you should find that the scores range from 0 to 13, with a concentration of scores at 5.

Activity 25

(c) You should have obtained the following percentages.

Score	Percentage of scores that are this high or higher (to 1 d.p.)
8	10.2%
9	4.1%
10	1.4%
11	0.4%
12	0.1%

(d) By the results of part (c), a score needs to be at least 9 to fall into the top 5% of scores. That is, the minimum score that would be regarded as showing evidence of ESP is 9.

(e) By the results of part (c), a score needs to be at least 11 to fall into the top 1% of scores. That is, the minimum score that would be regarded as showing evidence of ESP in this case is 11.

(The answers in parts (d) and (e) are the same as the answers based on just 100 scores on page 43, but this is just by luck! Some other sets of 100 scores would have given different results.)

Activity 26

(a) (i) In Activity 25(d) it was found that the 5% critical value is 9.

The solution to Activity 25(c) shows that approximately 4.1% of scores obtained simply by guessing will be 9 or more; that is, will lie in the 5% critical region.

So you would expect about 4.1% of subjects taking the test to achieve a score in the 5% critical region purely by chance.

(ii) The number of subjects taking the card-guessing test in a given presentation of MU123 is roughly

$$2000 \times 2 \times 0.90 = 3600.$$

So you would expect the number of subjects who achieve a score in the 5% critical region purely by chance to be approximately

$$3600 \times \frac{4.1}{100} \approx 148.$$

(b) (i) In Activity 25(e) it was found that the 1% critical value is 11.

The solution to Activity 25(c) shows that approximately 0.4% of scores obtained simply by guessing will be 11 or more; that is, will lie in the 1% critical region.

So you would expect about 0.4% of subjects taking the test to achieve a score in the 1% critical region purely by chance.

(ii) From part (a), the number of subjects taking the card-guessing test in a given presentation of MU123 is roughly 3600, so you would expect the number of subjects who achieve a score in the 1% critical region purely by chance to be approximately

$$3600 \times \frac{0.4}{100} \approx 14.$$

(You could check your answers to parts (a)(ii) and (b)(ii) by using the 'By chance' tab of the 'By chance alone' software to generate 3600 scores typical of those that might be obtained by guessing. You can do this by clicking 'Reset' and ticking 'Cumulate data', then generating three lots of 1000 scores followed by six lots of 100 scores. You can use the bar chart (or the percentage obtained by using 'Shade score') to see roughly how many of these scores are greater than or equal to 9, or greater than or equal to 11.)

(c) Probably neither the 5% criterion nor the 1% criterion is strict enough, as it is likely that with either of these criteria a reasonable number of subjects will achieve, purely by chance, a score good enough to be considered as evidence of ESP.

Activity 28

A sensible way to proceed with a subject who achieved a high score would be to ask him or her to take the test again several times. If he or she consistently maintained high scores, then and only then might you be looking for an explanation! You would want to consider explanations such as cheating, and whether you had carried out the experiment correctly, before concluding that your subject did indeed show evidence of ESP.

UNIT 12
Trigonometry

Introduction

In Unit 8 you met the idea of similar triangles, that is, triangles that are the same shape but not necessarily the same size. For example, similar triangles were used in Unit 8, Section 3, to find the height of a tree by using the length of its shadow.

Methods of using triangles to find unknown lengths and unknown angles have a long history, and the branch of mathematics that is concerned with such methods is called **trigonometry**.

The word trigonometry derives from the Greek words *trigon* for triangle and *metron* for measure.

Section 1 introduces the basic ideas of trigonometry, including the *sine*, *cosine* and *tangent* of an angle. Then these ideas are applied to problems that involve calculating unknown side lengths and unknown angles in right-angled triangles, a procedure known as *solving the triangle*.

Section 2 looks at the problem of solving triangles that do not necessarily have a right angle. This procedure has many applications in navigation, surveying and astronomy, and some of these applications are explored in this section, including estimating the speed of a glacier. Also in Section 2 the problem of finding the area of a triangle is revisited – how do you calculate the area if you know information other than the base and the height?

Section 3 is a change of direction. It turns out that the mathematics developed initially to solve triangles is also very useful in describing circular motion and other repetitive phenomena. Section 3 looks at this wider view of the use of trigonometry.

Radians are the default angle measure on many calculators and spreadsheets.

Finally, Section 4 introduces radians as an alternative to degrees as a measure of angles. You will see that, in a sense, radians are a more natural way to measure angles than degrees, and for this reason they are usually used in higher-level mathematics modules.

Activities 3, 8 and 32 on pages 63, 69 and 107, respectively, are in Section 3 of the MU123 Guide.

The MU123 Guide is needed for three of the activities in this unit.

1 Right-angled triangles

This section introduces the trigonometric ratios sine, cosine and tangent, and explains how they can be used in practical situations to solve geometric problems. Subsection 1.1 explains how the trigonometric ratios are defined and how you can find them using your calculator. Subsections 1.2 and 1.3 show you how these ratios can be used to find unknown lengths and unknown angles in right-angled triangles. In the final subsection you will see that for some special angles the trigonometric ratios can be calculated directly without using your calculator.

1.1 Sine, cosine and tangent

Let's start with a simple example of the kind of problem that can be solved by using trigonometry. In Unit 8 you saw a method for finding the height of a tall tree, which involved measuring the length of the shadow of the tree, and comparing it to the length of the shadow of a stick. However, there is another method, which can be used even if the sun isn't shining!

The idea is to walk a known distance away from the tree, and measure the angle θ from where you are standing to the top of the tree, as shown in Figure 1. An angle of this type, measured upwards from the horizontal, is called an **angle of elevation**, and it can be found by using a device called a *clinometer*, shown in Figure 2.

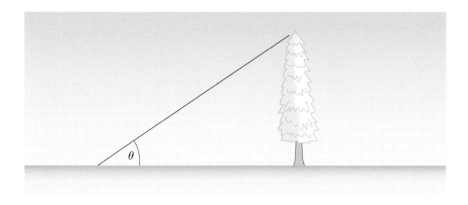

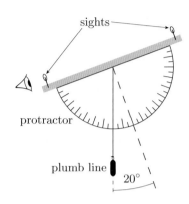

Figure I   The angle of elevation of a tree

Figure 2   A clinometer showing an angle of elevation of $20°$

Suppose that you walk 100 metres away from a particular tree, and the angle of elevation of the top of the tree from this distance turns out to be $20°$. The information that you know about the height of the tree is summarised in Figure 3. The vertical side of the right-angled triangle represents the tree, and the horizontal side represents the line between the foot of the tree and the point to which you walked. The lengths marked are in metres, with the height of the tree denoted by x.

For simplicity, it is assumed here that the angle is measured when the clinometer is on the ground and that the ground is horizontal.

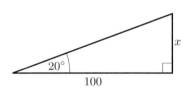

Figure 3   A diagram showing the information known about the height of the tree

The height of the tree can be worked out from this diagram, as it contains enough information for there to be only one answer for x. But how do you find x? This is where trigonometry comes in – it's all about the relationships between lengths and angles.

So let's look at the basic ideas of trigonometry, and then we'll come back to the problem of finding the height of the tree, and use trigonometry to solve it.

Basic trigonometry is all about the relationships between the lengths of the sides and the angles within right-angled triangles. As an illustration, consider the right-angled triangle shown in Figure 4 (overleaf). It has two acute angles as well as the right angle, and we will choose to focus on just one of these acute angles, the one marked θ in the diagram.

Remember that an *acute* angle is one between $0°$ and $90°$ (exclusive).

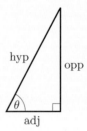

Figure 4   A right-angled triangle with chosen angle θ

One of the sides of the triangle is the hypotenuse (the side opposite the right angle), and you can distinguish the other two sides by using the fact that one of them is **opposite** the chosen angle θ, while the other is **adjacent** to it. The sides of the triangle have been marked hyp, opp and adj accordingly, for 'hypotenuse', 'opposite' and 'adjacent'.

Now look at Figure 5, which shows three triangles similar to the triangle in Figure 4. So all four triangles have the same three angles. The sides of these triangles are also marked hyp, opp and adj in relation to the angle θ.

Remember that *similar* triangles are the same shape but not necessarily the same size. So saying that two triangles are similar is the same as saying that one is a scaled (and possibly flipped) version of the other.

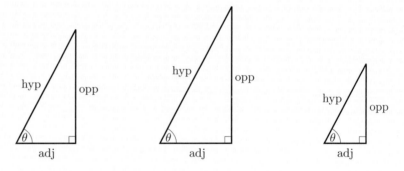

Figure 5   Three right-angled triangles similar to the triangle in Figure 4

The crucial fact which forms the foundation of trigonometry is that if you find the ratio of the lengths of two sides of a triangle and also the ratio of the lengths of the corresponding two sides of a similar triangle, then you get the same answer in each case. This fact applies to all similar triangles, not just right-angled ones, and it is illustrated by Figure 6. This figure shows a triangle with sides of lengths a, b and c, and a second, scaled triangle in which the side lengths are multiplied by the scale factor k. The ratio of the left slant side to the right slant side in the first triangle is b/c, and the ratio of the corresponding two sides in the second triangle is $(kb)/(kc)$, which is equal to b/c. So scaling a triangle does not affect the ratio of the lengths of any two of its sides.

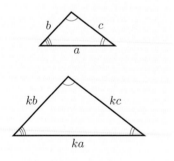

Figure 6   Two similar triangles

This means that for each of the triangles in Figures 4 and 5, the ratio of the lengths of the opposite and adjacent sides, that is

$$\frac{\text{opp}}{\text{adj}},$$

has the same value. And the same is true for the ratios of the lengths of the other pairs of sides,

$$\frac{\text{opp}}{\text{hyp}} \quad \text{and} \quad \frac{\text{adj}}{\text{hyp}}.$$

These three ratios are the key to solving problems involving the relationships between lengths and angles, and they are given the special names below.

Trigonometric ratios

Suppose that θ is an acute angle in a right-angled triangle in which the lengths of the hypotenuse, opposite and adjacent sides are represented by hyp, opp and adj, respectively, as in Figure 4.

The **sine** of the angle θ is

$$\sin \theta = \frac{\text{opp}}{\text{hyp}}.$$

The **cosine** of the angle θ is

$$\cos \theta = \frac{\text{adj}}{\text{hyp}}.$$

The **tangent** of the angle θ is

$$\tan \theta = \frac{\text{opp}}{\text{adj}}.$$

These expressions are read as:

> sine *thee*-ta,
> cos *thee*-ta,
> tan *thee*-ta.

A popular method of remembering these definitions is to take the initial letters from

Sine = Opp/Hyp,   Cosine = Adj/Hyp,   Tangent = Opp/Adj,

to make the acronym

SOH CAH TOA.

This acronym is read to rhyme with Krakatoa.

This acronym tells you the sides used in each ratio, and which side is divided by which. For example, SOH tells you that to find the sine of an angle in a right-angled triangle, you divide the length of the opposite side by the length of the hypotenuse.

Remember that in practical problems the lengths must be measured in the same units.

The sine, cosine and tangent of an acute angle θ each depend only on the size of the angle θ, and not on the particular right-angled triangle that θ is in – as you have seen, these values are the same for all such right-angled triangles. You can find the approximate values of the sine, cosine and tangent of any acute angle by drawing a suitable right-angled triangle and measuring its sides. For example, Figure 7 shows a right-angled triangle with an acute angle of 34°. This is an accurate scale drawing, and if you measure the sides then you will find that they are approximately 3.5 cm, 5.2 cm and 6.3 cm, as marked. The sides have also been marked opp, adj and hyp in relation to the angle of 34°.

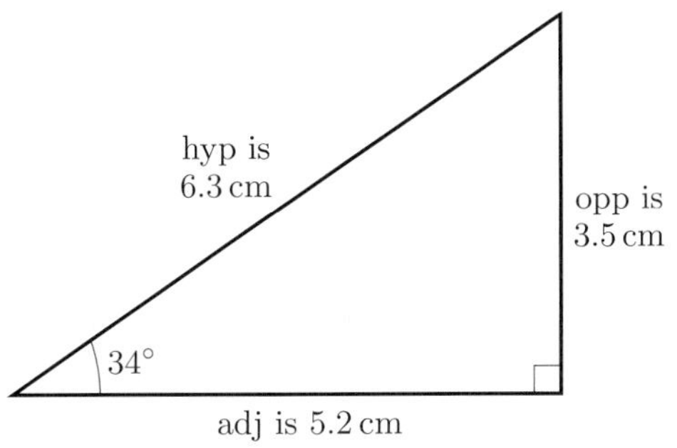

hyp is 6.3 cm

opp is 3.5 cm

34°

adj is 5.2 cm

Figure 7   A right-angled triangle with an angle of 34°

If you apply the definitions of sin, cos and tan to the triangle in Figure 7 (using the acronym SOH CAH TOA to help you remember them), then you obtain

$$\sin 34° = \frac{\text{opp}}{\text{hyp}} \approx \frac{3.5}{6.3} \approx 0.56,$$

$$\cos 34° = \frac{\text{adj}}{\text{hyp}} \approx \frac{5.2}{6.3} \approx 0.83,$$

$$\tan 34° = \frac{\text{opp}}{\text{adj}} \approx \frac{3.5}{5.2} \approx 0.67.$$

In the activity below, you are asked to find approximate values for the sine, cosine and tangent of the angle 20°.

Activity 1   Finding approximate values for trigonometric ratios

The diagram below shows a right-angled triangle with an acute angle of 20° and one side of length 10 cm.

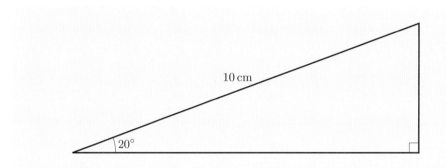

(a) Mark the sides of the triangle as opp, adj and hyp in relation to the angle 20°.

(b) By measuring the side lengths to the nearest millimetre, find the approximate values of sin 20°, cos 20° and tan 20°.

Because the longest side of any right-angled triangle is the hypotenuse, the opposite and adjacent side lengths are always less than the length of the hypotenuse. Thus the sine and cosine of an acute angle are always less than 1. However, the tangent of an acute angle can be less than 1 (as it is for 34° and 20°), or equal to 1, or greater than 1.

You are now ready to return to the problem of finding the height of the tree. The value of tan 20° that you found in Activity 1 can be used to solve this problem, at least approximately. The diagram giving the known information about the height of the tree is repeated in Figure 8, with the sides labelled opp, adj and hyp in relation to the angle of 20°. The lengths are in metres.

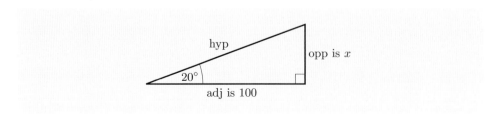

Figure 8   The diagram for the tree height problem

From this diagram,

$$\tan 20° = \frac{\text{opp}}{\text{adj}} = \frac{x}{100}.$$

But you already know the approximate value of $\tan 20°$, from Activity 1. So

$$\frac{x}{100} \approx \text{the value for } \tan 20° \text{ found in Activity 1.} \qquad (1)$$

In the activity below you are asked to use this equation to find the approximate height of the tree.

Activity 2 *Finding an approximate answer to the tree height problem*

Use equation (1) and the approximate value for $\tan 20°$ found in Activity 1 to find the approximate height of the tree.

Although approximate values for the trigonometric ratios of different angles can be obtained by drawing and measuring right-angled triangles, in practice it is much quicker to obtain accurate sine, cosine and tangent values from a calculator or computer. The next activity shows you how to do this.

Activity 3 *Trigonometric ratios on your calculator*

This activity is in Subsection 3.7 of the MU123 Guide.

For centuries, values of sines, cosines and tangents of acute angles were available only in mathematical tables, such as those shown in Figure 9.

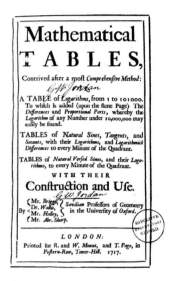

Figure 9 The title page of an eighteenth-century book of mathematical tables

Arguably the earliest table of trigonometric values is the table of lengths of chords in a circle in Claudius Ptolemy's *Almagest*, a book on mathematical astronomy, written in about AD 150 and known to us through later Arabic translations. In the *Almagest*, Ptolemy tabulated the lengths of the sides of many right-angled triangles, taking the hypotenuse to be of length 60.

Ptolemy's work became widely known in Europe after the publication in 1496 of the *Epitome of the Almagest*, by the German astronomers Georg Peurbach and Johannes Müller von Königsberg, known as Regiomontanus; for example, it was used by Copernicus and Galileo.

The first person to relate sines and cosines directly to angles in a triangle as we do today was the Austrian astronomer and mathematician Georg Joachim Rheticus, in his pamphlet *Canon doctrinae triangulorum* of 1551. Rheticus' masterwork, his immense *Opus palatinum de triangulis* of 1596, which ran to some 1500 pages, contained tables calculated to ten decimal places, which were of such accuracy that they were considered the standard until the early twentieth century.

The word *sine* has its origins in Sanskrit, coming to us through Arabic and Latin. The Latin word *sinus* appeared in European mathematics texts in the twelfth century.

In the next two subsections you will use sine, cosine and tangent values obtained from your calculator to solve problems involving right-angled triangles.

1.2 Finding unknown lengths

The following example shows you how to use the trigonometric ratios to find unknown lengths in two right-angled triangles.

Tutorial clip

Example 1   *Finding unknown lengths*

Find the lengths x and y in the triangles below, to three significant figures.

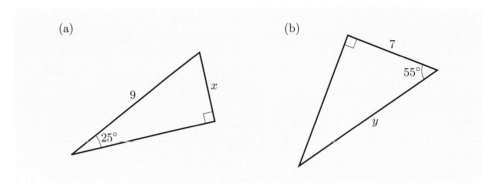

Solution

(a)   Label the sides of the triangle in relation to the given angle.

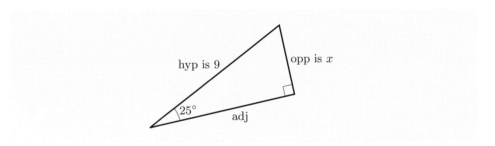

Use SOH CAH TOA. The unknown side x is opposite the angle of $25°$, and the known side is the hypotenuse, so the appropriate trigonometric ratio is sine.

From the diagram,

$$\sin 25° = \frac{\text{opp}}{\text{hyp}} = \frac{x}{9}, \quad \text{so} \quad x = 9\sin 25°.$$

A calculator gives $\sin 25° = 0.422\,618\ldots$, so

$$x = 9\sin 25° = 9 \times 0.422\ldots = 3.803\ldots.$$

Hence $x = 3.80$ (to 3 s.f.).

(b)

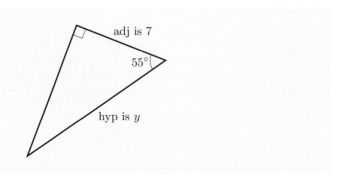

From the diagram,

$$\cos 55° = \frac{\text{adj}}{\text{hyp}} = \frac{7}{y}, \quad \text{so} \quad y\cos 55° = 7.$$

This gives

$$y = \frac{7}{\cos 55°} = 12.204\dots.$$

Hence $y = 12.2$ (to 3 s.f.).

As a check, notice that the value of y is greater than 7, as you would expect since y is the length of the hypotenuse.

Here are some similar questions for you to try. In each of them, you may find it helpful to draw your own diagram of the triangle, showing which sides are the opposite, adjacent and hypotenuse, as was done in Example 1.

Activity 4   *Finding unknown lengths*

For each of the following triangles, calculate the unknown length x to three significant figures.

(a)

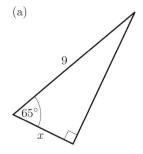

(b)

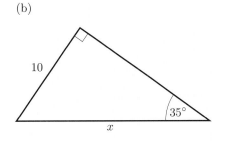

(c)

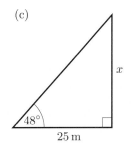

The triangle in part (a) is congruent to the triangle in Example 1(a). This illustrates that you can sometimes choose to use either sine or cosine to solve a problem.

In many geometric problems, drawing a clear diagram helps you to see how the problem can be solved. This is illustrated in the next example, which asks you to calculate the height of a kite above the ground.

Example 2   *Finding the height of a kite*

A child is flying a kite and holds the end of the string at a height of 0.9 metres above the ground. The length of the string is 55 metres. The string is taut and makes an angle of 70° with the horizontal, as shown in the figure below.

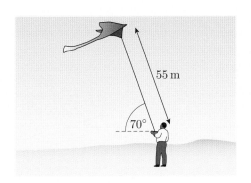

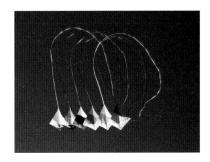

Figure 10   Stunt kites

(a) Calculate the height of the kite above the child's hand.

(b) Hence calculate the height of the kite above the ground.

Give your answers to the nearest 10 cm.

Solution

💭 Draw a diagram, mark the known measurements, and decide which lengths you need to find. 💭

This diagram is not to scale.

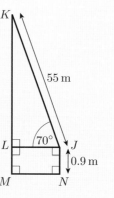

(a) The height of the kite above the child's hand is represented by the line segment KL. Now $\triangle KJL$ is a right-angled triangle, in which

$$\sin 70° = \frac{KL}{55}, \quad \text{so} \quad KL = 55 \sin 70° = 51.68\ldots.$$

Thus the height of the kite above the child's hand is 51.7 m (to the nearest 10 cm).

(b) From the diagram, the height of the kite above the ground is $KM = KL + LM$. So, by part (a),

$$KM = 51.68\ldots + 0.9 = 52.58\ldots.$$

Therefore the height of the kite above the ground is 52.6 m (to the nearest 10 cm).

The trigonometric ratios apply only to right-angled triangles. So sometimes you need to add construction lines to your diagram to form right-angled triangles before using these ratios, as illustrated in the next activity.

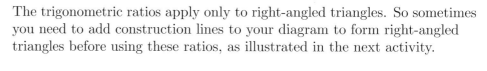

Activity 5   *Designing a herb garden*

Diagram (a) at the top of the next page shows a design for a herb garden in a wooden frame shaped like a regular pentagon. The struts from the centre of the pentagon to its vertices are each of length 1.5 m.

Diagram (b) shows one triangular section of the wooden frame with some of the measurements marked. Vertex A of the triangle corresponds to the centre of the pentagon, and B and C are vertices of the pentagon. A construction line AD has been added to split $\triangle ABC$ into two right-angled triangles.

Couldn't we just put a nice lawn here instead?

(a)

(b)

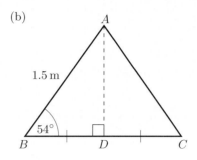

From Unit 8, each interior angle of a regular pentagon is 108°, so $\angle ABD = \frac{1}{2} \times 108° = 54°$.

What length of wood is needed for the edge labelled BC, correct to the nearest millimetre?

Trigonometric ratios can be useful in calculations involving the locations of objects such as ships or planes. Often the location of such an object is given by:

- the distance of the object from some known point;
- the direction of the object from the known point, measured as a **bearing**, that is, the number of degrees west or east of the north or south direction.

For example, Figure 11 shows a point B specified as 5 km from a point A in the direction 35° east of south of A. This direction is written concisely as S 35°E of A.

However, it can be more useful to specify how far north or south and how far east or west a point is from a known point. You can use the trigonometric ratios to calculate these distances, as in the following example.

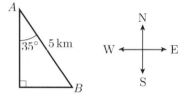

Figure 11 A point B that is 5 km in the direction 35° east of south of a point A

Figure 12 The dial of a compass used for navigation

Example 3 *Using bearings*

A ship is 10 km in the direction 30° west of north from a lighthouse. Calculate how many kilometres west and how many kilometres north the ship is from the lighthouse, correct to one decimal place.

Solution

Q First draw a diagram and label the unknown lengths. ☁

In the diagram, the point A represents the lighthouse and the point B represents the ship.

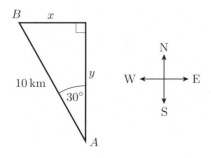

The hypotenuse of the right-angled triangle has length 10 km.

The distance x km that B lies to the west of A is the length of the side opposite the angle of 30°. Thus

$$\sin 30° = \frac{x}{10}, \quad \text{so} \quad x = 10 \sin 30° = 5.$$

Hence the ship is 5.0 km west of the lighthouse (correct to 1 d.p.).

Similarly, the distance that B lies to the north of A is the length y of the side adjacent to the angle of 30°. Thus

$$\cos 30° = \frac{y}{10}, \quad \text{so} \quad y = 10 \cos 30° = 8.66\ldots.$$

Hence the ship is 8.7 km north of the lighthouse (correct to 1 d.p.).

You can apply the same method to the following problem.

Activity 6 *Using bearings*

A plane travels a distance of 100 km in the direction 20° east of north. Calculate how far north it is from its starting position, to the nearest kilometre.

The solutions to the activities and examples in this subsection have depended on choosing the most appropriate trigonometric ratio to use. The next activity gives you some further practice in identifying these ratios.

Activity 7 *Choosing which trigonometric ratio to use*

For each of the following triangles, calculate the lengths x and y to three significant figures.

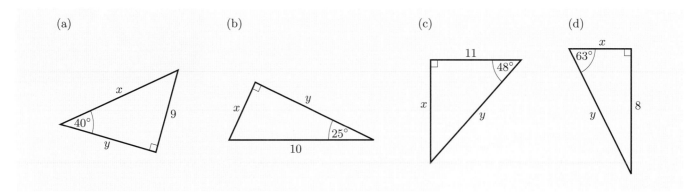

In each part of Activity 7, once you had found one of the unknown sides, you could have used Pythagoras' Theorem to find the other unknown side, instead of a second trigonometric ratio. However, it is usually better to use the values that you have been given, rather than values that you have calculated, in case you have made a numerical slip.

In this subsection you have seen how the three trigonometric ratios sine, cosine and tangent are defined in a right-angled triangle, and you have used these ratios to find unknown lengths in both practical and abstract problems. In the next subsection you will see how to use these ratios to find unknown angles.

1.3   Finding unknown angles

Not all problems involving triangles are to find an unknown length. Sometimes you want to find the size of an angle. For example, consider the diagram in Figure 13.

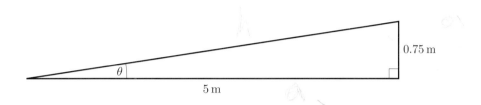

Figure 13   The angle of a ramp

This shows a ramp that extends over a length of 5 m, reaching a height of 0.75 m at its raised end. Suppose that you want to know the size of the angle θ, for example to determine whether the ramp is suitable for wheelchair users.

You can see from Figure 13 that the angle θ satisfies

$$\tan \theta = \frac{0.75}{5} = 0.15.$$

So the problem now is to find the angle θ whose tangent is 0.15.

If you know the tangent of an acute angle (or the sine or cosine of the angle), then you can use your calculator to find the angle. The notation used for the acute angle whose tangent is the number x is

$$\tan^{-1}(x).$$

Similarly, the notations used for the acute angle whose sine is x and for the acute angle whose cosine is x are

$$\sin^{-1}(x) \quad \text{and} \quad \cos^{-1}(x),$$

respectively.

Note that $\tan^{-1}(x)$ is not the same as $(\tan x)^{-1}$, which equals $1/\tan x$, and similar comments apply to $\sin^{-1}(x)$ and $\cos^{-1}(x)$.

The angles $\sin^{-1}(x)$, $\cos^{-1}(x)$ and $\tan^{-1}(x)$ are called the **inverse sine**, **inverse cosine** and **inverse tangent** of x, respectively. You will see in the next activity how to use your calculator to find such angles. For the wheelchair ramp problem, a calculator gives

$$\theta = \tan^{-1}(0.15) = 8.5° \text{ (to 2 s.f.)}.$$

So the ramp is at an angle of about 8.5°.

The next activity shows you how to find angles from trigonometric ratios using your calculator.

The expression $\tan^{-1}(x)$ is read as 'tan to the minus 1 of x' or as 'the inverse tangent of x'.

The inverse sine, inverse cosine and inverse tangent of x are also called the **arcsine**, **arccosine** and **arctangent** of x, with the alternative notations:
$$\arcsin(x) = \sin^{-1}(x),$$
$$\arccos(x) = \cos^{-1}(x)$$
and
$$\arctan(x) = \tan^{-1}(x).$$

Activity 8   *Finding angles from trigonometric ratios*

This activity is in Subsection 3.8 of the MU123 Guide.

Tutorial clip

The following example shows you how to find unknown angles in a right-angled triangle.

Example 4 *Finding unknown angles*

For each of the triangles below, find the angle θ to the nearest degree.

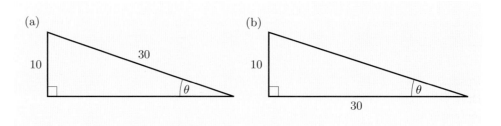

(a) (b)

Solution

(a) Here you know the length of the hypotenuse and the length of the side opposite the unknown angle.

In this triangle,
$$\sin \theta = \frac{10}{30} = \frac{1}{3}.$$

So θ is the acute angle whose sine is $\frac{1}{3}$.

Hence
$$\theta = \sin^{-1}\left(\tfrac{1}{3}\right).$$

A calculator gives $\sin^{-1}\left(\tfrac{1}{3}\right) = 19.471\ldots°$, so $\theta = 19°$ (to the nearest degree).

(b) Here you know the length of the side opposite the unknown angle and the length of the side adjacent to this angle.

In this triangle,
$$\tan \theta = \frac{10}{30} = \frac{1}{3}.$$

Hence
$$\theta = \tan^{-1}\left(\tfrac{1}{3}\right).$$

A calculator gives $\tan^{-1}\left(\tfrac{1}{3}\right) = 18.434\ldots°$, so $\theta = 18°$ (to the nearest degree).

Here are some similar questions for you to try.

Activity 9 *Finding unknown angles*

For each of the following triangles, find the labelled angle to the nearest degree.

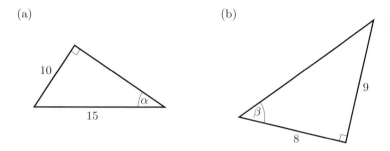

Practical problems often require you to use some of the geometric results that you met in Unit 8, as well as the trigonometric ratios, as the next example shows. This example also illustrates that it is important to convert all length measurements to the same unit before using trigonometric ratios.

Example 5 *Finding a glide angle*

In a hang-gliding competition, participants have to fly a horizontal distance of 3 km from a height of 300 m and land on a target. The glide angle is the angle between the horizontal and the downward path of the glider. If it is assumed that the glide angle is constant throughout the flight, what angle is required if the participant is to land at the target?

Solution

Convert the length measurements to the same unit and mark these on a clear diagram. Give the unknown angle a variable name. Do the same for other angles, where this is helpful.

In the diagram, the glider takes off from A and aims to land at B. The horizontal distance to be travelled is 3000 m and the vertical distance to descend is 300 m. The required glide angle is denoted by α and the angle at B is denoted by β.

Figure 14 Hang gliding

Use geometric results and trigonometry to find the required angle.

The angles α and β are equal, since they are alternate angles between two horizontal lines.

From the diagram, $\tan \beta = \dfrac{\text{opp}}{\text{adj}} = \dfrac{300}{3000} = 0.1$.

Hence $\beta = \tan^{-1}(0.1) = 5.71 \ldots °$.

So the required glide angle α is about $6°$.

The next activity also involves calculating an angle, and then interpreting the result.

Figure 15   An avalanche on a snowy mountainside

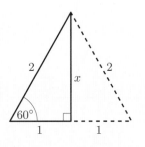

Figure 16   Dividing an equilateral triangle in half

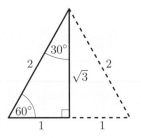

Figure 17   Height of an equilateral triangle

Activity 10   *Checking for an avalanche*

From a map, a skier knows that a hillside rises steadily through a vertical height of 150 m over a horizontal distance of 175 m. There is an avalanche risk if the slope of the snow is between 35° and 45°.

If it is assumed that the hillside is covered with a uniform layer of snow, is there an avalanche risk?

1.4   Useful trigonometric ratios and identities

In this subsection, you will see how the trigonometric ratios for the angles 30°, 45° and 60° can be worked out directly, without using your calculator. These values are quite memorable and useful to know. They can be calculated from triangles in which these angles occur.

For example, in an equilateral triangle, the interior angles are each 60°. Figure 16 shows an equilateral triangle with sides of length 2 units, in which a vertical line divides the base of the triangle into two equal parts, each of length 1. (Choosing the equilateral triangle to have sides of length 2 makes the calculations easier.)

From the right-angled triangle on the left-hand side of the equilateral triangle you can see that

$$\cos 60° = \frac{1}{2}.$$

The length, x, of the third side of this right-angled triangle can be calculated by using Pythagoras' Theorem:

$$1^2 + x^2 = 2^2, \quad \text{so} \quad x^2 = 4 - 1 = 3.$$

Hence $x = \sqrt{3}$ units, as shown in Figure 17. Since the side opposite the angle 60° is of length $\sqrt{3}$,

$$\sin 60° = \frac{\sqrt{3}}{2} \quad \text{and} \quad \tan 60° = \frac{\sqrt{3}}{1} = \sqrt{3}.$$

The right-angled triangle in Figure 17 can also be used to find the trigonometric ratios for 30°, the third angle in the triangle. You can see that the ratios are as follows:

$$\sin 30° = \frac{1}{2}, \quad \cos 30° = \frac{\sqrt{3}}{2} \quad \text{and} \quad \tan 30° = \frac{1}{\sqrt{3}}.$$

You can find the trigonometric ratios for the angle 45° by using a right-angled isosceles triangle in a similar way, in the next activity.

Activity 11   *Finding the sine, cosine and tangent of 45°*

For the triangle below, find the length x by using Pythagoras' Theorem, and then calculate $\sin 45°$, $\cos 45°$ and $\tan 45°$.

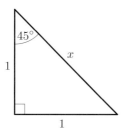

The trigonometric ratios for the angles 30°, 45° and 60° are used frequently, so they are listed in Table 1. If you study mathematics further, then you will find it useful to remember these values, or remember how to find them from the particular triangles discussed in this subsection.

There are various relationships between sines, cosines and tangents of angles. These relationships can help you to remember the values in Table 1, and they are often helpful in other ways.

In the next activity you will find two such relationships.

Table 1   Sine, cosine and tangent of special angles

θ	$\sin\theta$	$\cos\theta$	$\tan\theta$
30°	$\frac{1}{2}$	$\frac{\sqrt{3}}{2}$	$\frac{1}{\sqrt{3}}$
45°	$\frac{1}{\sqrt{2}}$	$\frac{1}{\sqrt{2}}$	1
60°	$\frac{\sqrt{3}}{2}$	$\frac{1}{2}$	$\sqrt{3}$

Activity 12   *Finding relationships between sines and cosines*

The diagram below shows a general right-angled triangle. Since its two acute angles add up to 90°, one is marked θ and the other is marked $90° - \theta$.

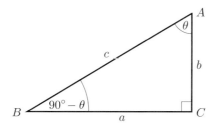

(a) Write down expressions for $\sin\theta$, $\cos\theta$, $\sin(90° - \theta)$ and $\cos(90° - \theta)$, in terms of the side lengths a, b and c.

(b) Use the results of part (a) to show that if θ is an acute angle, then

$$\cos\theta = \sin(90° - \theta) \quad \text{and} \quad \sin\theta = \cos(90° - \theta).$$

In Activity 12 you were asked to prove the following two results.

$$\cos\theta = \sin(90° - \theta)$$
$$\sin\theta = \cos(90° - \theta)$$

These equations are examples of *identities*, as they are true for every acute angle θ. They tell you that if two angles add up to 90°, then the sine of one angle is the cosine of the other, and vice-versa. For example,

$$\cos 30° = \sin 60°, \quad \cos 45° = \sin 45° \quad \text{and} \quad \cos 60° = \sin 30°.$$

This explains the repeated values that you can see in the sine and cosine columns of Table 1.

You can obtain another useful identity from the definitions of sine, cosine and tangent. The definitions are

$$\sin\theta = \frac{\text{opp}}{\text{hyp}}, \quad \cos\theta = \frac{\text{adj}}{\text{hyp}} \quad \text{and} \quad \tan\theta = \frac{\text{opp}}{\text{adj}}.$$

From these equations you can see that

$$\frac{\sin\theta}{\cos\theta} = \frac{\dfrac{\text{opp}}{\text{hyp}}}{\dfrac{\text{adj}}{\text{hyp}}} = \frac{\text{opp}}{\text{hyp}} \times \frac{\text{hyp}}{\text{adj}} = \frac{\text{opp}}{\text{adj}} = \tan\theta,$$

which gives the identity below.

$$\tan\theta = \frac{\sin\theta}{\cos\theta}$$

You might like to check this identity for some of the values in Table 1.

Finally, a very neat identity can be obtained by considering a right-angled triangle whose hypotenuse has length 1, as shown in Figure 18, and using Pythagoras' Theorem. In this triangle,

$$\sin\theta = \frac{\text{opp}}{\text{hyp}} = \frac{\text{opp}}{1} = \text{opp} \quad \text{and} \quad \cos\theta = \frac{\text{adj}}{\text{hyp}} = \frac{\text{adj}}{1} = \text{adj}.$$

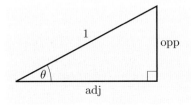

Figure 18 A right-angled triangle with hypotenuse of length 1

Thus, by Pythagoras' Theorem,

$$(\sin\theta)^2 + (\cos\theta)^2 = 1^2 = 1.$$

It is conventional to write $(\sin\theta)^2$ and $(\cos\theta)^2$ as $\sin^2\theta$ and $\cos^2\theta$, so the identity above is usually written as follows.

$$\sin^2\theta + \cos^2\theta = 1$$

Again, you might like to check this identity for some of the values in Table 1.

In Section 3 you will see that $\sin\theta$, $\cos\theta$ and $\tan\theta$ can also be defined for angles other than acute angles, and the identities above also hold for such angles.

2 Solving general triangles

There are many practical activities, such as surveying, navigating and designing buildings, where calculating unknown side lengths and angles in triangles is important. The process of finding some or all of the unknown side lengths or angles in a triangle is known as **solving the triangle**.

In Section 1 you saw how to solve a right-angled triangle. This section extends those ideas and explains how to solve triangles that do not necessarily have a right angle, and also how to find the area of a triangle when the height is not known. It considers only acute-angled triangles – an **acute-angled triangle** is one in which all three angles are acute. But you will see in Section 3 that the same techniques can also be used for triangles that have an obtuse angle.

As an illustration of the kind of problem that can be solved by finding lengths and angles in triangles, you will see how to use the techniques in this section to estimate how fast a glacier is moving. This problem was investigated in the television series *Rough Science*. The scientists on the programme were challenged to estimate the speed at which the Franz Josef glacier in New Zealand (Figure 19) was moving, and you can see how they tackled the problem in the next activity.

Figure 19 The Franz Josef glacier

Activity 13 *Learning about the speed of a glacier*

Watch the excerpt from the television programme *Rough Science* to see how the scientists estimated the speed of the glacier.

Video

The video is on the DVD.

The *Rough Science* programmes were made by the BBC on behalf of The Open University.

In the video you saw that the scientists took the following steps to find the speed of the glacier.

- First they made a large protractor to measure angles to a precision of 0.1°, as shown in Figure 20.

- Then they placed a flag on the glacier, shown in Figure 21, and marked two points 50 m apart on the mountain along the edge of the glacier, near the flag.

- The angles from each point to the flag were measured on consecutive days with the large protractor. This pinpointed the position of the flag on each day.

- Finally, they used the angle measurements, a scale diagram and trigonometry to estimate how far the glacier had moved in a day.

Figure 20 Using the large protractor

In this section you will see how to solve the glacier problem, using two important trigonometric rules for finding unknown side lengths and angles in general triangles, known as the *Sine Rule* and the *Cosine Rule*.

You will learn about these rules in the next two subsections, and in the third subsection you will see how to apply them to find the speed of the glacier.

Figure 21 The flag on the glacier

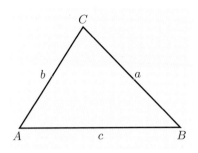

Figure 22   How to label a general triangle

2.1   The Sine Rule

In this subsection and the next you will meet rules that relate the angles and side lengths of any triangle. These rules are most easily stated using the notation shown in Figure 22. Here the vertices of a triangle are labelled A, B and C. The side lengths are labelled a, b and c in such a way that vertex A is opposite side length a, vertex B is opposite side length b, and vertex C is opposite side length c. The angles at vertices A, B and C can be denoted by $\angle A$, $\angle B$ and $\angle C$, or just by A, B and C.

The notation in Figure 22 is often used for a general triangle, as it helps you to remember which angle is related to which side, and it also makes the resulting formulas easier to remember. It will be used throughout this unit.

In Section 1 you saw how to solve right-angled triangles by using the trigonometric ratios sine, cosine and tangent, and in Unit 8 you saw that one way of making geometric problems easier to solve is to draw construction lines. So if you are trying to find a relationship between the sides and angles of the general triangle in Figure 22, then one approach is to draw a construction line to introduce right-angled triangles and use some of the facts that you already know about these.

Figure 23 shows a general triangle with three acute angles. A construction line has been drawn from C at right angles to the opposite side. A line like this, drawn at right angles to another line, is called a **perpendicular** and the process of drawing such a line is called **dropping a perpendicular**.

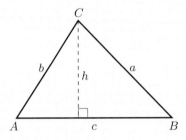

Figure 23   A general triangle with a perpendicular added

Let h be the length of the perpendicular. In the left-hand triangle you can use the fact that sine is opposite over hypotenuse to give

In this formula, A is short for $\angle A$.

$$\sin A = \frac{h}{b}, \quad \text{so} \quad h = b \sin A.$$

In the right-hand triangle you can get a similar expression for the sine of the angle B:

$$\sin B = \frac{h}{a}, \quad \text{so} \quad h = a \sin B.$$

The two expressions above for h are equal, so

$$b \sin A = a \sin B.$$

This equation can be rearranged to give the equation

$$\frac{a}{\sin A} = \frac{b}{\sin B}.$$

In a similar way, if you drop a perpendicular from the vertex A to the opposite side of the triangle, then you can show that

$$\frac{b}{\sin B} = \frac{c}{\sin C}.$$

Combining this equation with the one above gives the following rule.

Sine Rule

$$\frac{a}{\sin A} = \frac{b}{\sin B} = \frac{c}{\sin C}$$

or, equivalently,

$$\frac{\sin A}{a} = \frac{\sin B}{b} = \frac{\sin C}{c}$$

The second form of the Sine Rule is obtained from the first by taking reciprocals of each of the fractions.

The Sine Rule tells you that the ratio of a side length of a triangle to the sine of the angle opposite that side is the same no matter which side and its opposite angle you consider. So it can be used in the following way.

The Sine Rule was first given a systematic treatment by the thirteenth-century Persian mathematician and polymath Nasir al-Din al-Tusi, who was also one of the first people to treat trigonometry as a separate subject rather than as part of astronomy.

Using the Sine Rule

The Sine Rule can be used if you know one side length of a triangle and the opposite angle, and one further angle or side length.

For example, if you know the length a and the opposite angle A, and also the angle B, then you can find the length b by using the first equation in the Sine Rule,

$$\frac{a}{\sin A} = \frac{b}{\sin B},$$

and rearranging this equation to make b the subject.

The next two examples illustrate how this can be done.

Example 6 *Using the Sine Rule to find a side length*

Find the length of the side BC in the triangle below, to two significant figures.

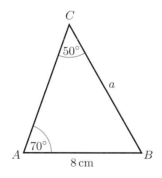

Solution

A side length and the opposite angle are known, together with one further angle, so the Sine Rule can be used.

The side AB of length 8 cm is opposite the 50° angle at C, so $c = 8$ and $C = 50°$. Also the side BC of unknown length is opposite the 70° angle at A, so the unknown length is a and $A = 70°$.

By the Sine Rule,
$$\frac{a}{\sin A} = \frac{c}{\sin C},$$
which gives
$$\frac{a}{\sin 70°} = \frac{8}{\sin 50°}, \quad \text{so} \quad a = \frac{8\sin 70°}{\sin 50°} = 9.813\ldots.$$
Hence the length BC is $9.8\,\text{cm}$ (to 2 s.f.).

In Example 6, the vertices and the sides were labelled as they are in the statement of the Sine Rule, and you may find it helpful to label your triangles in a similar way while you become familiar with the Sine Rule. When you feel confident using the Sine Rule, you can apply it directly without this labelling, as shown in the next example.

Tutorial clip

Example 7   *Using the Sine Rule without vertex labels*

Find the length x in the triangle below, to three significant figures.

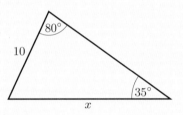

Solution

💭 A side length and the opposite angle are known, so the Sine Rule can be used. The side length 10 is opposite the angle of $35°$, and the unknown side length x is opposite the angle of $80°$. 💭

By the Sine Rule,
$$\frac{10}{\sin 35°} = \frac{x}{\sin 80°}, \quad \text{so} \quad x = \frac{10\sin 80°}{\sin 35°} = 17.169\ldots.$$
Hence $x = 17.2$ (to 3 s.f.).

Here is a similar question for you to try.

Activity 14   *Using the Sine Rule to find a side length*

Find the length x in the triangle below, to three significant figures.

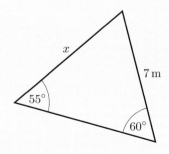

In this subsection you have seen that the Sine Rule is useful for solving a triangle when you know the length of a side and the angle opposite this side. As you have seen, if you also know one other angle, then you can use the Sine Rule to calculate the side length opposite this angle. If instead you know one further side length, then you can often use the Sine Rule to calculate the the angle opposite this side, but this is slightly more complicated and is covered in Section 3.

2.2 The Cosine Rule

Although the Sine Rule is useful in many cases, it can be used only if you know the length of a side and the opposite angle. If you know the lengths of two sides and the angle between them, as in Figure 24, then a different rule, called the *Cosine Rule*, can be used.

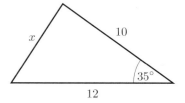

Figure 24 A triangle with two known sides and a known angle between them

Figure 25 shows a general triangle with three acute angles. Suppose that you want to find a formula for the side length a in terms of the side lengths b and c, and the angle A. To do this, you can start by dropping a perpendicular from C, as shown. The side of length c is then divided into two parts: if you call the length of one part y, then the other part has length $c - y$.

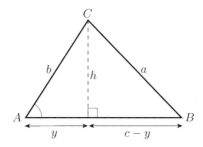

Figure 25 A general triangle with a perpendicular added

Applying Pythagoras' Theorem to each of the right-angled triangles gives

$$b^2 = y^2 + h^2, \tag{2}$$
$$a^2 = (c - y)^2 + h^2.$$

Expanding the brackets in the second of these equations gives

$$a^2 = c^2 - 2cy + y^2 + h^2.$$

The right-hand side of this equation contains the expression $y^2 + h^2$, which is equal to b^2 by equation (2). So the equation above can be rearranged as

$$a^2 = b^2 + c^2 - 2cy. \tag{3}$$

The length y in this equation can be replaced by using the fact that the right-angled triangle on the left in Figure 25 gives

$$\cos A = \frac{y}{b}, \quad \text{so} \quad y = b \cos A.$$

Substituting this expression for y in equation (3) gives the equation

$$a^2 = b^2 + c^2 - 2bc \cos A.$$

This equation is one form of the Cosine Rule. There are three forms of this rule, one for each of the three angles, as shown overleaf.

"HERE'S WHERE YOU MADE YOUR MISTAKE."

Book II of Euclid's *Elements* contains a geometric theorem equivalent to the Cosine Rule. It was put into its present useful form by the fourteenth-century Persian mathematician Jamshid Al-Kashi, and is still known in France as 'Le Théorème d'Al-Kashi'.

Cosine Rule

$$a^2 = b^2 + c^2 - 2bc\cos A,$$
$$b^2 = c^2 + a^2 - 2ca\cos B,$$
$$c^2 = a^2 + b^2 - 2ab\cos C.$$

These three equations look quite complicated, but there are some patterns in the way that the letters appear that will help you to remember them. For example, only one length appears on the left-hand side of each equation, and this length is related to the angle whose cosine appears on the right-hand side. The other two lengths appear only on the right-hand side in each case.

You will see in the next section that if $\angle C$ is a right angle, then $\cos C = 0$. In this case, the third form of the Cosine Rule simply states that $c^2 = a^2 + b^2$. This is Pythagoras' Theorem, as you would expect in a right-angled triangle. In fact, the Cosine Rule is similar to Pythagoras' Theorem, with an extra correction term because the opposite angle is not a right angle in general.

The next two examples illustrate how to use the Cosine Rule.

Example 8 *Using the Cosine Rule to find a side length*

Use the Cosine Rule to find the length AC in the triangle below, to two significant figures.

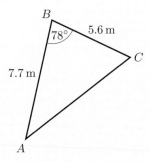

Solution

Label the sides with letters and identify which form of the Cosine Rule to use. The known angle is angle B, so use the second form.

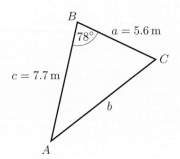

By the Cosine Rule,

$$b^2 = c^2 + a^2 - 2ca \cos B.$$

Substitute in the values and do the calculation.

Substituting $a = 5.6$, $c = 7.7$ and $B = 78°$ gives

$$b^2 = 7.7^2 + 5.6^2 - 2 \times 7.7 \times 5.6 \cos 78° = 72.719\ldots.$$

So $b = \sqrt{72.719\ldots} = 8.52\ldots.$ Hence the length AC is $8.5\,\text{m}$ (to 2 s.f.).

As with the Sine Rule, once you are familiar with the Cosine Rule you may prefer to apply it without labelling the vertices and sides of the triangle.

Tutorial clip

Example 9 *Using the Cosine Rule without vertex labels*

Find the length x in the triangle below, to two significant figures.

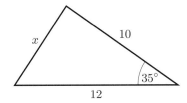

Solution

The lengths of two sides and the included angle are known, so use the Cosine Rule.

By the Cosine Rule,

$$x^2 = 10^2 + 12^2 - 2 \times 10 \times 12 \cos 35° = 47.403\ldots.$$

So $x = \sqrt{47.403\ldots} = 6.88\ldots = 6.9$ (to 2 s.f.).

Here is a similar question for you to try.

Activity 15 *Using the Cosine Rule to find a side length*

Find the length x in the triangle below, to two significant figures.

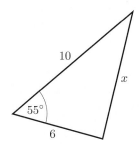

The Cosine Rule can also be used if you know the lengths of all three sides of a triangle and you want to find an angle, as in the following example.

Example 10 *Using the Cosine Rule to find an angle*

Find the angle θ in the triangle below, to the nearest degree.

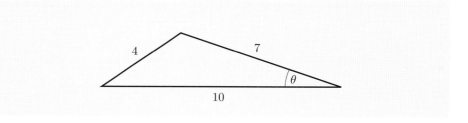

Solution

💭 The lengths of three sides are known, so use the Cosine Rule. 💭

By the Cosine Rule,

$$4^2 = 7^2 + 10^2 - 2 \times 7 \times 10 \cos\theta.$$

This equation simplifies to

$$16 = 149 - 140\cos\theta.$$

Making $\cos\theta$ the subject of the equation gives:

$$140\cos\theta = 133$$
$$\cos\theta = \frac{133}{140} = 0.95.$$

So $\theta = \cos^{-1}(0.95) = 18.194\ldots° = 18°$ (to the nearest degree).

You can use a similar method in the following activity.

Activity 16 *Finding all the angles in a triangle*

Use the Cosine Rule to calculate $\angle B$ of the isosceles triangle shown below, and deduce the other angles. Give your answers to the nearest degree.

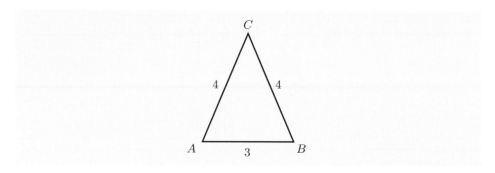

Summarising the methods of solving a triangle

In order to solve a triangle, you need to know two angles and one side length, or one angle and two side lengths, or three side lengths. You have now seen four methods of finding unknown lengths and angles in a triangle:

- Pythagoras' Theorem
- the trigonometric ratios sine, cosine and tangent
- the Sine Rule
- the Cosine Rule.

The process of choosing which of these methods to use can be summarised in the form of a decision tree, as shown in Figure 26.

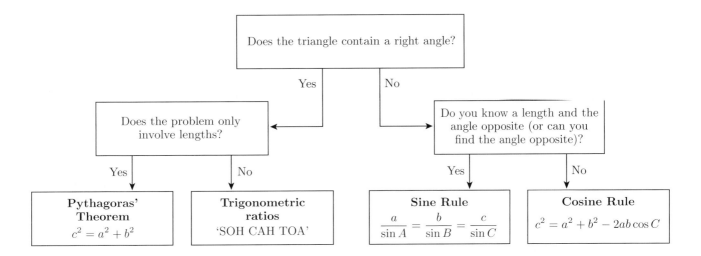

Figure 26 A decision tree showing methods of solving a triangle

You can try using the decision tree in the following activity.

Activity 17 *Choosing which way to solve a triangle*

For each of the following diagrams, decide which is the best method to use to find the unknown length x and the unknown angle θ, in either order. (You are not asked to find x and θ.)

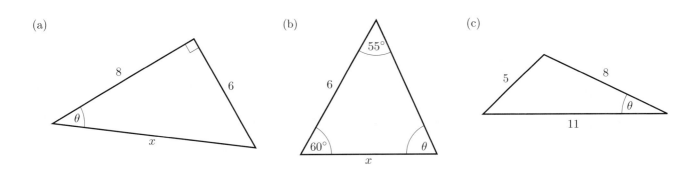

2.3   Finding the speed of the glacier

Now that you have met the Sine Rule and the Cosine Rule, you can estimate the speed of the glacier in the *Rough Science* programme.

The method used in the programme was to place a flag on the glacier and make observations of the direction of the flag from each end of a 50 m line on the ground beside the glacier, which the scientists called their *baseline*. These observations were made at the same time on two consecutive days, and they then used trigonometry to estimate how far the flag moved in a day.

The scientists in the programme used a different trigonometric approach from the one here – there are often different ways to tackle a problem!

In the next activity you are asked to find the distance of the flag from one end of the baseline on each of the two days.

Activity 18   *Finding the distance to the flag*

(a) On the first day the angles to the flag from each end of the 50 m baseline were 78.5° and 82.4°, as shown below. Calculate the length x to the nearest centimetre.

In this and the next figure the angles have not been drawn accurately, in order to indicate that the triangle for the second day is not congruent to the one for the first day.

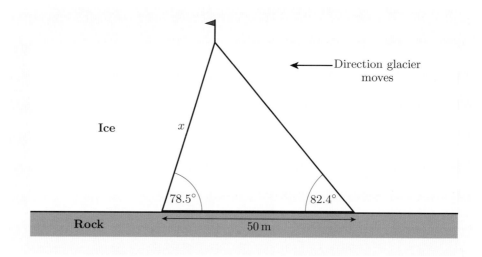

(b) On the second day the angles to the flag from each end of the 50 m baseline were 79.0° and 81.9°, as shown below. Calculate the length y to the nearest centimetre.

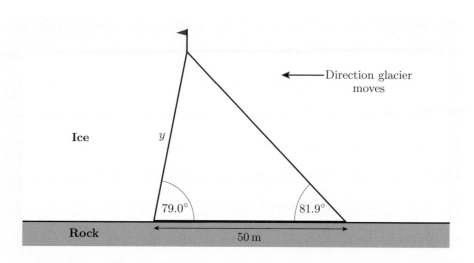

By combining the results from the two parts of Activity 18, you obtain the diagram shown in Figure 27.

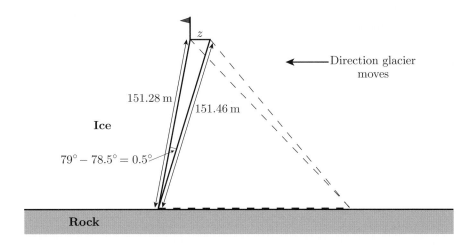

Figure 27   A diagram showing the movement of the flag

The triangle with solid lines in Figure 27 has two known sides and a known angle between these sides. So you can use the Cosine Rule to find the distance z that the flag moved.

Activity 19   *Finding the movement of the flag*

Use the Cosine Rule in Figure 27 to find the distance z that the flag moved in one day, to two significant figures.

In this activity you can use the rounded values of the side lengths and angles shown in Figure 27, since only a rough estimate of the speed of the glacier is required.

The answer found in Activity 19 agrees with the answer found in the video: the estimate of the speed of the glacier is 1.3 m per day.

2.4   A formula for the area of a triangle

In Unit 8, a formula was obtained for the area of a triangle in terms of the base and the height of the triangle. Using trigonometry you can derive a formula for the area of a triangle that can be used if you know the lengths of two sides and the included angle. As with the Sine Rule and Cosine Rule, we will derive this formula for a triangle with three acute angles, but it can also be used for triangles with an obtuse angle.

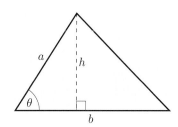

Figure 28   Finding the area of a triangle

For the triangle in Figure 28, the base is b and the height is h. So the area of the triangle is $\frac{1}{2}bh$, as given in Unit 8, Section 4. From the right-angled triangle on the left,

$$\sin\theta = \frac{h}{a}, \quad \text{so} \quad h = a\sin\theta.$$

Substituting this formula for h into $\frac{1}{2}bh$ gives the area of the triangle as

$$\tfrac{1}{2}bh = \tfrac{1}{2}b \times a\sin\theta = \tfrac{1}{2}ab\sin\theta.$$

This gives the following formula for the area of a triangle.

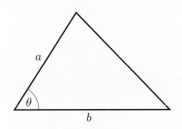

Figure 29   A triangle with two sides of lengths a and b and included angle θ

Area of a triangle

The area of a triangle with two sides of lengths a and b, and included angle θ, is

$$\text{area} = \tfrac{1}{2}ab\sin\theta.$$

This area formula is more useful in practical situations than the formula $\frac{1}{2}bh$. For example, in surveying it gives the area of a triangle of land in terms of quantities that a surveyor can readily measure. The areas of most pieces of land can be found by breaking them down into convenient triangular shapes and using this formula in each triangle.

You can use the formula in the following activity.

Activity 20   Finding the areas of triangles

Find the area of each of the following triangles, correct to three significant figures.

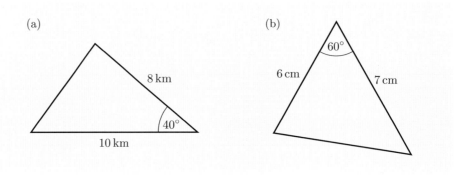

(a)

(b)

In many cases calculating the area of a triangle would be easier if there were a simple formula for the area of a triangle in terms of just the lengths of the three sides. Such a formula was derived by the Greek mathematician Heron around AD 62 and later found independently by Chinese mathematicians.

Heron of Alexandria taught physics and engineering, as well as mathematics. Heron's Formula is derived in Book 1 of his textbook *Metrica*.

Heron's Formula

The area of a triangle with sides of length a, b and c is

$$\text{area} = \sqrt{s(s-a)(s-b)(s-c)},$$

where $s = \tfrac{1}{2}(a+b+c)$.

Note that the lengths a, b and c appear symmetrically in the formula – this makes it more memorable.

The quantity s in Heron's Formula is called the **semi-perimeter** of the triangle because it is half the perimeter.

Heron's Formula can be proved by expressing one angle of the triangle in terms of the lengths of the sides and then using the formula $\frac{1}{2}ab\sin\theta$ for the area of the triangle. However, it takes considerable algebraic skill to write the final result in the neat form given in Heron's Formula.

In the next activity you are asked to use the two area formulas from this subsection to calculate the area of an equilateral triangle.

Activity 21 *Using area formulas*

For an equilateral triangle of side length 2:

(a) Calculate the area of the triangle using the formula: area $= \frac{1}{2}ab\sin\theta$.

(b) Calculate the semi-perimeter s of the triangle and then use Heron's Formula to calculate the area of the triangle.

Give your answers in surd form.

---

3 Trigonometric functions

So far in this unit the trigonometric ratios sine, cosine and tangent have always been applied to angles between $0°$ and $90°$. However, if you use your calculator to find $\sin 150°$, $\cos 1000°$ or even $\tan(-45°)$, then it gives the answers

$$\sin 150° = \tfrac{1}{2}, \quad \cos 1000° = 0.173\ldots, \quad \tan(-45°) = -1.$$

What do these values mean, and why are they needed?

In this section you will learn how to define the sine and cosine of every possible angle, and the tangents of most angles, and you will also see why defining these values is useful.

One reason why it is useful to define the sine and cosine of an angle greater than $90°$ is that some triangles have an obtuse angle, that is, an angle between $90°$ and $180°$. In order to solve such triangles, you may want to use the Sine Rule or the Cosine Rule: these apply to triangles with an obtuse angle in the same way as they apply to other triangles. But to do that you need to know what the sine and cosine of an obtuse angle are!

Since the definitions of sine and cosine given in Section 1 do not make sense for an obtuse angle, new definitions are needed. But once you know these new definitions, it is natural to define the sine and cosine of *any* angle, not just acute and obtuse ones.

The sines and cosines of general angles give rise to functions, called *trigonometric functions*, that turn out to be useful in situations that are not explicitly related to triangles. For example, these functions can be used to model many types of real-world behaviour with a repeating nature, such as the occurrence of high tides – as you will see.

3.1   Sine, cosine and tangent of a general angle

Unit 8, Section 1, introduced the idea that an angle is a measure of rotation, or amount of turning, that can be measured in degrees. There, angles were discussed that take values up to and including $360°$, that is, up to a rotation through one full turn. But it is possible to have a rotation through more than one full turn, so it makes sense to use general angles that measure more than $360°$. You can also have rotations that are clockwise or anticlockwise, and it is useful to distinguish between these.

> **Sign of an angle**
>
> A general angle is a measure of rotation around a point, measured in degrees. Positive angles give anticlockwise rotations, and negative angles give clockwise rotations.

Some examples of angles corresponding to rotations around the origin, from the positive x-axis, are shown in Figure 30. The arrow indicates whether the rotation is anticlockwise or clockwise.

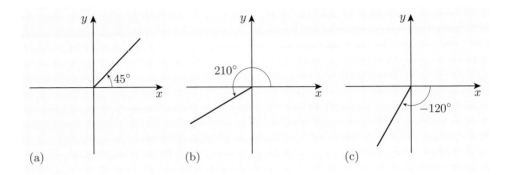

Figure 30 Some general angles

The sine and cosine of a general angle θ are defined by using a point P on the circle with radius 1 centred on the origin, which is called the **unit circle**. The position of the point P is determined by the angle θ; it is obtained by a rotation around the origin through the angle θ starting from the point on the x-axis with x-coordinate 1. If the angle θ is positive, then the rotation is anticlockwise; if the angle is negative, then the rotation is clockwise.

Some examples of how general angles give rise to points on the unit circle are shown in Figure 31.

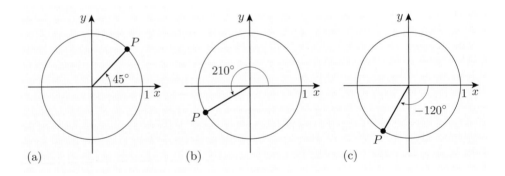

Figure 31 General angles and points on the unit circle

In Figure 31, the x- and y-axes divide the graph into four regions, each of which is known as a **quadrant**. These quadrants are numbered in order anticlockwise as shown in Figure 32, and they are useful for describing where points, such as those on the unit circle, lie.

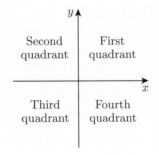

Figure 32 The four quadrants

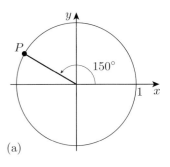

(a)

Activity 22 *Plotting general angles on the unit circle*

For each of the following angles, draw a sketch to illustrate how the point P on the unit circle is rotated through that angle from its starting position on the x-axis. Your sketches should be similar to those in Figure 31. In each case state the quadrant in which P lies.

(a) $60°$ (b) $225°$ (c) $390°$ (d) $-70°$

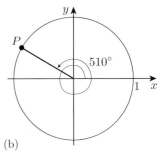

(b)

Figure 33   Angles of $150°$ and $510°$

It is possible that two different angles of rotation lead to the point P being in the same position. For example, as you can see in Figure 33, the point P is in the same position on the unit circle for the angle $510°$ as for the angle $150°$. This is because

$$510° = 150° + 360°,$$

so $510°$ gives exactly one full turn around the origin more than $150°$.

Figure 34 shows the point P after it has rotated through an acute angle θ, so P is in the first quadrant.

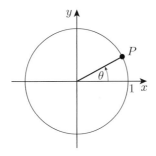

Figure 34   The point P after a rotation through an acute angle

If you drop a perpendicular from P to the x-axis, then you obtain a right-angled triangle with hypotenuse of length 1 in which one angle is θ, as shown in Figure 35.

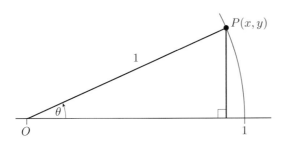

Figure 35   A right-angled triangle with angle θ

You can see that if P has coordinates (x, y), then

$$\sin\theta = \frac{y}{1} \quad \text{and} \quad \cos\theta = \frac{x}{1},$$

which give

$$x = \cos\theta \quad \text{and} \quad y = \sin\theta.$$

These two equations are the key to defining the sine and cosine of a general angle. This is done as follows.

> ### Sine and cosine of a general angle
>
> For a general angle θ, let P be the point on the unit circle obtained by a rotation of θ around the origin from the positive x-axis, and suppose that P has coordinates (x, y). Then
>
> $$\cos\theta = x \quad \text{and} \quad \sin\theta = y.$$

So the cosine and sine of a general angle θ are just the x- and y-coordinates of the point P whose position on the unit circle is determined by the angle θ, as shown in Figure 36.

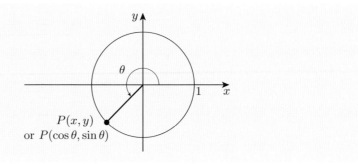

Figure 36   Defining $\cos\theta$ and $\sin\theta$

To illustrate this definition, consider the angle $\theta = 150°$. For this angle, the point P lies in the second quadrant, as shown in Figure 37.

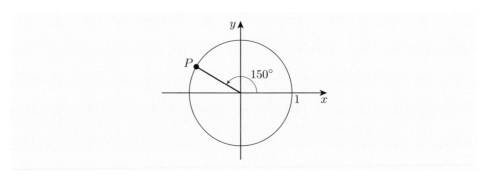

Figure 37   The point P obtained from the angle $150°$

To find $\sin\theta$ and $\cos\theta$ in this case, you need to find the coordinates of this point P. You can do this by using the right-angled triangle shown in Figure 38, which has one angle equal to $180° - 150° = 30°$.

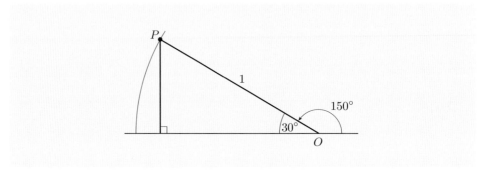

Figure 38   A right-angled triangle related to the angle $150°$

In the triangle in Figure 38, the hypotenuse is of length 1, so

$$\sin 30° = \frac{\text{opp}}{1} \quad \text{and} \quad \cos 30° = \frac{\text{adj}}{1}.$$

Hence

- the side opposite the angle of 30° has length $\sin 30° = \frac{1}{2}$,

- the side adjacent to the angle of 30° has length $\cos 30° = \frac{\sqrt{3}}{2}$.

Therefore the coordinates of the point P are $\left(-\frac{\sqrt{3}}{2}, \frac{1}{2}\right)$.

So, by the definitions of the sine and cosine of a general angle,

$$\cos 150° = -\frac{\sqrt{3}}{2} = -0.866\ldots \quad \text{and} \quad \sin 150° = \frac{1}{2} = 0.5.$$

You can check that your calculator gives these values for $\cos 150°$ and $\sin 150°$.

Note that the values of $\cos 150°$ and $\sin 150°$ were found by using the values of $\cos 30°$ and $\sin 30°$, respectively.

It is straightforward to write down the sine or cosine of an angle that is a multiple of 90°, because for such an angle the point P lies on one of the axes. For example, Figure 39 shows that $\cos 0° = 1$ and $\sin 0° = 0$.

Similarly, Figure 40 shows that $\cos 90° = 0$ and $\sin 90° = 1$.

Usually, you should simply use your calculator to find the sine and cosine of a general angle, just as you would do for an acute angle. But to make sure that you understand these definitions, it is worth working out some sines and cosines from basic principles. You are asked to do this in the following activity.

> You can find the values of $\sin 30°$ and $\cos 30°$ either by using your calculator or from Table 1 on page 73.

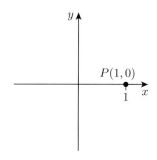

Figure 39 P is at $(1, 0)$ when $\theta = 0°$

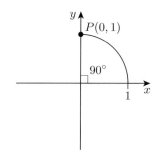

Figure 40 P is at $(0, 1)$ when $\theta = 90°$

Activity 23 *Finding sines and cosines from the definition*

(a) Find $\cos 225°$ and $\sin 225°$ (to four decimal places) by plotting the appropriate point P on the unit circle and using a suitable right-angled triangle. Check your answers with a calculator.

(b) Find $\cos(-180°)$ and $\sin(-180°)$ by plotting the appropriate point P on the unit circle. Check your answers with a calculator.

Now that you know the definition of the sine and cosine of any angle, the next question is: How can you define the tangent of a general angle? To answer this question, recall the relationship between the sine, cosine and tangent of an acute angle found in Subsection 1.4. In any right-angled triangle with an acute angle θ,

$$\tan \theta = \frac{\sin \theta}{\cos \theta}.$$

This equation can be used to *define* the tangent of a general angle.

Tangent of a general angle

For a general angle θ,

$$\tan \theta = \frac{\sin \theta}{\cos \theta}, \quad \text{provided that } \cos \theta \neq 0.$$

> Remember that division by 0 is not allowed.

For example,

The sines and cosines of 150° and 90° were found just before Activity 23.

$$\tan 150° = \frac{\sin 150°}{\cos 150°} = \frac{\frac{1}{2}}{-\frac{\sqrt{3}}{2}} = -\frac{1}{\sqrt{3}} = -0.577\ldots.$$

You can check this value on a calculator.

However, $\tan 90°$ cannot be defined because $\cos 90° = 0$.

Activity 24   Finding tangents from the definition

Use your answers to Activity 23 to find $\tan 225°$ and $\tan(-180°)$.

Earlier in the subsection, the sine and cosine of a general angle θ were defined geometrically in terms of the position of a point P on the unit circle. There is also a geometric interpretation of the tangent of θ. This interpretation will be useful in the next subsection when we draw graphs of the sine, cosine and tangent functions.

First consider the situation when the angle θ is acute, so the point P is in the first quadrant, as shown in Figure 41. A vertical line has been drawn through the point on the x-axis with coordinate 1, and the line from the origin through P has been extended to meet this vertical line, at the point Q. A new right-angled triangle $\triangle OQN$ has thus been formed in which the side adjacent to the angle θ has length 1. In this triangle,

$$\tan \theta = \frac{\text{opp}}{\text{adj}} = \frac{\text{opp}}{1} = \text{opp},$$

so the y-coordinate of Q is $\tan \theta$.

The name tangent arises from the fact that in this diagram the line that passes through the point $(1, 0)$ and the point Q is a *tangent* to the unit circle; that is, it meets this circle at exactly one point.

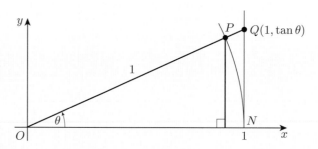

Figure 41   The geometric interpretation of $\tan \theta$ when θ is acute

As the angle θ increases, the point Q moves up the vertical line, so $\tan \theta$ increases. As θ reaches the value 90°, the line from the origin through P becomes vertical. At this point $\tan 90°$ is not defined.

For values of θ between 90° and 180°, the line through the origin and P once again meets the vertical line on the right, though now the point of intersection is *below* the x-axis, as shown in Figure 42. It can be shown, by considering the triangles in the diagram, that the y-coordinate of Q is again $\tan \theta$, though the details are not given here.

It can also be shown that this interpretation works for any angle θ where $\tan \theta$ is defined; that is, the value of $\tan \theta$ is always the y-coordinate of the point Q. You will see an animation illustrating this fact in the next subsection.

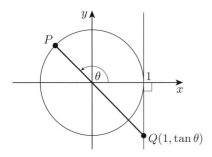

Figure 42   The geometric interpretation of $\tan\theta$ when θ is obtuse

3.2   Graphs of sine, cosine and tangent

In Subsection 3.1 you saw how the sine, cosine and tangent of any angle are defined – except when division by zero is involved. So you can think of each of the expressions

$$\sin\theta, \quad \cos\theta \quad \text{and} \quad \tan\theta$$

as a 'rule' that takes an input value θ and produces an output value. In Unit 6, Section 3, you saw that a rule of this type, which transforms an input value into an output value, is often called a 'function'. For this reason, sine, cosine and tangent are often called **trigonometric functions**.

To gain a better understanding of a function, it is often helpful to plot its graph, as you saw with quadratics in Unit 10. Let's begin by plotting the graphs of sine, cosine and tangent in the range $0°$ to $90°$. This can be done by using the values in Table 2, which were obtained from a calculator and are stated to two decimal places.

Table 2   Values of trigonometric functions

θ	$0°$	$10°$	$20°$	$30°$	$45°$	$60°$	$70°$	$80°$	$90°$
$\sin\theta$	0.00	0.17	0.34	0.50	0.71	0.87	0.94	0.98	1.00
$\cos\theta$	1.00	0.98	0.94	0.87	0.71	0.50	0.34	0.17	0.00
$\tan\theta$	0.00	0.18	0.36	0.58	1.00	1.73	2.75	5.67	–

Using these values, the following graphs can be drawn. Only a few significant points are shown on the graphs.

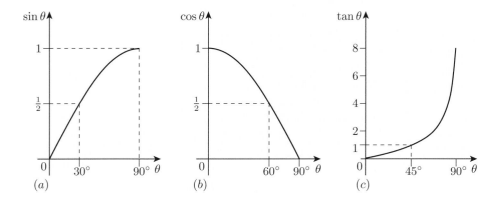

Figure 43   Graphs of sine, cosine and tangent functions for $0° < \theta < 90°$

In Unit 14 the variable y *will* be used on the vertical axis for such trigonometric graphs.

In Figure 43, the input variable θ is on the horizontal axis. The vertical axes are labelled with the names of the functions, in order to emphasise which function is involved and also to avoid using the variable y, which had a different meaning earlier in this section as one of the coordinates of the point P.

You can see that, as the angle θ increases from 0 to 90°:

- the value of $\sin\theta$ increases from 0 to 1;

- the value of $\cos\theta$ decreases from 1 to 0;

- the value of $\tan\theta$ increases from 0 and takes values that are arbitrarily large as the angle θ approaches 90°.

These changes take place because, as the point P moves anticlockwise round the part of the unit circle in the first quadrant (see Figure 34 on page 89), the vertical coordinate of P, which is equal to $\sin\theta$, increases from 0 to 1, and the horizontal coordinate of P, which is equal to $\cos\theta$, decreases from 1 to 0. Also the point Q (see Figure 41 on page 92) moves upwards from the point $(1, 0)$, arbitrarily far as θ approaches 90°.

But what do these graphs look like for other values of θ? In fact, the other parts of these graphs have similar shapes to the parts that are plotted in Figure 43, but these other parts are positioned differently in relation to the axes. The following activity allows you to see how these graphs are generated as the point P moves on the unit circle in the way described in the previous subsection.

Dynamic trigonometry

Activity 25   *Using animated graphs of trigonometric functions*

Carry out the computer activity to explore the graphs of sine, cosine and tangent for different ranges of angles.

In Activity 25 you explored the graphs of the sine, cosine and tangent functions between −360° and 360°. In fact, the graphs repeat endlessly along the horizontal axis. The parts of the graphs corresponding to values of θ between −360° and 720° are shown in Figures 44, 45 and 46.

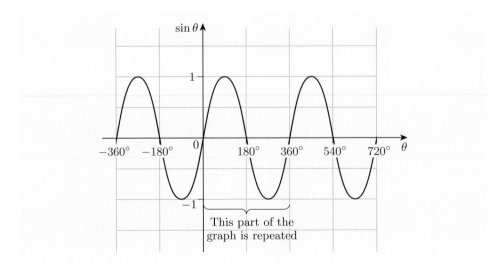

Figure 44   The graph of the sine function

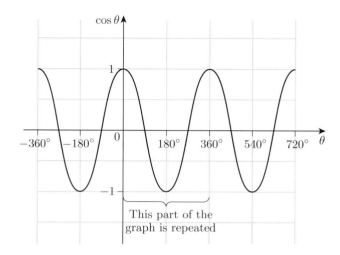

Figure 45   The graph of the cosine function

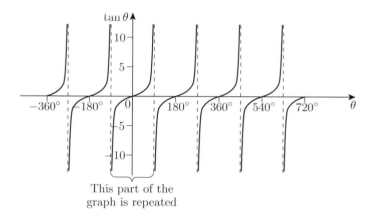

Figure 46   The graph of the tangent function

The graphs of these three trigonometric functions have various properties, such as symmetry characteristics, which can be useful when you are working with sines, cosines and tangents. Let's have a look at some of these properties.

Periodicity

A key feature of these graphs is that their shapes repeat in a regular way. The sine and cosine graphs repeat every 360° and we say that these functions are *periodic*, with **period** 360°. This is what you would expect because as the angle θ increases the position of the point P on the unit circle repeats every 360°. The tangent function is also periodic but with a smaller period, of 180°. So the values of the tangent function repeat twice as often as the values of the sine and cosine functions.

Because of this property of periodicity, an equation such as $\sin\theta = 0.5$ has infinitely many solutions, and not just the solution $\sin^{-1}(0.5) = 30°$. For example, $\sin 390° = \sin 30° = 0.5$ because $390° = 360° + 30°$. Another solution is 150°, since $\sin 150° = 0.5$ as you saw in Subsection 3.1.

In Unit 14 you will see how to find all the solutions of equations such as $\sin\theta = 0.5$.

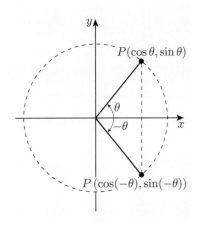

Figure 47 $\cos(-\theta) = \cos(\theta)$

Remember that the *magnitude* of a number is its value without its negative sign, if it has one.

Mirror symmetry

The sine and cosine graphs have *mirror symmetry* in any vertical line through a peak or trough on the graph. For example, the graph of the cosine function (part of which is shown in Figure 45) has mirror symmetry in the vertical axis. This property means that any angle and its negative have the same cosine value. This is what you would expect, because if the point P is rotated around the origin from the positive x-axis by an angle of either θ or $-\theta$, as in Figure 47, then the resulting x-coordinate is the same. Facts like this can be written down as trigonometric identities; this fact gives

$$\cos(-\theta) = \cos(\theta)$$

for any angle θ. For example, $\cos(-30°) = \cos 30°$.

Rotational symmetry

Each of the three graphs has *rotational symmetry* about any point where the graph crosses the θ-axis – if you rotate the graph through a half-turn about such a point, then it lies exactly on top of where it was before. For example, the sine graph (part of which is shown in Figure 44) has rotational symmetry about the origin. This means that any angle θ and its negative $-\theta$ have sine values that have the same magnitude, but one of the sine values is negative while the other is positive. Exactly the same is true of the tangent graph; these two facts give the identities

$$\sin(-\theta) = -\sin(\theta) \quad \text{and} \quad \tan(-\theta) = -\tan(\theta)$$

for any angle θ. For example, $\sin(-30°) = -\sin 30°$.

Asymptotes

The graph of the tangent function differs from the other two graphs in that it is broken up into separate pieces and it takes values that are arbitrarily large. The breaks in the graph correspond to the values of θ where $\cos\theta$ is zero, such as $\theta = 90°$.

For angles just below $90°$, you can see that $\tan\theta$ is very large and positive. This is because $\tan\theta = \sin\theta/\cos\theta$, and $\sin\theta$ is close to 1 whereas $\cos\theta$ is very small and positive (if you divide a number close to 1 by a very small number, then the answer is a very large number). Similarly, for angles just above $90°$, you can see that $\tan\theta$ is very large and negative.

This behaviour is described by saying that the tangent graph has an **asymptote** at $\theta = 90°$. Informally, an asymptote is a line that a graph approaches but never reaches. Asymptotes are often indicated by dashed lines, as in Figure 46.

Activity 26   *The asymptotes of the tangent graph*

Write down the values of θ between $360°$ and $720°$ at which the asymptotes of the tangent graph occur.

Relationships between the sine and cosine graphs

Another key fact that you saw in Activity 25 is that the sine and cosine graphs have the same basic shape. Various relationships between sines and cosines can be obtained from this fact.

For example, try the following 'thought experiment'. Imagine walking from left to right along the sine graph, starting from the origin. As the angle increases from $0°$, the height you are above the horizontal axis increases from 0 to 1, then decreases from 1 through 0 to -1, and then increases from -1 to 0 again, and so on.

If you performed the same thought experiment with the cosine graph, again walking from left to right but this time starting at $-90°$, then the heights would follow exactly the same pattern. This is because the graph of the cosine function is obtained by shifting the graph of the sine function to the left by a distance of $90°$ on the θ-axis. The corresponding trigonometric identity is

$$\sin\theta = \cos(-90° + \theta)$$

for any angle θ. For example, $\sin 60° = \cos(-90° + 60°) = \cos(-30°)$.

Similarly, if you walked along the cosine graph starting from $90°$, but this time from right to left, then the same pattern of heights would occur. In this case, the resulting trigonometric identity is

$$\sin\theta - \cos(90° - \theta) \tag{4}$$

for any angle θ. For example, $\sin 60° = \cos(90° - 60°) = \cos 30°$.

You have already seen that the identity $\sin\theta = \cos(90° - \theta)$ holds for acute angles, in Subsection 1.4. So now you know that it holds for *all* angles.

Similarly, the identity

$$\cos\theta = \sin(90° - \theta)$$

for any angle θ, can be seen from the sine and cosine graphs by using a thought experiment similar to those above; you might like to try this.

Another way to see identity 4 is to plot

$$y = \sin\theta \quad \text{and} \quad y = \cos(90 - \theta)$$

on Graphplotter. One graph will lie on top of the other, illustrating that

$$\sin\theta = \cos(90° - \theta)$$

for all the values of θ plotted on the graph.

Two other trigonometric identities

In Subsection 1.4 the identity

$$\tan\theta = \frac{\sin\theta}{\cos\theta}$$

was shown to hold for all acute angles. In fact it holds for all angles θ, except where $\cos\theta = 0$, since it was used to *define* $\tan\theta$ for non-acute angles!

Finally, the identity

$$\sin^2\theta + \cos^2\theta = 1$$

also holds for every angle θ. For example, suppose that P is the point on the unit circle corresponding to an obtuse angle θ. As shown in Figure 48, the line from the origin to P has length 1 and it is the hypotenuse of a right-angled triangle. The length of the vertical side of the triangle is $\sin\theta$ (because $\sin\theta$ is positive). Since the x-coordinate of P is negative, the length of the horizontal side of the triangle can be found by multiplying the x-coordinate of P by -1. So the length of the horizontal side is $-\cos\theta$. Then, by Pythagoras' Theorem,

$$(\sin\theta)^2 + (-\cos\theta)^2 = 1^2, \quad \text{so} \quad \sin^2\theta + \cos^2\theta = 1.$$

A similar argument holds for angles in the other quadrants, so the identity is true for all values of θ.

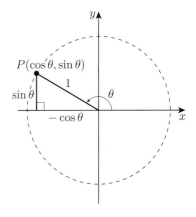

Figure 48   A right-angled triangle

Modelling real-world phenomena

The sine, cosine and tangent functions can be used in modelling many real-world phenomena; you will meet some examples in Unit 14. As the unit circle is used in the definition of sine and cosine, it may not surprise you that circular motion can be analysed mathematically using sines and cosines. If you go on to study higher-level modules, then you will see that this is exploited to analyse the circular motion of many types of objects, from satellites to children's roundabouts and spinning tops.

What is perhaps a little more surprising is that sines and cosines can be used to describe any periodic phenomenon such as the heights of tides, sea temperatures during the year, the motion of waves or the time when the Sun rises during the year. The video in the following activity explains how circular motion is used to predict tides. It shows how rotating circles can generate complicated periodic graphs that are similar to the graphs that show the heights of tides. The video contains an excerpt from the television series *Local Heroes* about Arthur Doodson (1890–1968), a mathematician who specialised in the prediction of tides and who designed a machine that used rotating wheels to predict the tides at ports all over the world.

Doodson first became interested in tides when he worked at the University of Liverpool. The River Mersey has the second highest tidal range in Britain – the difference between low and high tide at Liverpool can be as much as 10 metres. This has made it harder to build modern container-handling facilities there than at other ports with less variable water levels. The largest tidal range in Britain (and the second largest in the world) is in the Bristol Channel.

 Video

The video is on the DVD.

Activity 27   *Modelling the tides*

Watch the video 'Modelling the tides' to see how the heights of tides can be predicted using a mechanical model.

So far in this section you have seen how the sine, cosine and tangent of any angle are defined, and you have also explored the graphs of these functions and seen one way they can be used. The next subsection shows you how the Sine Rule and Cosine Rule can be applied to a triangle that contains an obtuse angle.

3.3   Solving obtuse-angled triangles

In Section 2, you used the Sine Rule and Cosine Rule to solve acute-angled triangles. It is possible to show that these rules, along with the formula for the area of a triangle in Subsection 2.4, also hold for obtuse-angled triangles – an **obtuse-angled triangle** is one that contains an obtuse angle. These three results also hold in a right-angled triangle, but there is never any need to use them in such a triangle as it is simpler to use the trigonometric ratios sine, cosine and tangent and Pythagoras' Theorem.

The proofs are similar to the geometric proofs that you saw in Section 2 for acute-angled triangles.

This means that you can find unknown lengths and unknown angles in *any* triangle, providing that you have enough information about the other sides and angles. This is particularly useful in applications such as surveying.

When you use the Sine Rule or the Cosine Rule in a triangle with an obtuse angle, you might need to find the sine or cosine of the obtuse angle. You can use your calculator to do this in exactly the same way as for acute angles.

In Subsection 2.2 you saw that you can use the Cosine Rule to find either an unknown side or an unknown angle in a triangle. To find an unknown angle, you first use the Cosine Rule to find the value of the cosine of the angle, and then you use this value to find the angle itself. If the angle that you are trying to find happens to be obtuse, then the cosine will be negative, but you can still use the inverse cosine key on your calculator to find the angle in the usual way. For example, if you enter $\cos^{-1}(-0.5)$, then you will obtain the answer $120°$.

Remember that the cosine is negative for angles between $90°$ and $180°$.

The next activity illustrates a practical application of the Cosine Rule in an obtuse-angled triangle. If you are designing a garden, then one of the first steps is to draw a scale diagram of the boundary. To make sure that the angles and lengths on the diagram are accurate, you can use a process known as *triangulation*. This involves identifying some key points on the boundary of the garden and then measuring the distance from each of these points to two known fixed points, such as the corners of a building.

Figure 49 shows the boundary of a garden. The distances of the boundary point B from the two fixed points A and C at the corners of the house are marked, as is the width of the house. You can use the Cosine Rule to find the angle at A in the triangle ABC, and you can then use this angle to help you to draw an accurate scale diagram.

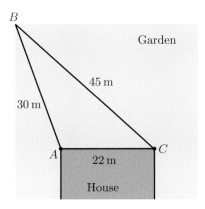

Figure 49 Measurements in a garden

Activity 28 Finding an angle using the Cosine Rule

Use the Cosine Rule to find the value of $\cos A$ in Figure 49, and hence find the angle A to the nearest degree.

It was mentioned at the end of Subsection 2.1 that you can sometimes use the Sine Rule to find unknown angles. The method is similar to the method based on the Cosine Rule: you use the Sine Rule to find the sine of the unknown angle, and then you use this value to find the angle itself. The sine of the angle is always a positive number between 0 and 1, since an angle in a triangle is always between $0°$ and $180°$. However, there is a complication when you try to use the sine of the angle to find the angle.

Think back to the way that the sine of an angle is defined: it is the y-coordinate of the corresponding point P on the unit circle. Figure 50(a) shows an acute angle and its corresponding point P. If you reflect the point P in the y-axis, as shown in Figure 50(b), then its y-coordinate remains the same, but it corresponds to a different angle, namely the obtuse angle $180° - \theta$, as you can see from the diagram. So the two angles θ and $180° - \theta$ have the same sine value.

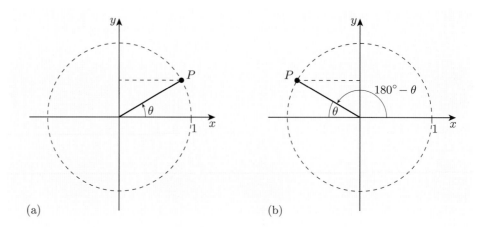

(a)   (b)

Figure 50   Two angles that have the same sine value

So, for example, the acute angle $30°$ and the obtuse angle $150°$ have the same sine value, because $150° = 180° - 30°$. Similarly, $60°$ and $120°$ have the same sine value, and so on. You might like to try finding the sines of some other pairs of angles of the form θ and $180° - \theta$ on your calculator.

So if you know the sine of an angle in a triangle, for example by using the Sine Rule, then there are two possibilities for the angle. It could be either the acute angle θ that you find by using the inverse sine key on your calculator, or the obtuse angle $180° - \theta$. This means that you can use the Sine Rule to find an angle only if you know enough information about the angle to be able to decide which of the two possibilities is correct. For example, you might simply be told whether the angle is acute or obtuse, as in the next example.

Example 11   Using the Sine Rule to find an angle

Find the angle C, to the nearest degree, in the triangle below, given that it is obtuse.

The angle C in the diagram *looks* obtuse, but remember that you should not assume that a geometric diagram has a property just because it looks as if it does. You can only use properties that are explicitly marked or stated.

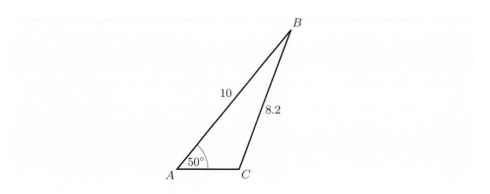

Solution

A side length and the opposite angle are known, so use the Sine Rule.

By the Sine Rule,

$$\frac{\sin 50°}{8.2} = \frac{\sin C}{10}, \quad \text{so} \quad \sin C = \frac{10\sin 50°}{8.2} = 0.9342\ldots.$$

A calculator gives

$$\sin^{-1}(0.9342\ldots) = 69.09\ldots° = 69° \text{ (to the nearest degree).}$$

So the two possible values for C are $69°$ and $180° - 69° = 111°$.

But C is an obtuse angle, so $C = 111°$ (to the nearest degree).

This solution uses the second form of the Sine Rule,
$$\frac{\sin A}{a} = \frac{\sin B}{b} = \frac{\sin C}{c},$$
given on page 77.

Note that you can subtract the rounded value $69°$ from $180°$, rather than subtracting the full-calculator-precision value and then rounding. You will get the same answer either way.

In Example 11, you saw that the Sine Rule gave two values for C, namely $69°$ and $111°$, and the acute angle was disregarded because C is an obtuse angle.

In fact, two different triangles can be drawn with the measurements given in Example 11. Both triangles have an angle of $50°$, an opposite side of length 8.2 and a further side of length 10. However, the other two angles of the first triangle are approximately $69°$ and $61°$, whereas those of the second triangle are approximately $111°$ and $19°$. These two triangles are shown in Figure 51.

The third angle in a triangle can be found by subtracting the two known angles from $180°$.

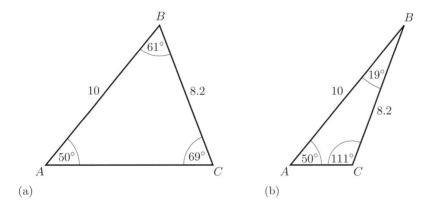

Figure 51 Two triangles can be formed from the given measurements

This fact may not have surprised you! The initial measurements were in the order angle-side-side (ASS) and you know from Unit 8, Subsection 3.1, that this combination of an angle and two sides isn't always sufficient to determine a triangle uniquely. If you use the Sine Rule to find an unknown angle in such a triangle, then it is important to check which of the two possible values for the angle is required.

Activity 29 *Finding an unknown angle using the Sine Rule*

(a) Use the Sine Rule to find the value of $\sin A$, to four decimal places, for the triangle below.

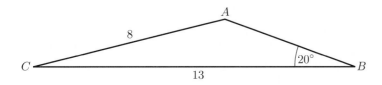

(b) The angle A is obtuse. What is its value, to the nearest degree?

If you know the value of one of the angles of a triangle and it is at least 90°, then since the angles in a triangle add up to 180° both the other angles must be acute. So in this case, if you use the Sine Rule to find one of these other angles, then you need to find only the acute angle solution, that is, the value given by your calculator.

In this section you have seen how to define the sines, cosines and tangents of general angles measured in degrees. In the next section you will see a different method of measuring angles.

4 Radians

This section is concerned with another way of measuring angles, different from degrees. The number of degrees in a full turn, 360, is a matter of convention that has its roots in ancient Babylonian mathematics. This convention has persisted for so many centuries because it has worked well and there was no good reason for changing to another measurement system when applying trigonometry in practical situations such as surveying.

However, when mathematicians studied circular motion and other periodic phenomena, it became apparent that the equations involved are often simpler if you use a different unit for measuring angles, called a *radian*. In higher-level mathematics modules, angles are almost always measured in radians.

4.1 Defining a radian

You can understand what a radian is by thinking about arcs on the circumference of a circle. Figure 52 shows such an arc, and the corresponding angle at O, the centre of the circle. The angle at the centre is said to be **subtended** by the arc. The definition of a radian is as follows.

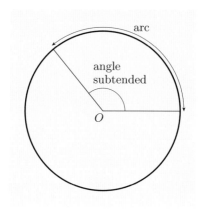

Figure 52   The angle subtended by an arc

> **Radians**
>
> One **radian** is the angle subtended at the centre of a circle by an arc that is the same length as the radius.

This definition is illustrated in Figure 53.

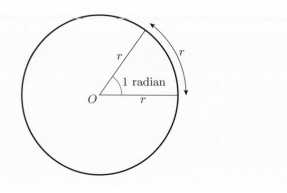

Figure 53   An angle of one radian

From this definition, you can find the number of radians in a full turn. The circumference of the circle in Figure 53 has length $2\pi r$, and each arc of length r subtends an angle of 1 radian. So the number of radians in a full turn is

$$\frac{2\pi r}{r} = 2\pi.$$

In other words, $360°$ is the same angle as 2π radians.

2π radians $= 360°$.

This gives

$$1 \text{ radian} = \frac{360°}{2\pi} = \frac{180°}{\pi}.$$

Since

$$\frac{180}{\pi} = 57.295\ldots,$$

one radian is approximately $57°$.

Because a full turn is 2π radians, the number of radians in a simple fraction of a full turn can be conveniently expressed in terms of π. It is usual to leave these numbers in this form, rather than finding decimal approximations. For example, a half-turn is an angle of π radians, and a quarter-turn is an angle of $\frac{1}{2}\pi$ radians, also written as $\frac{\pi}{2}$ radians or $\pi/2$ radians. Reasoning in this way, we can build up Table 3.

The expression $\pi/2$ is usually read as 'pi by two'.

Table 3 A conversion table for common angles

Angle in degrees	Angle in radians
$0°$	0
$30°$	$\pi/6$
$45°$	$\pi/4$
$60°$	$\pi/3$
$90°$	$\pi/2$
$180°$	π
$360°$	2π

For example, $30°$ is one twelfth of a full turn, so $30°$ is $2\pi/12 = \pi/6$ radians.

Since

$$1 \text{ radian} = \frac{180°}{\pi},$$

the factor $180/\pi$ can be used to convert an angle measured in radians into degrees, and vice versa.

Converting between degrees and radians

$$\text{angle in radians} = \frac{\pi}{180} \times \text{angle in degrees},$$

$$\text{angle in degrees} = \frac{180}{\pi} \times \text{angle in radians}.$$

Here are some examples of these types of conversions.

Example 12 *Converting between degrees and radians*

(a) Convert 270° to radians.

(b) Convert 5π/6 radians to degrees.

Solution

(a) Applying the degrees-to-radians conversion formula gives
$$\text{angle in radians} = \frac{\pi}{180} \times 270 = \frac{3\pi}{2}.$$
So 270° = 3π/2 radians.

(b) Applying the radians-to-degrees conversion formula gives
$$\text{angle in degrees} = \frac{180}{\pi} \times \frac{5\pi}{6} = 150.$$
So 5π/6 = 150°.

Here are some similar questions for you to try.

Activity 30 *Converting between degrees and radians*

(a) Convert the following angles from degrees to radians.

   (i) 75°   (ii) 225°

(b) Convert the following angles from radians to degrees.

   (i) 3π/4 radians   (ii) 4π/5 radians

4.2 Formulas involving radians

Some formulas related to circles have a simpler form if angles are measured in radians rather than degrees.

An example is the formula for the length of an arc on the circumference of a circle of radius r, in terms of the angle θ subtended. You know that

   an arc that subtends an angle of 1 radian has length r.

Hence

   an arc that subtends an angle of θ radians has length $r\theta$.

> **Length of an arc of a circle**
>
>   arc length = $r\theta$,
>
> where r is the radius of the circle and θ is the angle subtended by the arc, measured in radians.

An arc of a circle is sometimes called a **circular arc**, and it can occur as part of another shape. The **centre** and **radius** of a circular arc are the centre and radius of the circle whose circumference it is part of. The next example involves a curved section of road whose edges are circular arcs.

Example 13 *Planning a road barrier*

The diagram below shows a plan for a bend $ABCD$ in a new road. AB and CD are circular arcs with centre O. A barrier is to be placed along CD. What is the length of this barrier, to the nearest metre?

Figure 54 The road is long, with many a winding turn

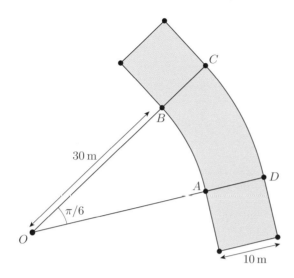

Solution

⬡ Find the radius of the arc and the angle that it subtends at the centre of the circle. ⬡

The radius of the arc CD is the length $OA + AD$, which is 40 metres.

The arc CD subtends an angle of $\pi/6$ radians at the centre of the circle.

⬡ Use the formula for arc length. ⬡

So the length of the arc CD is $r\theta$, where $r = 40$ and $\theta = \pi/6$.

Hence the length of the arc CD in metres is

$$40 \times \frac{\pi}{6} = \frac{20\pi}{3} = 20.94\ldots$$

So the length of the barrier is $21\,\text{m}$ (to the nearest metre).

Another formula that's simpler when radians are used is the formula for the area of a sector. As you saw in Unit 8, Subsection 4.3, a *sector* of a circle is the part of the circle lying between two radii, as shown in Figure 55.

Figure 55 A sector of a circle

Here's how to find this formula. First, the area of a sector is proportional to the angle θ of the sector. Next, if the angle of the sector is π radians, a half-turn, then the sector is a semicircle, which has area $\frac{1}{2}\pi r^2$. That is,

an angle of π radians gives a sector of area $\frac{1}{2}\pi r^2$.

Hence

an angle of 1 radian gives a sector of area $\frac{1}{2}r^2$,

so

an angle of θ radians gives a sector of area $\frac{1}{2}r^2\theta$.

This result is summarised overleaf.

> **Area of a sector of a circle**
>
> $$\text{area of sector} = \tfrac{1}{2}r^2\theta,$$
>
> where r is the radius of the circle and θ is the angle of the sector, measured in radians.

The following example uses the formula for the area of a sector to find the area of the road bend in Example 13.

Example 14   Finding the area of the bend in the road

Calculate the area of the road bend $ABCD$ in Example 13.

Solution

💭 Identify the area that is required and work out how you can find it from the areas of shapes that you know how to calculate. 💭

The area of $ABCD$ can be found by subtracting the area of the sector OAB from the area of the sector OCD.

💭 Use the formula for the area of a sector. 💭

For the sector OCD, the radius r is 40 metres and the angle is $\pi/6$. So the area in square metres of the sector OCD is

$$\tfrac{1}{2} \times 40^2 \times \frac{\pi}{6} = \frac{400\pi}{3} = 418.879\ldots.$$

For the sector OAB, the radius r is 30 metres and the angle is $\pi/6$. So the area in square metres of the sector OAB is

$$\tfrac{1}{2} \times 30^2 \times \frac{\pi}{6} = 75\pi = 235.619\ldots.$$

Hence the area in square metres of the bend in the road is

$$\text{area of sector } OCD - \text{area of sector } OAB$$
$$= 418.879\ldots - 235.619\ldots$$
$$= 183.259\ldots$$
$$= 183 \text{ (to the nearest integer)}.$$

So the area of the bend is approximately 183 square metres.

The next activity involves using the formulas for arc length and the area of a sector to calculate lengths and areas in a gothic window. An example of a gothic window is shown in Figure 56.

The angles given in the activity are measured in degrees, so before you can use the formulas, the first step is to convert from degrees to radians.

Activity 31   Finding lengths and areas in a gothic window

The following diagram shows a gothic window. Each of the two curves at the top is a circular arc whose centre is the lowest point of the other circular arc.

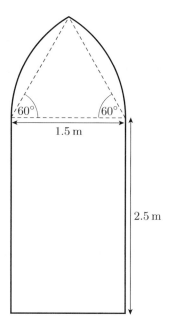

Figure 56 A gothic window

(a) Convert 60° to radians.

(b) Calculate the length of metal edging that is required to fit around the entire perimeter of the window, in metres, to two decimal places.

(c) Calculate the area of the window, in square metres, to two decimal places, using the following steps.

   (i) Calculate the area of the triangle formed by the three dashed lines.

   (ii) Calculate the area of the sector formed by the horizontal dashed line, one slant dashed line and one of the circular arcs.

   (iii) Hence calculate the area of the window above the horizontal dashed line.

   (iv) Calculate the area of the whole window.

When the size of an angle is given in radians, the word 'radians' is often omitted. For example, you might say that the size of an angle is $\pi/3$, rather than $\pi/3$ radians. So if you see the size of an angle given with no degrees mentioned, then you can assume that it is measured in radians.

This convention is particularly useful when you are using trigonometry and the angles are measured in radians. For example, $\sin(\pi/3)$ means the sine of the angle that measures $\pi/3$ radians.

You can use your calculator to find the trigonometric ratios of angles measured in radians, but first it is important to check that your calculator is set to measure angles in radians rather than degrees. The next activity shows you how to do that.

In Unit 14, you will need to find the trigonometric ratios of angles measured in radians.

Activity 32 *Using radians on your calculator*

This activity is in Subsection 3.9 of the MU123 Guide.

In Subsection 1.4 you discovered that you could work out the trigonometric ratios of some commonly-used angles without using your calculator. Table 4 shows the trigonometric ratios of these angles, with the radian measures included as well. The table also includes the angles $0°$ and $90°$, whose trigonometric ratios you learned about in Section 3.

Table 4   Sine, cosine and tangent of special angles

θ in degrees	θ in radians	$\sin\theta$	$\cos\theta$	$\tan\theta$
$0°$	0	0	1	0
$30°$	$\frac{\pi}{6}$	$\frac{1}{2}$	$\frac{\sqrt{3}}{2}$	$\frac{1}{\sqrt{3}}$
$45°$	$\frac{\pi}{4}$	$\frac{1}{\sqrt{2}}$	$\frac{1}{\sqrt{2}}$	1
$60°$	$\frac{\pi}{3}$	$\frac{\sqrt{3}}{2}$	$\frac{1}{2}$	$\sqrt{3}$
$90°$	$\frac{\pi}{2}$	1	0	$-$

Fortunately there are several patterns in Table 4 that make the values easier to remember. For example, you saw in Activity 12 on page 73 how the sine and cosine values of certain angles are related. There is also a neat pattern for remembering the values of $\sin\theta$ in the table, which is given in Table 5. Remember, as well, that you can quickly work out the trigonometric ratios of $30°$, $45°$ and $60°$ by drawing appropriate right-angled triangles, as you saw in Subsection 1.4.

Table 5   A pattern in the table

θ	θ	$\sin\theta$
$0°$	0	$\frac{\sqrt{0}}{2} = 0$
$30°$	$\frac{\pi}{6}$	$\frac{\sqrt{1}}{2} = \frac{1}{2}$
$45°$	$\frac{\pi}{4}$	$\frac{\sqrt{2}}{2} = \frac{1}{\sqrt{2}}$
$60°$	$\frac{\pi}{3}$	$\frac{\sqrt{3}}{2}$
$90°$	$\frac{\pi}{2}$	$\frac{\sqrt{4}}{2} = 1$

As you continue your mathematical studies you will find that trigonometry has many applications: solving triangles is a skill that will often be useful, and the trigonometric functions will appear in a variety of topics, some of which are only distantly related to the geometry of triangles. You will meet some examples in Unit 14.

Learning checklist

After studying this unit, you should be able to:

- define the sine, cosine and tangent of an acute angle and relate these to the sides of a right-angled triangle
- use inverse sine, inverse cosine and inverse tangent to find angles
- state and derive the sine, cosine and tangent of some special angles
- solve triangles using the Sine Rule and the Cosine Rule as appropriate
- calculate the areas of triangles from two side lengths and the included angle, or from three side lengths
- find the sine, cosine and tangent of any angle on a calculator, where these are defined
- appreciate the relationship between the sine and cosine functions, and periodic motion, in particular circular motion
- use radians as a measure of angle, and convert between radians and degrees
- calculate the lengths of arcs of circles and the areas of sectors of circles using radians.

Solutions and comments on Activities

Activity 1

(a) The marked triangle is shown below.

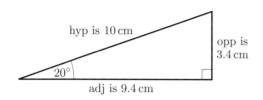

(b) The sides of the triangle measure approximately 10 cm, 3.4 cm and 9.4 cm. Using SOH CAH TOA gives

$$\sin 20° = \frac{\text{opp}}{\text{hyp}} \approx \frac{3.4}{10} \approx 0.34,$$

$$\cos 20° = \frac{\text{adj}}{\text{hyp}} \approx \frac{9.4}{10} \approx 0.94,$$

$$\tan 20° = \frac{\text{opp}}{\text{adj}} \approx \frac{3.4}{9.4} \approx 0.36.$$

Activity 2

The approximate value for $\tan 20°$ found in Activity 1 is 0.36, so the equation is

$$\frac{x}{100} \approx 0.36$$

which gives

$$x \approx 0.36 \times 100 = 36.$$

So the height of the tree is approximately 36 m.

Activity 4

(a) The unknown side is adjacent to the angle of 65°, and the given side is the hypotenuse, so the appropriate trigonometric ratio is cosine. Thus

$$\cos 65° = \frac{x}{9}, \quad \text{so} \quad x = 9 \cos 65°.$$

Using a calculator gives $x = 3.80$ (to 3 s.f.).

(b) The given side is opposite the angle of 35°, and the unknown side is the hypotenuse, so the appropriate trigonometric ratio is sine. Thus

$$\sin 35° = \frac{10}{x}, \quad \text{so} \quad x = \frac{10}{\sin 35°}.$$

Using a calculator gives $x = 17.4$ (to 3 s.f.).

(c) The unknown side is opposite the angle of 48°, and the given side is adjacent to this angle, so the appropriate trigonometric ratio is tangent. Thus

$$\tan 48° = \frac{x}{25}, \quad \text{so} \quad x = 25 \tan 48°.$$

Using a calculator gives $x = 27.76\ldots$, so the length is 27.8 m (to 3 s.f.).

Activity 5

From the symmetry of the triangle, $BD = DC$, so $BC = 2BD$.

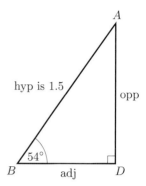

In the right-angled triangle $\triangle ABD$, the hypotenuse AB is 1.5 m and the side adjacent to the angle 54° is BD. Hence

$$\cos 54° = \frac{BD}{1.5}, \quad \text{so} \quad BD = 1.5 \cos 54°.$$

Hence

$$BC = 2 \times 1.5 \cos 54° = 1.7633\ldots.$$

Thus the length of BC is 1.763 m, or 1763 mm (to the nearest millimetre).

Activity 6

In the diagram below, the unknown distance is labelled x.

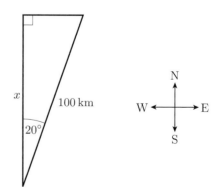

The unknown length is adjacent to the given angle. Thus

$$\cos 20° = \frac{x}{100}, \quad \text{so} \quad x = 100 \cos 20° = 93.969\ldots.$$

Hence the plane is 94 km north of its starting position (to the nearest kilometre).

Activity 7

(a) The given length 9 is opposite the angle 40°
and the unknown x is the length of the
hypotenuse. Thus

$$\sin 40° = \frac{9}{x}, \quad \text{so} \quad x = \frac{9}{\sin 40°} = 14.001\ldots.$$

Hence $x = 14.0$ (to 3 s.f.).

The unknown y is adjacent to the angle 40°. Thus

$$\tan 40° = \frac{9}{y}, \quad \text{so} \quad y = \frac{9}{\tan 40°} = 10.725\ldots.$$

Hence $y = 10.7$ (to 3 s.f.).

(b) The length of the hypotenuse is 10 and the
unknown x is opposite the angle 25°. Thus

$$\sin 25° = \frac{x}{10}, \quad \text{so} \quad x = 10\sin 25° = 4.226\ldots.$$

Hence $x = 4.23$ (to 3 s.f.).

The unknown y is adjacent to the angle 25°. Thus

$$\cos 25° = \frac{y}{10}, \quad \text{so} \quad y = 10\cos 25° = 9.063\ldots.$$

Hence $y = 9.06$ (to 3 s.f.).

(c) The given length 11 is adjacent to the given
angle 48° and the unknown x is opposite this
angle. Thus

$$\tan 48° = \frac{x}{11}, \quad \text{so} \quad x = 11\tan 48° = 12.21\ldots.$$

Hence $x = 12.2$ (to 3 s.f.).

The unknown y is the hypotenuse. Thus

$$\cos 48° = \frac{11}{y}, \quad \text{so} \quad y = \frac{11}{\cos 48°} = 16.43\ldots.$$

Hence $y = 16.4$ (to 3 s.f.).

(d) The given length 8 is opposite the given
angle 63° and the unknown x is adjacent to this
angle. Thus

$$\tan 63° = \frac{8}{x}, \quad \text{so} \quad x = \frac{8}{\tan 63°} = 4.076\ldots.$$

Hence $x = 4.08$ (to 3 s.f.).

The unknown y is the hypotenuse. Thus

$$\sin 63° = \frac{8}{y}, \quad \text{so} \quad y = \frac{8}{\sin 63°} = 8.978\ldots.$$

Hence $y = 8.98$ (to 3 s.f.).

Activity 9

(a) In this triangle, you know the length of the
side opposite the angle α and the length of the
hypotenuse. So

$$\sin \alpha = \frac{10}{15} = \frac{2}{3}.$$

Thus α is the acute angle whose sine is $\frac{2}{3}$. A
calculator gives $\sin^{-1}(\frac{2}{3}) = 41.8\ldots°$, so the

unknown angle is 42° (to the nearest degree).

(b) In this triangle, you know the length of the
side opposite the angle β and the length of the side
adjacent to it. So

$$\tan \beta = \frac{9}{8}.$$

Thus β is the acute angle whose tangent is $\frac{9}{8}$. A
calculator gives $\tan^{-1}(\frac{9}{8}) = 48.3\ldots°$, so the
unknown angle is 48° (to the nearest degree).

Activity 10

Let α represent the angle that the snow slope
makes with the horizontal.

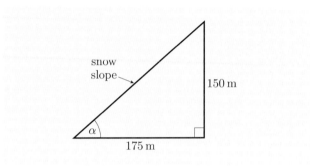

From the diagram, $\tan \alpha = \frac{150}{175} = \frac{6}{7}$.

So $\alpha = \tan^{-1}(\frac{6}{7}) = 40.6\ldots°$.

Since $35° < \alpha < 45°$, there is a risk of an avalanche.

(Note that many other factors may contribute to
the risk of an avalanche!)

Activity 11

The length of the hypotenuse, x, can be calculated
by applying Pythagoras' Theorem:

$$x^2 = 1^2 + 1^2 = 2, \quad \text{so} \quad x = \sqrt{2}.$$

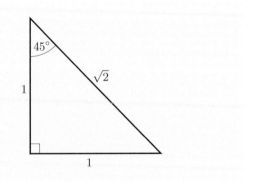

So the hypotenuse has length $\sqrt{2}$ and the adjacent
and opposite sides have length 1. Thus

$$\sin 45° = \frac{1}{\sqrt{2}}, \quad \cos 45° = \frac{1}{\sqrt{2}}, \quad \tan 45° = \frac{1}{1} = 1.$$

Activity 12

(a) In this triangle,
$$\sin\theta = \frac{\text{opp}}{\text{hyp}} = \frac{a}{c}, \quad \cos\theta = \frac{\text{adj}}{\text{hyp}} = \frac{b}{c}.$$
Also,
$$\sin(90° - \theta) = \frac{\text{opp}}{\text{hyp}} = \frac{b}{c}, \quad \cos(90° - \theta) = \frac{\text{adj}}{\text{hyp}} = \frac{a}{c}.$$

(b) By the equations in part (a),
$$\cos\theta = \frac{b}{c} = \sin(90° - \theta)$$
and
$$\sin\theta = \frac{a}{c} = \cos(90° - \theta).$$

Activity 14

The side length 7 m is opposite the angle of 55°, and the unknown side length x is opposite the angle of 60°. By the Sine Rule,
$$\frac{7}{\sin 55°} = \frac{x}{\sin 60°},$$
so
$$x = \frac{7\sin 60°}{\sin 55°} = 7.400\ldots.$$
Thus $x = 7.40$ m (to 3 s.f.).

Activity 15

The unknown side length x is opposite the angle of 55°, and this angle is between two known side lengths. So we can apply the Cosine Rule to the triangle to give
$$x^2 = 6^2 + 10^2 - 2 \times 6 \times 10 \cos 55° = 67.170\ldots.$$
Thus $x = \sqrt{67.170\ldots} = 8.19\ldots = 8.2$ (to 2 s.f.).

Activity 16

We first calculate $\angle B$ using the Cosine Rule. The side opposite $\angle B$ has length 4, and this appears on the left-hand side of the equation, with the other two lengths on the right-hand side:
$$4^2 = 3^2 + 4^2 - 2 \times 3 \times 4 \cos B,$$
so
$$16 = 25 - 24 \cos B.$$
Hence
$$\cos B = \frac{25 - 16}{24} = \frac{9}{24} = 0.375.$$
A calculator gives $\cos^{-1}(0.375) = 67.975\ldots$, so $\angle B = 68°$ to the nearest degree.

As the triangle is isosceles, $\angle A = \angle B$. So $\angle A = 68°$ to the nearest degree.

The third angle can be found by using the fact that the angles of a triangle add up to 180°. Using the unrounded value of $\angle B$, we obtain the following value for $\angle C$:
$$180 - 2 \times 67.975\ldots = 44.048\ldots.$$
So $\angle C = 44°$ to the nearest degree.

Activity 17

(a) This is a right-angled triangle, so go down the left-hand side of the decision tree. The problem of finding x involves only lengths, so the best method to use is Pythagoras' Theorem.

To find θ use a trigonometric ratio – in this case you can find θ from the equation $\tan\theta = 6/8$.

(b) This is not a right-angled triangle, so follow the right-hand side of the decision tree. The known side length, 6, is not opposite a known angle, but you can calculate the angle θ to be $180° - 55° - 60° = 65°$. (This is the case indicated in brackets in the decision tree.)

Now you know a side length, 6, opposite a known angle, 65°, so you can use the Sine Rule to calculate x.

(c) Again, this is not a right-angled triangle, so follow the right-hand side of the decision tree. No angles are given, so the Sine Rule does not apply. But you know three side lengths, so you can find θ by using the Cosine Rule.

Activity 18

(a) The unknown length x is opposite a known angle, but the given length, the baseline 50 m, is opposite an unknown angle. So the first task is to calculate the angle opposite the baseline. Since the angles in a triangle add up to 180°, the angle opposite the baseline is $180° - 78.5° - 82.4° = 19.1°$.

Now use the Sine Rule:
$$\frac{50}{\sin 19.1°} = \frac{x}{\sin 82.4°},$$
so
$$x = \frac{50\sin 82.4°}{\sin 19.1°}.$$
Using a calculator gives $x = 151.46$ m (to the nearest centimetre).

(b) Proceeding in a similar manner on the second day, start by calculating the third angle in the triangle, which is $180° - 79.0° - 81.9° = 19.1°$.

Now use the Sine Rule:
$$\frac{50}{\sin 19.1°} = \frac{y}{\sin 81.9°},$$
so
$$y = \frac{50\sin 81.9°}{\sin 19.1°}.$$
Using a calculator gives $y = 151.28$ m (to the nearest centimetre).

Activity 19

The angle opposite the unknown length z is the difference between the angles measured from the left-hand end of the baseline on day 1 and day 2, that is, $79° - 78.5° = 0.5°$.

By the Cosine Rule,

$$z^2 = 151.46^2 + 151.28^2$$
$$- 2 \times 151.46 \times 151.28 \cos 0.5°$$
$$= 1.777\ldots.$$

So $z = \sqrt{1.777\ldots} = 1.33\ldots.$ Hence $z = 1.3\,\text{m}$ (to 2 s.f.).

Activity 20

(a) By the area formula, the area of the triangle in km^2 is

$$\tfrac{1}{2} \times 8 \times 10 \sin 40° = 25.71\ldots.$$

Thus the area is $25.7\,\text{km}^2$ (to 3 s.f.).

(b) By the area formula, the area of the triangle in cm^2 is

$$\tfrac{1}{2} \times 6 \times 7 \sin 60° = 18.18\ldots.$$

Thus the area is $18.2\,\text{cm}^2$ (to 3 s.f.).

Activity 21

(a) Since the side length of the equilateral triangle is 2 and each angle is $60°$, the area is

$$\tfrac{1}{2} \times 2 \times 2 \sin 60° = 2 \times \frac{\sqrt{3}}{2} = \sqrt{3}.$$

(b) Each side has length 2, so the semi-perimeter is $s = \tfrac{1}{2}(2 + 2 + 2) = 3$. By Heron's Formula, the area is

$$\sqrt{s(s-a)(s-b)(s-c)}$$
$$= \sqrt{3(3-2)(3-2)(3-2)}$$
$$= \sqrt{3},$$

as in part (a).

Activity 22

(a) P lies in the first quadrant.

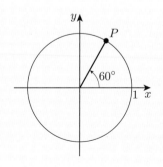

(b) P lies in the third quadrant.

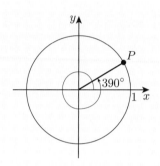

(c) P lies in the first quadrant.

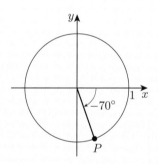

(d) P lies in the fourth quadrant.

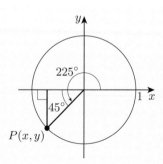

Activity 23

(a)

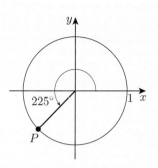

The hypotenuse of the right-angled triangle in the diagram has length 1, so

$$\sin 45° = \frac{\text{opp}}{1} \quad \text{and} \quad \cos 45° = \frac{\text{adj}}{1}.$$

Hence the side opposite the angle of $45°$ has length

$$\sin 45° = \frac{1}{\sqrt{2}},$$

and the side adjacent to the angle of $45°$ has length

$$\cos 45° = \frac{1}{\sqrt{2}}.$$

(You can find the values of $\sin 45°$ and $\cos 45°$ either by using your calculator or from Table 1 on page 73.)

Therefore the coordinates of the point P are

$$\left(-\frac{1}{\sqrt{2}}, -\frac{1}{\sqrt{2}}\right).$$

So, by the definitions of the sine and cosine of a general angle,

$$\cos 225° = -\frac{1}{\sqrt{2}} = -0.7071 \text{ (to 4 d.p.)}$$

and

$$\sin 225° = -\frac{1}{\sqrt{2}} = -0.7071 \text{ (to 4 d.p.)}.$$

These values agree with those given by a calculator.

(b)

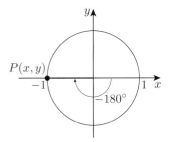

Since P has coordinates $(-1, 0)$,

$$\cos(-180°) = -1 \quad \text{and} \quad \sin(-180°) = 0.$$

These values agree with those given by a calculator.

Activity 24

By the solution to Activity 23(a),

$$\tan 225° = \frac{\sin 225°}{\cos 225°} = \frac{-\frac{1}{\sqrt{2}}}{-\frac{1}{\sqrt{2}}} = 1.$$

By the solution to Activity 23(b),

$$\tan(-180°) = \frac{\sin(-180°)}{\cos(-180°)} = \frac{0}{-1} = 0.$$

Activity 26

The asymptotes of the tangent graph occur when $\cos\theta = 0$.

So for the portion of the tangent graph between $360°$ and $720°$, the asymptotes of this graph are $\theta = 450°$ and $\theta = 630°$.

Activity 28

The dimensions of the triangle are shown below.

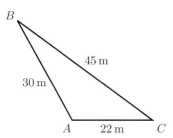

By the Cosine Rule,

$$a^2 = b^2 + c^2 - 2bc \cos A,$$

so

$$\cos A = \frac{b^2 + c^2 - a^2}{2bc}$$

$$= \frac{22^2 + 30^2 - 45^2}{2 \times 22 \times 30}$$

$$= -0.4856\ldots.$$

Using a calculator gives

$$\cos^{-1}(-0.4856\ldots) = 119.05\ldots°.$$

So $A = 119°$ (to the nearest degree).

Activity 29

(a) By the Sine Rule,

$$\frac{\sin A}{13} = \frac{\sin 20°}{8}.$$

Thus

$$\sin A = \frac{13 \sin 20°}{8} = 0.555\,78\ldots,$$

so $\sin A = 0.5558$ (to 4 d.p.).

(b) Using a calculator gives

$$\sin^{-1}(0.555\,78\ldots) = 33.76\ldots°.$$

So, to the nearest degree, the two possible angles are $34°$ and $180° - 34° = 146°$.

Since A is obtuse, the value of A is $146°$.

Activity 30

(a) (i) Applying the degrees-to-radians conversion formula gives

$$\text{angle in radians} = \frac{\pi}{180} \times 75 = \frac{5\pi}{12}.$$

So $75° = 5\pi/12$ radians.

(ii) Applying the degrees-to-radians conversion formula gives

$$\text{angle in radians} = \frac{\pi}{180} \times 225 = \frac{5\pi}{4}.$$

So $225° = 5\pi/4$ radians.

(b) (i) Applying the radians-to-degrees conversion formula gives

$$\text{angle in degrees} = \frac{180}{\pi} \times \frac{3\pi}{4} = 135.$$

So $3\pi/4$ radians $= 135°$.

(ii) Applying the radians-to-degrees conversion formula gives

$$\text{angle in degrees} = \frac{180}{\pi} \times \frac{4\pi}{5} = 144.$$

So $4\pi/5$ radians $= 144°$.

Activity 31

(a) Applying the degrees-to-radians conversion formula gives

$$\text{angle in radians} = \frac{\pi}{180} \times 60 = \frac{\pi}{3}.$$

So $60° = \pi/3$ radians.

(Alternatively, you could have looked up the angle $60°$ in Table 3 on page 103.)

(b) The length of each of the two arcs in the diagram is given by $r\theta$, where $r = 1.5$ and $\theta = \pi/3$. So the length of each arc in metres is

$$1.5 \times \pi/3 = 0.5\pi.$$

Hence the total length of edging required is

$$2 \times 0.5\pi + 2 \times 2.5 + 1.5 = \pi + 6.5$$
$$= 9.64 \,\text{m (to 2 d.p.).}$$

(c) (i) The area of the triangle is given by the formula

$$\text{area} = \tfrac{1}{2}ab\sin\theta,$$

with $a = b = 1.5$ and $\theta = 60°$. So it is

$$\tfrac{1}{2} \times 1.5^2 \times \frac{\sqrt{3}}{2} = \frac{9\sqrt{3}}{16} = 0.974\ldots \,\text{m}^2.$$

(ii) The area of the sector is given by the formula

$$\text{area} = \tfrac{1}{2}r^2\theta,$$

with $r = 1.5$ and $\theta = \pi/3$. So it is

$$\tfrac{1}{2} \times 1.5^2 \times \frac{\pi}{3} = \frac{3\pi}{8} = 1.178\ldots \,\text{m}^2.$$

(iii) There are two sectors visible in the diagram of the window, and their overlap is the triangle formed by the dashed lines. So the area of the window above the horizontal dashed line is

$$2 \times \text{area of sector} - \text{area of triangle}$$
$$= 2 \times 1.178\ldots - 0.974\ldots$$
$$= 1.381\ldots \,\text{m}^2.$$

(Alternatively, you could subtract the area of the triangle from the area of one sector to find the area of one of the two thin segments at the top of the window. Then you could calculate the area of the window above the horizontal dashed line by adding twice the area of the segment to the area of the triangle.)

(iv) The area of the window below the horizontal dashed line is

$$1.5 \times 2.5 = 3.75 \,\text{m}^2,$$

so the area of the whole window is

$$1.381\ldots + 3.75 = 5.13 \,\text{m}^2 \text{ (to 2 d.p.).}$$

Exponentials

Introduction

People sometimes talk about things growing exponentially – the population of the world or the number of people with a particular disease, for example. What exactly does this mean?

The idea of exponential growth can be understood by thinking about chain letters (or, more commonly nowadays, chain emails or chain text messages). A typical chain letter contains a message that the recipient is asked to send on to, say, five other people. For example, the message in one spoof chain letter asked recipients to 'help a dying child get into the Guinness Book of World Records' by sending their business cards to a certain address, and recipients were asked to forward this message to several other people.

To encourage recipients of a chain letter to continue the chain, they may be promised good luck if they cooperate (the 'carrot approach') or threatened with bad luck if they don't (the 'stick approach').

If each letter in a chain is sent to five recipients, each of whom sends a letter to five new people, who in turn each send it on to five more people, then the growth in the number of letters is remarkable:

> first round: 5 letters;
>
> second round: $5 \times 5 = 5^2 = 25$ letters;
>
> third round: $5 \times 25 = 5^3 = 125$ letters;
>
> fourth round: $5 \times 125 = 5^4 = 625$ letters;

and so on.

If all the recipients respond as asked, and each person enters the chain only once, then the twentieth round consists of 5^{20} letters, which is nearly 100 trillion – about 10 000 times the number of people in the world. Even if only a certain proportion of recipients respond, then the number of letters grows extremely rapidly. For example, if three out of the five recipients respond on each occasion, then the twentieth round consists of 3^{20} letters, which is more than three billion – about half of the number of people in the world.

This type of growth, where the numbers increase by the same factor at each stage, is called *exponential growth*. Exponential growth can be extremely rapid, but 'exponential growth' does not *mean* 'rapid growth' – it is a common misconception that the two mean the same. Exponential growth can also be slow, if the factor by which the numbers increase is small. And some types of growth are rapid but not exponential. So be aware that when you see or hear the term 'exponential growth' used in an everyday context, its user may not intend the clearly-defined mathematical meaning given in this unit.

You will learn about exponential growth in this unit, and also about *exponential decay*, which is closely related to exponential growth but involves decreasing quantities rather than increasing ones.

In Sections 1 and 2 you will learn exactly what is meant by exponential growth and decay, and you will see a range of examples of this type of change. You will also see how you can use models based on this type of change to make predictions. In Section 3 you will explore the graphs of the equations that describe exponential growth and decay, and you will be introduced to the important mathematical constant e, which has a value of

If you send this
to 5 more people,
something major
that you've been
wanting will happen!

PS don't break the chain,
or you'll be sorry ...

A well wisher

Figure I Typical examples of the carrot and stick approaches in chain letters, emails or text messages

roughly 2.718 and a special place in mathematics. Finally, in Sections 4 and 5 you will meet the idea of *logarithms*. You will see that these are closely related to the ideas covered in the earlier parts of the unit, and learn about some of their uses.

The calculator section of the MU123 Guide is needed for two of the activities in this unit. If you do not have the MU123 Guide to hand when you reach these activities, then you can omit them and return to them later. However, you will need to work through these activities before you study Subsections 5.2 and 5.3.

Activities 21 and 25, on pages 153 and 156, respectively, are in the MU123 Guide.

1 Exponential growth and decay

In this section you will learn about exponential growth and decay by considering a number of examples.

1.1 Doubling and halving

The activity below asks you to think about growth in a particular situation.

Activity 1 *Guessing the height of a pile of paper*

Imagine tearing a long strip of paper in half and placing one half on top of the other, then tearing the two pieces in half again and stacking them to make a pile of four pieces, then repeating the process to make a stack of eight pieces, and so on. Suppose that you continue until you have carried out the process 50 times in all. What do you think the height of your paper pile might be, roughly?

Here is another puzzle that reveals something about the surprisingly powerful effect of doubling.

Activity 2 *Thinking about doubling*

Imagine a pond containing water lilies (Figure 2). Suppose that the area of the pond covered by the lily pads doubles every day. It takes 30 days for the lily pads to completely cover the pond. After how many days did the lily pads cover exactly half of the pond?

Figure 2 Lily pads in a pond

Another striking illustration of the effect of repeated doubling comes from a legend. It is said that the ruler of an ancient land was so delighted with the newly invented game of chess that he decided to reward its inventor. Rashly, he asked the inventor to name his own reward. The inventor cunningly asked the ruler for the following: for the first square of the chessboard (Figure 3, overleaf), he should receive one grain of rice, then two grains for the second square, four grains for the third square, and so on, doubling the number of grains each time until all 64 squares were accounted for.

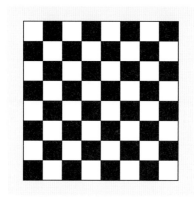

Figure 3 A chessboard, with 64 squares

The ruler foolishly agreed to this arrangement. However, his state treasurer subsequently discovered that it would be impossible to give the inventor the reward.

You can work out the number of grains of rice on the successive squares of the chessboard as follows. Let's number the squares from 0 to 63, so that square 0 contains the first grain of rice, square 1 contains the number of grains after 1 doubling, square 2 contains the number of grains after 2 doublings, and so on. Then

the number of grains on square 0 is 1;
the number of grains on square 1 is 1×2;
the number of grains on square 2 is $1 \times 2 \times 2 = 2^2$;
the number of grains on square 3 is $1 \times 2 \times 2 \times 2 = 2^3$;

and so on. In general,

the number of grains on square n is $1 \times 2^n = 2^n$.

The total number of grains of rice comes to

$$1 + 2 + 2^2 + 2^3 + 2^4 + \cdots + 2^{63}.$$

This is a lot of rice! In fact, it is much more than the amount that would be produced in one harvest, at modern yields, if all the Earth's arable land could be devoted to growing rice.

You have now seen several illustrations of the effect of repeated doubling. Repeated doubling always produces the type of growth called exponential growth.

To understand exactly what 'exponential growth' means, think back to the first illustration, the pile of paper. The height in metres of the initial pile was 0.0001, and each successive height was calculated by multiplying the previous height by the same number, namely 2.

Exponential growth is growth that arises from repeated multiplication by the same number. The number that you start with is called the **starting number**, and the number that you multiply by is called the **scale factor** (or *multiplication factor*). For exponential growth, the scale factor must be greater than 1, so that when you multiply you obtain an increase rather than a decrease.

You have already met the idea of a scale factor in various different contexts earlier in the module.

In the example of the paper pile, the starting number is 0.0001, since this is the height in metres of the initial pile of one strip of paper, and the scale factor is 2, since the height of the pile is multiplied by 2 at each step. As you saw in the solution to Activity 1, the successive heights in metres of the pile of paper are as follows:

the initial height is the starting number, 0.0001;
after 1 step, the height is 0.0001×2;
after 2 steps, the height is $0.0001 \times 2 \times 2 = 0.0001 \times 2^2$;
after 3 steps, the height is $0.0001 \times 2 \times 2 \times 2 = 0.0001 \times 2^3$;

and so on. In general,

after n steps, the height in metres is 0.0001×2^n.

A formula for exponential growth with any starting value and any scale factor can be worked out in the same way. If the starting value is a and the scale factor is b, then:

the initial value is the starting number, a;
after 1 step, the value is $a \times b = ab$;
after 2 steps, the value is $a \times b \times b = ab^2$;
after 3 steps, the value is $a \times b \times b \times b = ab^3$;

and so on. In general,

after n steps, the value is ab^n.

These ideas about exponential growth are summarised in the box below.

Exponential growth

Suppose that a positive quantity changes in steps, where its value at each step is obtained from its value at the previous step by multiplying by the same constant, which is greater than 1. Then the quantity is said to **grow exponentially**. The constant is called the scale factor.

If the starting number is a and the scale factor is b, then the value after n steps is ab^n.

The word *exponential* arises from the fact that the number of steps, n, is in the *exponent* in the formula ab^n.

Remember that *exponent* is another name for *power* or *index*.

Figure 4 shows the height in metres of the paper pile at the beginning of the process and after each of the first ten steps. You can see that the growth starts slowly, but keeps increasing and soon becomes very rapid indeed. This is typical of exponential growth.

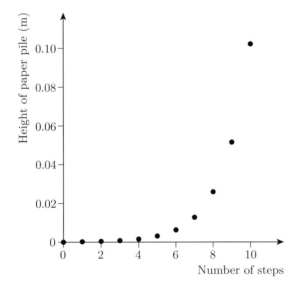

Figure 4   The height of the paper pile after each of the first ten steps

However, as you saw in the introduction to the unit, exponential growth does not necessarily mean very fast growth, contrary to how the term is often used in the media. If the scale factor were, say, 1.000 001, then the quantity would grow only very slowly, but the growth would still be exponential growth.

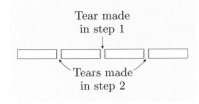

Tear made in step 1

Tears made in step 2

Figure 5   Tears in the paper strip at right angles to the long edges

Now let's think about the paper-tearing process from a different point of view. Suppose that you always tear the paper strips exactly in half, and always at right angles to the long edges of the initial strip of paper, as illustrated in Figure 5. Consider the length of the pieces of paper after each step. Suppose that you start with a strip of paper 0.7 metres long. Then the lengths, in metres, of the strips after each step are as follows:

the initial length is 0.7;

after 1 step, the length is $0.7 \times \frac{1}{2}$;

after 2 steps, the length is $0.7 \times \frac{1}{2} \times \frac{1}{2} = 0.7 \times \left(\frac{1}{2}\right)^2$;

after 3 steps, the length is $0.7 \times \frac{1}{2} \times \frac{1}{2} \times \frac{1}{2} = 0.7 \times \left(\frac{1}{2}\right)^3$;

and so on. In general,

after n steps, the length of the pieces of paper in metres is $0.7 \times \left(\frac{1}{2}\right)^n$.

This formula is of the same form as the formula for exponential growth. It arises from a starting number, 0.7, repeatedly multiplied by a scale factor, $\frac{1}{2}$. The only difference is that here the scale factor is less than 1 (but still positive), so at each step the size *decreases* rather than increases. This is an example of *exponential decay*.

> ### Exponential decay
>
> Suppose that a positive quantity changes in steps, where its value at each step is obtained from its value at the previous step by multiplying by the same scale factor, which is between 0 and 1 (exclusive). Then the quantity is said to **decay exponentially**.
>
> If the starting number is a and the scale factor is b, then the value after n steps is given by the same formula as for exponential growth, namely ab^n.

Figure 6 shows the lengths of the pieces of paper at the beginning of the process and after each of the first ten steps. You can see that the decay is rapid at first, but gets slower and slower as the length gets closer to zero. This is typical of exponential decay.

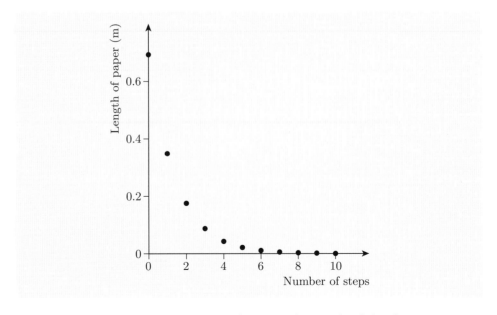

Figure 6   The length of the pieces of paper after each of the first ten steps

In the examples of exponential growth and decay that you have seen in this subsection, the scale factor was either 2 (corresponding to doubling) or $\frac{1}{2}$ (corresponding to halving). The scale factor in exponential change can be any positive number at all (except 1, which would give no change), and you will see some examples of exponential growth and decay with different scale factors in the next subsection.

1.2 Multiplying by a scale factor

In real-life examples of exponential growth and decay, scale factors are often given in the form of percentage increases or decreases. So this subsection starts by reminding you how to obtain the scale factor corresponding to a percentage increase or decrease. This idea is essential to your understanding of the rest of the unit.

Suppose, for example, that you want to increase the price of an item costing £18 by 15%. Since $100\% + 15\% = 115\%$, this means that the new price is 115% of the old price. So you can calculate the new price by multiplying the old price by the fraction $\frac{115}{100}$, which is equal to 1.15. The new price is

You saw how to work with percentage increases and decreases in Examples 14 and 15 on pages 41–42 of Unit 1.

$$£18 \times 1.15 = £20.70.$$

By the same principle:

to increase a number by 27%, multiply it by the scale factor 1.27;
to increase a number by 80%, multiply it by the scale factor 1.80, or simply 1.8;

and so on.

$1.27 = 27$
$1.05 = 5\%$
$1.005 = 0.5\%$

Care is needed with percentage increases of less than 10%. For example, if you want to increase a number by 6%, then you do *not* multiply it by the scale factor 1.6. You want to increase it to 106% of its original value, so you multiply by the fraction $\frac{106}{100}$, which is equal to 1.06.

The principle above also applies to percentage decreases. Suppose that you want to apply a 15% discount to the price of an item costing £18. Since $100\% - 15\% = 85\%$, the new price is 85% of the old price. So you can calculate the new price by multiplying the old price by the fraction $\frac{85}{100}$, which is equal to 0.85. The new price is

$$£18 \times 0.85 = £15.30.$$

By the same principle:

to decrease a number by 27%, multiply it by the scale factor 0.73 (since $100\% - 27\% = 73\%$);
to decrease a number by 80%, multiply by the scale factor 0.2 (since $100\% - 80\% = 20\%$);

and so on.

Scale factors for percentage increases and decreases

To increase a number by $r\%$, multiply it by $\dfrac{100 + r}{100} \left(= 1 + \dfrac{r}{100} \right)$.

To decrease a number by $r\%$, multiply it by $\dfrac{100 - r}{100} \left(= 1 - \dfrac{r}{100} \right)$.

You can practise converting percentage increases and decreases to scale factors in the next two activities.

Activity 3 *Finding the scale factors for percentage increases and decreases*

(a) A market stallholder buys leather purses for £4.25 each and applies a 65% mark-up to work out his selling price. By what scale factor must he multiply the buying price to work out the selling price? Use this scale factor to calculate the selling price.

(b) The same stallholder is offering a 30% discount on £7 shirts. By what scale factor must he multiply the usual price to work out the discounted price? Use this scale factor to work out the discounted price.

Activity 4 *More practice with scale factors*

(a) Write down the scale factor corresponding to each of the following percentage increases and decreases.

  (i) 10% increase (ii) 3% increase (iii) 0.5% increase

  (iv) 15% decrease (v) 2% decrease (vi) 1.5% decrease

(b) Write down the percentage increase or decrease corresponding to each of the following scale factors.

  (i) 1.08 (ii) 0.91 (iii) 1.072

In each part of Activity 3, a number had to be multiplied by a scale factor only once. However, there are some practical situations where a number is repeatedly multiplied by a scale factor, leading to exponential growth or decay.

A common example is the growth in the value of a sum of money invested for a number of years at a fixed annual rate of interest. Usually the interest earned at the end of the first year is added to the initial investment, so in the second year interest is earned not just on the initial investment, but also on the amount of the first interest payment. Then the interest earned in the second year is also added to the value of the investment, and so on. The interest accrued in this way is called **compound interest**.

The value of the investment after one year is calculated by multiplying by the appropriate scale factor. The value of the investment after a greater number of years is calculated by repeatedly multiplying by the same scale factor, as illustrated in the example below.

Example 1 *Calculating the value of an investment*

A sum of £240 is invested in a deposit account that gives a 4% per year rate of return. There are no further transactions.

(a) How much will the investment be worth after the following times?

  (i) 1 year (ii) 2 years (iii) 10 years

(b) Suppose that £V is the value of the investment after n years. Write down a formula for V in terms of n.

Solution

(a) (i) The rate of return is 4% per year, so by the end of 1 year the value of the investment will have increased by a scale factor of 1.04.

The value of the investment after 1 year is

$$£240 \times 1.04 = £249.60.$$

(ii) The value of the investment after 2 years is 1.04 times its value after 1 year.

The value after 2 years is

$$£240 \times 1.04 \times 1.04 = £240 \times 1.04^2$$
$$= £259.58 \text{ (to the nearest penny)}.$$

(iii) The value after 10 years is

$$£240 \times 1.04 \times 1.04 \times 1.04 \times 1.04 \times 1.04$$
$$\times 1.04 \times 1.04 \times 1.04 \times 1.04 \times 1.04$$
$$= £240 \times 1.04^{10}$$
$$= £355.26 \text{ (to the nearest penny)}.$$

(b) A formula for the value $£V$ of the investment after n years is

$$V = 240 \times 1.04^n.$$

Here are two activities involving compound interest for you to try.

Activity 5 *Working out compound interest*

Suppose that you invest $£1800$ at a fixed rate of 4.5% per year.

(a) How much will your investment be worth after the following times?

　(i) 1 year　　(ii) 3 years　　(iii) 10 years

(b) Calculate the total interest earned since the money was invested, after each of the times in part (a).

(c) Suppose that $£V$ is the value of the investment, and $£W$ is the total amount of interest earned, after n years. Write down a formula for V in terms of n, and a formula for W in terms of n.

Activity 6 *Working out how much money to invest*

Suppose that you want to invest some money for a newborn baby so that she receives a gift of $£1000$ in 18 years' time. You have found an investment product that guarantees to pay compound interest of 5% per year for the whole of this period. You want to know how much money you must invest now in order to achieve your target.

(a) Suppose that the amount that you invest now is $£M$. Write down an expression for the value of the investment in 18 years' time, in terms of M.

(b) Hence write down an equation that M must satisfy if you are to achieve your target, and solve it to find how much money you must invest, to the nearest penny.

I used to be a banker but after a while I started to lose interest!

1.3 Discrete and continuous exponential growth and decay

In most of the examples of exponential growth and decay that you have seen in this unit so far, the change happened in steps, so the size of the quantity jumped from one value to the next, where each value was the previous value multiplied by the same scale factor. For example, the height of the pile of paper started at $0.0001\,\text{m}$, then it jumped to $0.0002\,\text{m}$ (two times the first value), then to $0.0004\,\text{m}$ (two times the value before), and so on.

However, consider the growth of the lily pads mentioned in Activity 2. The area of the pond covered by the lily pads doubled every day, so plotting the area covered after each day would give a graph like the one shown in Figure 7. Here n is the number of days and A is the area covered by the lily pads, measured in some suitable units, such as square metres.

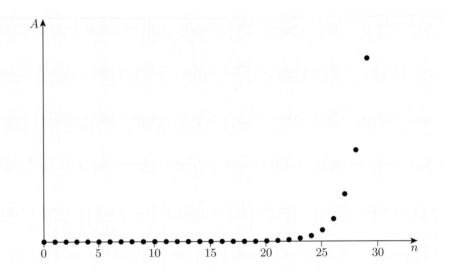

Figure 7   The area A covered by the lily pads after n days

As you know, each point on the graph in Figure 7 is given by a formula of the form

$$A = S \times 2^n,$$

where S is the area covered by the lily pads at the start of the 30 days, in the same units as A.

The area covered by the lily pads would not have grown in jumps, however – it would have grown continuously. The graph of its growth would have been something like the graph shown in Figure 8.

The curve in Figure 8 has exactly the same equation as the sequence of dots in Figure 7, namely

$$A = S \times 2^n. \tag{1}$$

The only difference is that the curve corresponds to the variable n taking *any* value, rather than just integer values. You saw in Unit 3 that you can raise a positive number to *any* power, not just powers that are integers.

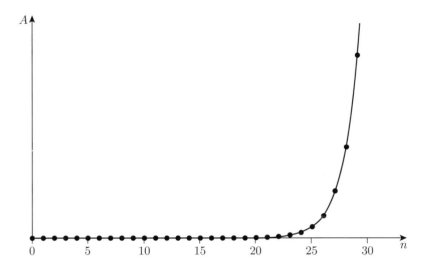

Figure 8 The area A covered by the lily pads after n days, as a continuous graph

You can use equation (1) to work out the area covered by the lily pads after $26\frac{1}{2}$ days, or 23.7 days, or any fractional number of days that you like (provided that you know the value of the initial area S): you substitute the appropriate number for n into the expression on the right-hand side of the equation and evaluate it. Your calculator will handle exponents that are not whole numbers in just the same way as whole-number exponents.

The definitions of exponential growth and decay that you saw in Subsection 1.1 can be extended to include the type of change illustrated in Figure 8, as follows.

Exponential growth and decay

A variable y is said to **change exponentially** with respect to a variable x if the relationship between x and y is given by an equation of the form

$$y = ab^x,$$

where a and b are positive constants, with b not equal to 1.

If $b > 1$, then y **grows exponentially**.

If $0 < b < 1$, then y **decays exponentially**.

If the change happens in steps (x takes values from a range of equally spaced numbers, such as the non-negative integers), then it is **discrete exponential change** (also called **geometric change**).

If the change happens continuously (x takes values from an interval of real numbers, such as the non-negative real numbers), then it is **continuous exponential change**.

The growth in the height of the paper pile is an example of *discrete* exponential growth. The height h metres of the pile is given by the formula

$$h = 0.0001 \times 2^n,$$

where n is the number of steps and takes the values $0, 1, 2, \ldots$.

In contrast, the growth in the area covered by the lily pads is an example of *continuous* exponential growth. The area A is given by the formula

$$A = S \times 2^n,$$

where n is the time in days since the growth started, and takes any value that is a non-negative real number (perhaps up to some maximum value).

A curve like the one in Figure 8 – that is, a curve that is the graph of an equation of the form $y = ab^x$, where a and b are positive constants with b not equal to 1 – is called an **exponential curve**. If $b > 1$, as in Figure 8, then the curve is called an **exponential growth curve**. If $0 < b < 1$, then it is called an **exponential decay curve**.

Of course, the lily pad example is not very realistic, but many examples of real-life growth and decay can be modelled by exponential growth or decay curves. You will see some examples in the next two subsections.

1.4 Using continuous exponential models

Any model based on an equation of the form in the pink box on page 125 is called an **exponential model**. In particular, a model based on discrete exponential change is called a *discrete exponential model*, and similarly a model based on continuous exponential change is called a *continuous exponential model*. Usually you can choose a discrete or continuous exponential model according to which seems to best suit a situation.

An example of a situation that can be modelled by a continuous exponential model is the amount of a prescription drug in a patient's bloodstream. The concentration of the drug in the patient's bloodstream peaks shortly after it is administered, and then gradually falls as the drug is broken down or eliminated from the body. The concentration tends to drop steeply at first, but more slowly later, giving rise to a graph something like the one in Figure 9. This graph covers the period of time after the concentration of a particular drug in a patient's bloodstream peaks.

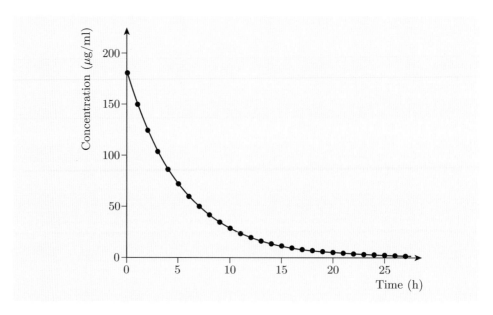

Figure 9 The concentration of a drug in a patient's bloodstream

A microgram (μg) is one millionth of a gram. The abbreviation mcg is sometimes used instead of μg.

In Figure 9, the peak concentration of the drug in the patient's bloodstream is 180 micrograms per millilitre (μg/ml). The curve models the subsequent decline in the concentration, and the dots model the concentrations after whole numbers of hours. In this particular graph, the concentration represented by each dot is obtained from the concentration represented by the previous dot by multiplying by the scale factor 0.83, so the equation of the curve is

$$C = 180 \times 0.83^t,$$

where t is the time in hours and C is the concentration of the drug in the patient's bloodstream, in μg/ml.

Because the scale factor by which the concentration falls each hour is 0.83, and $83\% = 100\% - 17\%$, the percentage by which the concentration falls each hour is 17%.

It is important to remember that a graph like the one in Figure 9 is only a *model* for the decline in the concentration of a drug in a patient's bloodstream. The actual concentration at a particular time may not lie exactly on the curve.

As with all models, you should interpret any results obtained from an exponential model in an appropriate way. For example, you should not quote results too precisely, but should round them appropriately, as models give only approximate predictions. It is also important to make sure that the model used is appropriate for the situation. For example, the speed of the decline of a drug in a patient's bloodstream may vary from person to person.

In the next activity you are asked to use a model similar to the one discussed above to estimate the concentration of a drug in a patient's bloodstream after some different periods of time, including some that are not whole numbers of hours.

Activity 7   *Calculating the concentration of a drug in a patient's bloodstream*

A dose of a particular drug is administered to a patient, and the concentration of the drug in the patient's bloodstream peaks at 90 nanograms per millilitre (ng/ml) shortly afterwards. The concentration then decreases by 14% per hour. Let C ng/ml be the concentration t hours after the concentration peaked.

A nanogram (ng) is one billionth of a gram; that is, $1/10^9$ of a gram.

(a) Find the scale factor by which the concentration of the drug decreases every hour. Hence write down a formula for C in terms of t.

(b) Use your formula to find the expected concentration of the drug, to the nearest 5 ng/ml, at the following times after the concentration peaked.

   (i) 4 hours   (ii) 30 minutes

(c) Suppose that the peak concentration of the drug occurs 40 minutes after the drug was administered. Find the expected concentration of the drug in the patient's bloodstream two hours after it was administered, to the nearest 5 ng/ml.

Now suppose that you know the peak concentration of a drug in a patient's bloodstream, and the concentration one hour after this peak concentration. These two values can be estimated by using blood tests. You can use the two values to work out the scale factor by which the concentration of the drug decreased in the hour after the peak concentration was reached. If you assume that the concentration of the drug will continue to decrease by the same scale factor every hour, then you can use this scale factor to write down a formula for the concentration of the drug any number of hours after the peak concentration.

For example, suppose that the peak concentration of a drug in a patient's bloodstream is $20\,\mu\text{g/ml}$, and the concentration after one hour is $14\,\mu\text{g/ml}$. Then over that hour the concentration of the drug changed by the scale factor

$$\frac{14}{20} = 0.7.$$

If the concentration of the drug continues to decrease by the same scale factor every hour, then the concentration $C\,\mu\text{g/ml}$ at the time t hours after the concentration peaked is given by the formula

$$C = 20 \times 0.7^t.$$

Activity 8   Finding a scale factor

Suppose that the peak concentration of a drug in a patient's bloodstream is $36\,\mu\text{g/ml}$, and one hour later the concentration has dropped to $27\,\mu\text{g/ml}$. Assume that the concentration decreases by the same scale factor every hour, and let $C\,\mu\text{g/ml}$ be the concentration t hours after the concentration peaked.

(a) Find the scale factor by which the concentration decreases each hour.

(b) Hence write down a formula for C in terms of t.

(c) Use your formula to work out the expected concentration 1 hour and 15 minutes after the peak concentration, to the nearest $\mu\text{g/ml}$.

As mentioned at the beginning of this subsection, you can usually choose a discrete exponential model or a continuous exponential model according to which seems to best suit a situation. You would choose a discrete exponential model if it is appropriate to model the quantity with change that takes place in steps *with the same scale factor at each step*. You would choose a continuous exponential model if it is appropriate to model the quantity with exponential change that happens continuously.

Even if a quantity does not change continuously, it is often appropriate to model it with a continuous exponential model. For example, suppose that the population of a new housing estate is increasing by about 15% every year. The size of population does not change continuously, as it jumps from one whole number of people to another whole number of people, rather than going through all the numbers in between. However, it is appropriate to model the size of the population with a continuous exponential model – as for any model, you would round any results obtained to a suitable degree of precision. Using a continuous exponential model allows you to estimate the size of the population at any time during the year, whereas using a discrete exponential model, based on steps at intervals of a year, allows you to estimate it only after whole numbers of years.

What you should remember is that the adjectives 'discrete' and 'continuous' refer not to the possible values taken by the quantity modelled, but to the values taken by the variable x in the equation $y = ab^x$ that is used in the model, as you will see if you look back at the pink box on page 125. (However, the adjective 'discrete' does not fully describe the nature of the values taken by the variable x in discrete exponential change, as they must be not just discrete, but *equally-spaced*.)

1.5   Exponential models from data

In Unit 6 you saw how to use Dataplotter to fit the best straight line to a set of data points. This process is called **linear regression**.

There is a similar process, called **exponential regression**, that can be used to fit the best exponential curve to a set of data points. Many computer spreadsheets and graphics calculators can carry out exponential regression (and linear regression). You will not be expected to carry out exponential regression in this module, but you should be aware that it can be done.

As an illustration, Table 1 gives some estimated data for the population of the world. Figure 10(a) shows a scatterplot of these data, and you can see that the points would be better modelled with a curve than with a straight line. Exponential curves frequently provide good models for the growth of populations – which can be of humans, animals or anything else – since populations often increase by a particular percentage every year. (For some types of population it can be appropriate to consider the percentage change over some other unit of time, instead of a year. For example, for a population of bacteria you might consider the percentage change every hour.)

Table 1   Estimated data for the population of the world

Year	Population
1850	1.260×10^9
1900	1.650×10^9
1920	1.860×10^9
1930	2.070×10^9
1950	2.520×10^9
1960	3.042×10^9
1990	5.282×10^9
2000	6.086×10^9
2009	6.786×10^9

Source: The first five data pairs come from United Nations (1999) *The World at Six Billion*; the remaining four data pairs come from the US Census Bureau.

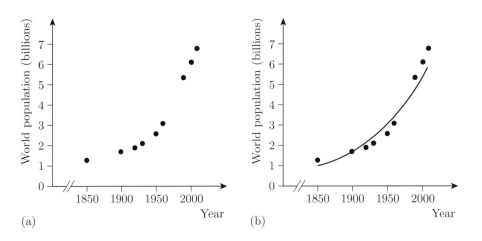

Figure 10   (a) A scatterplot of the data from Table 1. (b) The same scatterplot with the exponential regression curve superimposed.

Applying exponential regression to the data points in Table 1 shows that the exponential regression curve for these data has equation

$$y = 0.659\,543 \times 1.011\,47^x,$$

where x is the year, y is the size of the population, and the constants are given to six significant figures. This curve is shown in Figure 10(b). It is not a very close fit to the data points, but it is better than a straight line.

Activity 9   *Thinking about an exponential regression curve*

(a) What evidence is there from Figure 10(b) to show that, in recent years, the population of the world has been growing more quickly than the historical trend would suggest?

(b) Can you offer any possible explanation for this?

Figure 11   There are large flocks of ring-necked parakeets in south-east England.

If you look carefully at the scatterplot in Figure 10(a), you can see that if you were to draw a curve *exactly* through the points, it would get more and more steep until about 1990, when it would start to become slightly less steep. So it looks as if an exponential model for the population of the world is not appropriate in the long term. In fact, most exponential models are appropriate only for limited periods of time, as they eventually predict growth that is so rapid that it cannot happen in practice.

You need to be careful when you use an exponential model for a population that changes seasonally, as many animal populations do. For example, suppose that a survey has been carried out every September to estimate the size of a particular flock of ring-necked parakeets (Figure 11) in south-east England, and that the results of the survey are as shown on the graph in Figure 12(a). The equation of the exponential regression curve for these data points is

$$y = 10.5032 \times 1.28440^x,$$

where x is the time in years since 1 September 2000, y is the number of parakeets, and the constants are given to six significant figures.

This equation models the number of parakeets every September, but it is unlikely to model the number of parakeets at other times of the year. This is because the size of the flock would probably not follow a smooth curve, but might decline over the winter and then increase in the breeding season, perhaps as shown in Figure 12(b).

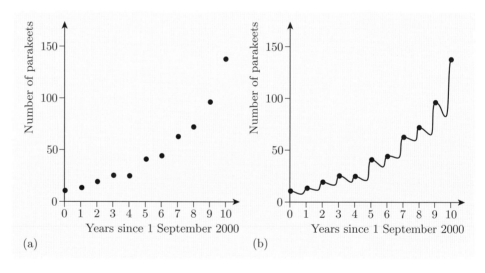

Figure 12   (a) A scatterplot showing the estimated number of parakeets every September from 1 September 2000. (b) A possible graph for the number of parakeets at all times of the year.

For similar reasons to those for the flock of parakeets, if the lily pads discussed in Subsection 1.3 tend to grow more quickly at some times of the day than at others, then it might be more appropriate to model their growth by a discrete exponential model like that shown in Figure 7 on page 124, rather than by a continuous exponential model like that shown in Figure 8 on page 125.

So the model is valid only for whole numbers of years after 1 September 2000 – that is, only for values of x that are non-negative integers. Because of this, it is appropriate to treat this model as a *discrete* exponential model, with the size of the flock changing in steps from September of one year to September of the next year.

As always with models, any results obtained from models like those in this subsection need to be interpreted appropriately. For example, the model for the number of parakeets predicts that after 11 years the number of parakeets in the flock will be 164.825.... This number should be rounded, as you cannot have a fractional number of parakeets! You could round it to 165, but since these sorts of models are often rather imprecise, a prediction of 'roughly 160' parakeets might be more appropriate.

In this section you have learned what it means for a quantity to grow or decay exponentially, and you have seen how to find and use formulas describing this type of change. You have also learned about the difference between discrete and continuous exponential change.

2 Working with exponential growth and decay

In this section you will see some further useful ways to work with exponential growth and decay.

2.1 Growth and decay to particular sizes

In the last section you used formulas for exponential growth and decay to work out answers to problems of the following type: How large will a quantity be after a particular time (or after a particular number of steps, in the case of discrete exponential growth)?

However sometimes you want to know the answer to a different type of problem: How much time (or how many steps) will it take until a quantity reaches a particular size?

For example, you might want to use an exponential model for the decline in the concentration of a drug in a patient's bloodstream to estimate the time when the concentration will fall to a particular level, so that a decision can be made about when the next dose of the drug should be administered. One way to make such an estimate is to obtain an accurate graph of the equation that describes the decline in the concentration (for example, using Graphplotter), and read the appropriate value from the graph. You are asked to do this in the next activity.

Activity 10 *Predicting the time when a drug concentration will fall to a particular level*

Graphplotter

Suppose that the decline in the concentration of a drug in a patient's bloodstream is modelled by the equation

$$C = 30 \times 0.78^t,$$

where $C\,\mu$g/ml is the concentration t hours after the concentration peaked.

In parts (a)–(c) below you are asked to use Graphplotter to obtain the graph of this equation and estimate when the concentration will fall to a particular level.

(a) Open Graphplotter, and make sure that the 'One graph' tab is selected. Click the 'Options' tab and make sure that 'Grid', 'Axes' and 'Trace' are all selected, and all the other options are not selected. Click the 'Functions' tab to return to the main panel.

(b) Choose the equation $y = ab^x + c$ from the drop-down list. Set $a = 30$ and $b = 0.78$, and keep $c = 0$. Set the values of x min, x max, y min and y max to give the range 0 to 20 on the x-axis and the range 0 to 35 on the y-axis.

(c) Use the Trace facility to find the time, to the nearest half-hour, when the concentration falls to $10\,\mu$g/ml.

Figure 13   Typical advice to runners is to increase running distance by no more than 10% each week.

Another way to find the time, or number of steps, until a quantity that is changing exponentially reaches a particular level is to use **trial and improvement**. You start by guessing an answer and testing it, and then you repeatedly adjust your guess until you find the answer that you are looking for.

For example, consider the case of an athlete who has been running 20 km every week, but plans a new training schedule in which each week she will increase her running distance by 10% over the previous week. An increase of 10% corresponds to a scale factor of 1.1, so this means that in week 1 of her new schedule she will run a distance of $20 \times 1.1\,\mathrm{km} = 22\,\mathrm{km}$, in week 2 she will run $20 \times 1.1^2\,\mathrm{km} = 24.2\,\mathrm{km}$, and so on. In general, the distance in kilometres that she will run in week n is given by the expression

$$20 \times 1.1^n. \tag{2}$$

The athlete wants to know the week of the schedule in which she will first be due to run more than 65 km, as at that point she plans to cease the schedule and stick to 65 km per week for a few weeks. The number of this week in the schedule is the smallest value of n for which

$$20 \times 1.1^n > 65.$$

The example below illustrates how you can use trial and improvement to find this value of n.

Example 2   *Using trial and improvement*

If the distance in kilometres run by an athlete in week n of a training schedule is given by expression (2), find the week number in which she is first due to run more than 65 km.

Solution

Guess a sensible value for the week number n, substitute it into the formula to calculate the corresponding running distance, then repeatedly adjust your guess until you find the answer. It can be helpful to set out the process in a table.

Guess for week number	Distance run in km (to the nearest 0.1 km)	Evaluation
20	$20 \times 1.1^{20} \approx 134.5$	Much too big
10	$20 \times 1.1^{10} \approx 51.9$	Too small
15	$20 \times 1.1^{15} \approx 83.5$	Too big
13	$20 \times 1.1^{13} \approx 69.0$	Still greater than 65
12	$20 \times 1.1^{12} \approx 62.8$	Less than 65

Since the athlete is due to run 62.8 km in week 12 and 69.0 km in week 13, the first week in which she is due to run more than 65 km is week 13.

The example above involves discrete exponential change, but you can also use trial and improvement in situations that are modelled by continuous exponential change, such as some changing populations. You are asked to try this in the next activity, which involves the number of Elvis Presley impersonators!

It has been reported that when Elvis Presley died on 16 August 1977, he had approximately 170 impersonators, but thirty years later, in 2007, the number had risen to roughly 85 000. In fact, it has been calculated that the number of Elvis impersonators is increasing by about 23% per year.

Figure 14 Is it the real Elvis, or one of his many impersonators?

The assumption that the population of the world will remain constant is of course unrealistic. There is more on this point in the text below the activity.

Activity 11 *Calculating the time until everyone is an Elvis impersonator*

Suppose that the number of Elvis impersonators was 170 on 16 August 1977, and has been increasing by 23% per year since that date.

(a) Write down the scale factor by which the number of Elvis impersonators is increasing each year, and hence write down a formula for the number of Elvis impersonators t years after 16 August 1977.

(b) Check that your formula gives the answer 85 000, approximately, for the number of Elvis impersonators 30 years after 16 August 1977.

(c) Use trial and improvement to find, roughly (to within two years), the time that it would take for Elvis impersonators to account for the entire population of the world, if the population of the world remains at the size it is today, which is about 7 billion. Hence find, roughly, the calendar year in which you would expect this to happen.

Clearly Activity 11 is only a bit of foolish fun, but it nevertheless illustrates a limitation of exponential models that was mentioned in the last section – they are often unlikely to be appropriate in the long term. Of course it won't happen that eventually the entire population of the world will be Elvis impersonators! In fact, it is probably unlikely that the annual growth rate of 23% in the number of Elvis impersonators will continue for many more years. So this exponential model for the growth in the number of Elvis impersonators might be realistic for a number of years, but it will not be a good model in the long term. Any exponential growth model eventually predicts growth so rapid that it cannot happen in practice.

You might also have noticed that the assumption in the question that the population of the world will remain the same is also unrealistic. In fact, as you saw in the last section, the population of the world is growing quite rapidly. At the time of writing, the population of the world is estimated to be increasing at a rate of about 1.13% per year. Although it may increase less rapidly in future, current predictions suggest that it could be as high as 9 billion in 2050. So even if the growth rate of the number of Elvis impersonators were to remain at 23% per year, if you want to compare the number of Elvis impersonators with the total number of people in the world, then you need to take into account the growth rate of the population of the world.

Trial and improvement can be a useful way of finding an answer to a mathematical problem when you don't know a better method. However, it can be time-consuming, especially if the answer that you are trying to find might be any value from an interval of real numbers (as opposed to just integer values, for example), and you want to find it fairly accurately. Later in the unit you will learn a quicker method that can be used to answer questions of the type considered in this subsection. It involves the idea of *logarithms*.

2.2   Growth and decay over different lengths of time

In this subsection you will learn about a useful property of exponential growth and decay.

As an illustration, consider again the paper pile discussed in Subsection 1.1. Its height doubles at each step, so if you know the height after a particular step, and you want to know the height after one more step, then you multiply by 2. Similarly, if you know the height after a particular step, and you want to know the height after *two* more steps, then you multiply by 2 twice – that is, you multiply by 2^2. And to work out the height of the pile from its height *three* steps earlier, you multiply by 2^3, and so on. In general, to work out the height of the pile from its height i steps earlier, you multiply by 2^i. In other words, every i steps the height of the paper pile changes by the scale factor 2^i.

You can see that the fact in the box below is true for discrete exponential change in general.

> ### Discrete exponential change over different numbers of steps
>
> Suppose that a quantity changes by the scale factor b at each step.
>
> Then every i steps it changes by the scale factor b^i.

Annual percentage rates (APRs), which you have probably seen quoted in relation to loans such as credit card debts, are worked out using this fact. Suppose that you have a debt on which you are charged interest at 2% per month, and you do not repay any of the money owing. After each month the interest is added to the debt, and then the interest for the next month is calculated on the total amount owing. That is, the interest is *compounded* each month.

You met the idea of compound interest in Subsection 1.2, although there the discussion was from the point of view of an investor, whereas here it is from the point of view of a debtor.

In the case of the debt discussed above, the compound interest is 2% per month, so your debt increases by the scale factor 1.02 each month. Over a year (12 months) your debt is increased by this scale factor 12 times, so, by the property in the box above, altogether your debt increases by the scale factor

$$1.02^{12} \approx 1.27.$$

In other words, the annual interest rate that you are being charged is about 27%. This number, 27%, is the *annual percentage rate*, or APR.

Notice that the APR of 27% is greater than 12 times the monthly rate of 2%. This is because the interest is compounded. This example illustrates why it is important to consider the APR when you pay interest, rather than just the monthly rate, for example. Small monthly rates of interest may lead you to believe that you are getting a good deal, whereas in fact the annual rate of interest can be higher than you think.

APRs provide the best way to compare loan offers from lenders who charge interest in different ways, such as every year, or every six months. For example, suppose that you were offered the opportunity to transfer the debt discussed above to a different lender, at 26% annual interest. This is a slightly better option, since the 2% monthly rate charged by the current lender is equivalent to an annual rate of 27%.

Here is another example that illustrates how to calculate an APR.

Example 3 *Calculating an APR*

Calculate the APR for an interest rate of 4.5%, charged quarterly (that is, every three months), giving your answer as a percentage to one decimal place.

Solution

An interest rate of 4.5% charged quarterly corresponds to a scale factor of 1.045 quarterly. This gives a scale factor of

$$1.045^4 = 1.193 \text{ (to 3 d.p.)}$$

per year, which gives an interest rate of 19.3% (to 1 d.p.) per year. That is, the APR is approximately 19.3%.

Activity 12 *Calculating APRs*

(a) Calculate the APR for each of the following interest rates, as a percentage to one decimal place.

  (i)   An interest rate of 17.5%, charged annually

  (ii) An interest rate of 8.5%, charged every six months

  (iii) An interest rate of 1.4%, charged monthly

(b) If you have three loan offers, with the three interest rates in part (a), which would you choose?

There is a version of the property in the pink box on page 134 that is useful when you are dealing with *continuous* exponential change.

To illustrate it, let's consider a particular continuous exponential model. The value of a car tends to drop more in the early years of its existence than in the later years, and the decline in the value can often be modelled by a continuous exponential model. The decline in the value of a car (or any item) is known as **depreciation**.

For example, the exponential curve in Figure 15 (overleaf) models the value of a car whose value at purchase is £20 000 and which depreciates by 20% per year; that is, by a scale factor of 0.8 per year. The equation of the curve is

$$v = 20\,000 \times 0.8^t,$$

where v is the value of the car in £ after t years. The dots on the curve model the values of the car after whole numbers of years.

In practice, graphs like the one in Figure 15 are usually appropriate models only for cars that are at least a year old, as the value of a new car tends to drop by a much higher percentage in its first year than in subsequent years.

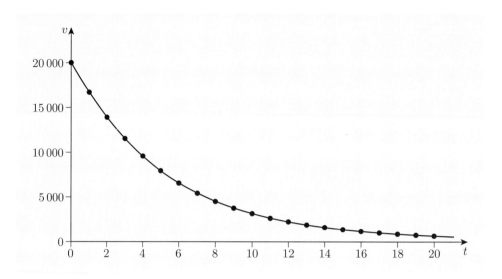

Figure 15   The graph of the equation $v = 20\,000 \times 0.8^t$. The variable t represents the number of years, and v is the value of the car in £.

You know that the value of the car at each dot is 0.8 times its value at the previous dot. So, from what you saw earlier in this subsection, if you know the value of the car after any whole number of years, and you want to work out its value i years later, where i is any whole number, then you multiply by 0.8^i.

But what if you know the value of the car at some point in time, not necessarily after a whole number of years, and you want to work out its value after some further length of time, which is again not necessarily a whole number of years? In fact, you can work out the new value in exactly the same way as above – if the length of time is 1.5 years, say, then you just multiply the old value by $0.8^{1.5}$. This even works for negative periods of time: if you want to know the value of the car 2.25 years, say, *before* a particular time, then you multiply by $0.8^{-2.25}$. The reason why this works is explained shortly, but first here is an example to illustrate how you can apply this idea in practice.

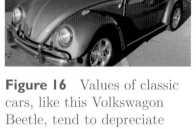

Figure 16   Values of classic cars, like this Volkswagon Beetle, tend to depreciate more slowly than those of other cars, and may even *appreciate* (increase).

Figure 17   A Volkswagon Beetle whose value has certainly depreciated significantly!

Example 4   *Working out some values of a car*

A car depreciates at the rate of 17% per year. Its value three and a half years after purchase was £10 920. How much, to the nearest ten pounds, was it worth at the following times?

(a) 1.5 years later   (b) At purchase

Solution

The car depreciates at the rate of 17% per year, so its values change by the scale factor 0.83 each year.

(a) 1.5 years after the value of the car was £10 920, its new value was

$$£10\,920 \times 0.83^{1.5} = £8260 \text{ (to the nearest £10).}$$

(b) The value of the car at purchase was

$$£10\,920 \times 0.83^{-3.5} = £20\,960 \text{ (to the nearest £10).}$$

Here is a similar activity for you to try.

Activity 13   *Working out some values of a car*

A car depreciates at the rate of 16% per year. Its value one year after purchase was £15 450. How much, to the nearest ten pounds, was it worth at the following times?

(a) 0.25 years later   (b) 2.75 years *after purchase*   (c) At purchase

---

The useful fact used in Example 4 and Activity 13 can be summarised as follows.

Continuous exponential change over different time periods

Suppose that a quantity is subject to continuous exponential change by the scale factor b every year.

Then over any time interval of length i years, it changes by the scale factor b^i.

(The same is true if time is measured in any other unit, such as weeks, days or minutes.)

To see why this is true, consider, for example, the car mentioned on page 135, whose depreciation is modelled by the equation

$$v = 20\,000 \times 0.8^t,$$

where v is the value of the car in £ after t years. Consider two points in time that are i years apart, say t years after purchase and $t + i$ years after purchase. The values in £ of the car at these two times are

$$20\,000 \times 0.8^t \quad \text{and} \quad 20\,000 \times 0.8^{t+i},$$

respectively. By an index law that you met in Unit 3, the second value of the car can be rewritten as

$$20\,000 \times 0.8^t \times 0.8^i,$$

The index law used here is
$$a^m \times a^n = a^{m+n}.$$

so you can see that it is 0.8^i times the first value. Exactly the same argument will hold whatever the annual scale factor and starting value are.

So if a quantity is subject to continuous exponential change over time, then it doesn't have just one scale factor associated with its change: *different lengths of time correspond to different scale factors.* For example, if a quantity changes by the scale factor 1.3 every day, then

over any week (7 days) it changes by the scale factor $1.3^7 \approx 6.27$,

over any hour ($\frac{1}{24}$ day) it changes by the scale factor $1.3^{1/24} \approx 1.01$,

and so on.

Activity 14   *Working out scale factors over different lengths of time*

A population of pigeons in a city is thought to be increasing at a rate of 80% per decade.

(a) By what scale factor does the number of pigeons grow each decade?

(b) By what scale factor does the number of pigeons grow each year? Give your answer to four significant figures.

(c) By what percentage increase does the number of pigeons grow each year? Give your answer to one decimal place.

Figure 18   Urban pigeons

The fact in the pink box on page 137 is true even if the unit of time over which the initial scale factor is measured is not a standard one: it could be 4 weeks, or 12.7 years, and so on. For example, if a quantity changes by the scale factor b every 4 weeks, then over any time interval of length 10 weeks (which is 2.5 times 4 weeks) the quantity changes by the scale factor $b^{2.5}$.

In this section you have seen how to use either a graphical method or trial and improvement to calculate the length of time (or number of steps) that a quantity that is changing exponentially will take to reach a particular value. You will see a better method, involving logarithms, for solving problems like this in Section 5. You have also seen how to calculate scale factors for exponential change over different lengths of time (or over different numbers of steps).

3 Exponential curves

In this section you will explore the graphs of functions with rules of the form

$$y = ab^x,$$

You learned about the meaning of b^x, where b and x are not necessarily integers, in Unit 3.

where a and b are constants, with b positive. The constant b must be positive because if b is negative then b^x has no meaning for non-integer values of x, and if b is zero then b^x has no meaning for non-positive values of x. As you saw in Subsection 1.3, a function whose rule is of the form above, with $a > 0$ and $b \neq 1$, corresponds to exponential change from the starting value a by the scale factor b, and its graph is called an *exponential curve*.

We start by looking at a more restricted family of functions: those with rules of the form

$$y = b^x,$$

In some texts, the term 'exponential function' has a less restricted definition than that given here. For example, the term might be used to refer to any function with a rule of the form $y = ab^x$, where a and b are constants, with b positive.

where b is a positive constant. A function of this form with $b \neq 1$ is called an **exponential function**. It corresponds to exponential change from the starting value 1, since its rule is of the more general form $y = ab^x$ with $a = 1$.

3.1 Graphs of equations of the form $y = b^x$

This subsection is about the graphs of exponential functions. Before you explore these graphs, let's first compare a particular exponential function with two functions of other types. Here are the rules of three different functions, each of which can be used to model a positive quantity y that increases as a positive quantity x increases:

$$y = 2x, \quad y = x^2, \quad y = 2^x.$$

These three functions are commonly confused with each other, so it is important that you are able to distinguish between them. In the next activity you are asked to compare how fast the y-values of these three functions increase.

Activity 15 *Comparing growth models*

(a) Look at the three functions at the bottom of the opposite page. State whether each is linear, quadratic or exponential.

(b) The table below shows some of the y-values of each function for $x = 0, 1, 2, 3, 4, 5, 6$. Calculate the missing y-values and write them in the table. Then compare how the y-values of each function increase as x increases from 0 to 6. Which function has the greatest increase, and which has the smallest?

x	0	1	2	3	4	5	6
$y = 2x$	0		4		8	10	
$y = x^2$	0		4		16	25	
$y = 2^x$	1		4		16	32	

In Activity 15 you should have found that the growth of $y = 2^x$ outstripped the growth of $y = x^2$, which itself outstripped the growth of $y = 2x$. In fact, the growth of any exponential function $y = b^x$ with $b > 1$ will always eventually outstrip the growth of any quadratic function $y = ax^2 + bx + c$ with $a > 0$, which itself will always eventually outstrip the growth of any linear function.

The exponential function that you looked at in Activity 15 was the one with the simple rule $y = 2^x$. To explore the graphs of exponential functions, let's start with this function.

The exponential function $y = 2^x$

We will plot a graph of the equation $y = 2^x$ by constructing a table of values. The values of y for some positive values of x have already been found in Activity 15, so let's now find the values of y for some negative values of x.

You could do this by using your calculator, but so that you can understand why the answers are as they are, let's instead use the definition of what it means to raise a number to a negative power, which you saw in Unit 3. The definition is summarised by the index law

$$a^{-n} = \frac{1}{a^n}.$$

This gives

$$2^{-1} = \frac{1}{2^1} = \tfrac{1}{2} = 0.5,$$

$$2^{-2} = \frac{1}{2^2} = \tfrac{1}{4} = 0.25,$$

$$2^{-3} = \frac{1}{2^3} = \tfrac{1}{8} = 0.125,$$

$$2^{-4} = \frac{1}{2^4} = \tfrac{1}{16} = 0.0625,$$

and so on. If you think about how this pattern continues, you'll see that the values will get smaller and smaller, but they will never reach zero.

Table 2 shows the values of y for integer values of x between -4 and 4.

Table 2   A table of values for the equation $y = 2^x$

x	-4	-3	-2	-1	0	1	2	3	4
y	0.0625	0.125	0.25	0.5	1	2	4	8	16

The values of 2^x where x is not an integer lie on a smooth curve between the values of 2^x where x is an integer. You learned the meaning of these values in Unit 3. For example,

$$2^{\frac{1}{2}} = \sqrt{2}, \quad 2^{\frac{3}{2}} = \left(\sqrt{2}\right)^3 \quad \text{and} \quad 2^{-\frac{1}{2}} = \frac{1}{2^{\frac{1}{2}}} = \frac{1}{\sqrt{2}}.$$

If you plot the nine points given by Table 2 and join them with a smooth curve, then you obtain the graph in Figure 19. It is an exponential *growth* curve, as you would expect, because the equation $y = 2^x$ corresponds to exponential change (from the starting value 1) by the scale factor 2, which is greater than 1.

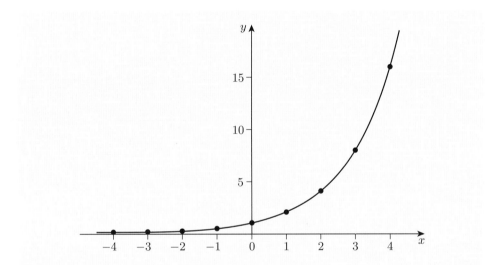

Figure 19   The graph of $y = 2^x$

There are several features worth noticing about this graph. First, the y-intercept is 1. This is because substituting $x = 0$ into the equation $y = 2^x$ gives $y = 2^0$, and you saw in Unit 3 that raising any number to the power 0 gives 1.

The heights of the dots on and to the right of the y-axis are the values of 2^x when $x = 0, 1, 2$ and so on. These values start at 1, when $x = 0$, and then repeatedly double, so, as you would expect, they increase rapidly.

The heights of the dots to the left of the y-axis are the values of 2^x when $x = -1, -2, -3$, and so on. As you have seen, these values get smaller and smaller as x decreases, but never reach zero.

The graph of $y = 2^x$ lies entirely above the x-axis. Although it never reaches the x-axis, it does get closer and closer to it. This behaviour is described by saying that the x-axis is an *asymptote* of the graph.

Now let's consider the graph of another simple exponential function.

You met the word 'asymptote' in Unit 12, in connection with the graph of the tangent function. You saw that the tangent function has infinitely many asymptotes, each of which is a vertical line. An asymptote can be a horizontal or vertical line, or even a slant line.

The exponential function $y = \left(\frac{1}{2}\right)^x$

To plot the graph of the equation $y = \left(\frac{1}{2}\right)^x$, we begin by constructing a table of values. You can find the values of y for negative values of x by using the index laws

$$a^{-1} = \frac{1}{a} \quad \text{and} \quad (a^m)^n = a^{mn}. \tag{3}$$

The first of these two index laws is a special case of the index law

$$a^{-n} = \frac{1}{a^n}.$$

These give

$$\left(\tfrac{1}{2}\right)^{-1} = \left(2^{-1}\right)^{-1} = 2^1 = 2,$$
$$\left(\tfrac{1}{2}\right)^{-2} = \left(2^{-1}\right)^{-2} = 2^2 = 4,$$
$$\left(\tfrac{1}{2}\right)^{-3} = \left(2^{-1}\right)^{-3} = 2^3 = 8,$$
$$\left(\tfrac{1}{2}\right)^{-4} = \left(2^{-1}\right)^{-4} = 2^4 = 16,$$

and so on. You can see that these values will grow rapidly.

Table 3 shows the values of y for integer values of x between -4 and 4.

Table 3   A table of values for the equation $y = \left(\frac{1}{2}\right)^x$

x	-4	-3	-2	-1	0	1	2	3	4
y	16	8	4	2	1	0.5	0.25	0.125	0.0625

Notice that the y-values in Table 3 are just the same as the y-values in Table 2, but in reverse order. This is because for any number x,

$$\left(\tfrac{1}{2}\right)^x = (2^{-1})^x = 2^{-x},$$

by index laws (3) again.

The values of $\left(\frac{1}{2}\right)^x$ where x is not an integer lie on a smooth curve between the values of $\left(\frac{1}{2}\right)^x$ where x is an integer.

If you plot the nine points given by Table 3 and join them with a smooth curve, then you obtain the graph in Figure 20. It is an exponential *decay* curve, as you would expect, because the equation $y = \left(\frac{1}{2}\right)^x$ corresponds to exponential change (from the starting value 1) by the scale factor $\frac{1}{2}$, which is between 0 and 1.

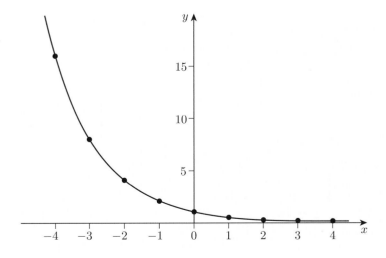

Figure 20   The graph of $y = \left(\frac{1}{2}\right)^x$

There are several features worth noticing about this graph, too. Like the graph of $y = 2^x$, the graph of $y = \left(\frac{1}{2}\right)^x$ has y-intercept 1. The reason is the same: raising any number to the power 0 gives 1, so, in particular, $\left(\frac{1}{2}\right)^0 = 1$.

The heights of the dots on and to the right of the y-axis are the values of $\left(\frac{1}{2}\right)^x$ when $x = 0, 1, 2$, and so on. These values start at 1, when $x = 0$, and then repeatedly halve, so they get smaller and smaller, but never reach zero.

The heights of the dots to the left of the y-axis are the values of $\left(\frac{1}{2}\right)^x$ when $x = -1, -2, -3$, and so on. As you have seen, these values grow rapidly as x decreases.

Like the graph of $y = 2^x$, the graph of $y = \left(\frac{1}{2}\right)^x$ lies entirely above the x-axis, and has the x-axis as an asymptote. As x increases, the values of $y = \left(\frac{1}{2}\right)^x$ get closer and closer to the x-axis but never reach it.

Other exponential functions

You have now looked in detail at the graphs of the equations $y = 2^x$ and $y = \left(\frac{1}{2}\right)^x$. In the next activity you are asked to use Graphplotter to investigate the graphs of some other exponential functions.

Graphplotter

Activity 16   *Investigating graphs of equations of the form $y = b^x$*

Use Graphplotter, with the 'One graph' tab selected. Click the 'Autoscale' button to ensure that the axis scales are at their default values. Tick the y-intercept checkbox on the Options page, and untick the Trace checkbox, if it is ticked.

(a) Choose the equation $y = ab^x + c$ from the drop-down list. Make sure that $a = 1$ and $c = 0$, and keep a and c set to these values throughout the activity, since the aim is to explore the graphs of equations of the form $y = b^x$.

(b) Make sure that $b = 2$, and check that you have obtained the graph of $y = 2^x$, as expected.

(c) Vary the value of b (remembering that it must be *positive*) and write down what you discover about the effect that this has on the graph. In particular, try setting $b = 1$.

(d) What do you notice about the y-intercept of the graph for different values of b? Can you explain why this happens?

You should have found in Activity 16 that in both the range $0 < b < 1$ (which gives decay curves) and the range $b > 1$ (which gives growth curves), the closer the value of b is to 1, the flatter is the graph. This makes sense, because b is the scale factor, so the closer it is to 1, the less change you get when you multiply a number by b, so the slower is the growth or decay. You should have seen that when $b = 1$ the graph is completely flat!

You should also have observed that all the graphs in Activity 16 have y-intercept 1: the reason for this is given in the solution to Activity 16. You might have noticed, too, that all of the graphs lie entirely above the x-axis, and all of them, except the straight-line graph obtained by putting $b = 1$, have the x-axis as an asymptote.

You can see some of these features of the graphs of exponential functions in the four graphs in Figure 21. Graphs (a) and (b) illustrate $0 < b < 1$

(decay curves) and graphs (c) and (d) illustrate $b > 1$ (growth curves). You can see that the values of b closer to 1 give the flatter graphs. Notice also that all four graphs have y-intercept 1 and the x-axis as an asymptote.

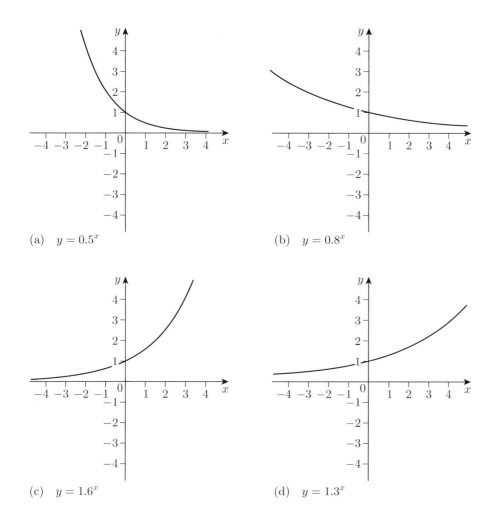

(a) $y = 0.5^x$

(b) $y = 0.8^x$

(c) $y = 1.6^x$

(d) $y = 1.3^x$

Figure 21 Graphs of equations of the form $y = b^x$

3.2 Graphs of equations of the form $y = ab^x$

In this subsection you will look at the graphs of equations of the form $y = ab^x$, where b is positive.

 Graphplotter

Activity 17 *Investigating graphs of equations of the form $y = ab^x$*

Use Graphplotter, with the 'One graph' tab selected. Tick the y-intercept checkbox on the Options page, if it is not already ticked.

(a) Choose the equation $y = ab^x + c$ from the drop-down list, if it is not already selected. Make sure that $c = 0$, and keep c set to 0 throughout this activity, since the aim is to explore the graphs of equations of the form $y = ab^x$.

(b) Set $b = 2$ and vary the value of a. Write down what you discover about the effect that this has on the graph. Look in particular at the y-intercept.

(c) Repeat part (b) for one or two other (positive) values of b.

In Activity 17, you should have found that, regardless of the value of b, the y-intercept is equal to the value of a. This is because substituting $x = 0$ in the equation $y = ab^x$ gives $y = ab^0 = a \times 1 = a$. Some examples of graphs of equations of the form $y = ab^x$ are shown in Figure 22, and you can see that in each case the y-intercept is the value of a.

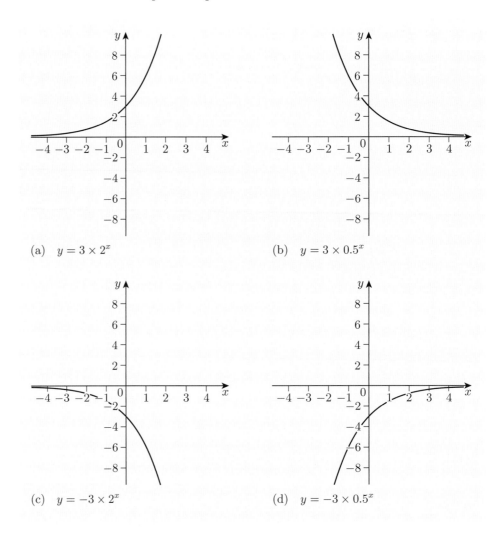

(a) $y = 3 \times 2^x$

(b) $y = 3 \times 0.5^x$

(c) $y = -3 \times 2^x$

(d) $y = -3 \times 0.5^x$

Figure 22 Graphs of equations of the form $y = ab^x$

You should also have found in Activity 17 that positive values of a produce exponential growth and decay curves (provided that $b \neq 1$). This is as you would expect, because if a is positive and $b \neq 1$ then the equation $y = ab^x$ corresponds to exponential change by the scale factor b from the starting value a.

You should have found that the larger the value of a, the steeper the curve. This is because the graph of $y = ab^x$ is obtained from the graph of $y = b^x$ by multiplying each y-value by a, which moves the corresponding points on the curve up or down vertically. The larger the size of the y-value before it is multiplied by a, the more the corresponding point moves, which causes the steepness of the curve to increase.

Negative values of a produce curves of a type that you have not seen so far. The shapes of these curves are the shapes of exponential growth or decay curves reflected in the x-axis. To see why this happens, think about changing the value of a in the equation $y = ab^x$ to its negative. This changes all the y-values to their negatives, and the effect is that the graph is changed to its mirror image, reflected in the x-axis. You might like to use the 'Two graphs' tab in Graphplotter to explore pairs of graphs of the

You saw other examples of this mirror-image effect in Unit 10, when you considered what happens to a parabola with an equation of the form $y = ax^2$ when you change the value a to its negative.

form $y = ab^x$, where the two graphs have the same value of b and values of a that are negatives of each other.

It is important to appreciate that reflecting an exponential growth curve in the x-axis does not give the shape of an exponential decay curve, and similarly that reflecting an exponential decay curve in the x-axis does not give the shape of an exponential growth curve. So curves with equations of the form $y = ab^x$ where a is negative are *not* exponential growth or decay curves. For example, Figure 22(a) shows an exponential growth curve, and Figure 22(c) shows its reflection in the x-axis. Although the graph in Figure 22(c) is decreasing, it becomes *steeper* as you run your eye from left to right, whereas an exponential decay curve, like that in Figure 22(b), becomes *flatter*.

You should have found that for negative values of a, as well as for positive values, the larger the magnitude of a, the steeper the curve.

Finally, you might have noticed that if a is positive then the graph of $y = ab^x$ lies entirely above the x-axis, while if a is negative then the graph lies entirely below the x-axis. All the graphs, except those produced by putting $b = 1$, have the x-axis as an asymptote.

Activity 18   *Choosing values of a and b that give exponential decay*

Without looking at any of the graphs in this unit, write down a value of a and a value of b such that the graph of $y = ab^x$ is an exponential decay curve.

You will have noticed that Graphplotter allows you to explore functions of the form $y = ab^x + c$. From your experience of graphs in earlier units, you should know that the graph of $y = ab^x + c$ will be the same shape as the graph of $y = ab^x$, but shifted vertically by the amount c. The shift is upwards if c is positive and downwards if c is negative. This happens because adding the constant c to the right-hand side of the equation $y = ab^x$ just changes all the y-values by c units, which causes the graph to move up or down. You might like to try this on Graphplotter.

So, for example, since the graph of $y = ab^x$ has the x-axis as an asymptote, the graph of $y = ab^x + c$ has the horizontal line with equation $y = c$ as an asymptote (provided that $a \neq 0$ and $b \neq 1$).

Here is a summary of what you have learned about the graphs of functions of the form $y = ab^x$ in the last two subsections.

Graphs of equations of the form $y = ab^x$

- If $a > 0$ then the graph lies entirely above the x-axis. If also

  $b > 1$,   then the graph is an exponential growth curve;
  $0 < b < 1$,   then the graph is an exponential decay curve;
  $b = 1$,   then the graph is a horizontal line.

- If $a < 0$ then the graph lies entirely below the x-axis and is neither an exponential growth curve nor an exponential decay curve.

- The x-axis is an asymptote (except when $a = 0$ or $b = 1$).

- The y-intercept is a.

- The closer the value of b is to 1 (and the closer the value of a is to 0) the flatter is the graph.

3.3 Euler's number e

In Subsection 3.1 you investigated the graphs of exponential functions, which are functions with rules of the form

$$y = b^x,$$

where b is positive. You saw that all the graphs go through the point $(0, 1)$. You also saw that if $b > 1$ then the graph is an exponential growth curve, and the larger the value of b, the steeper the graph. Some examples are shown in Figure 23.

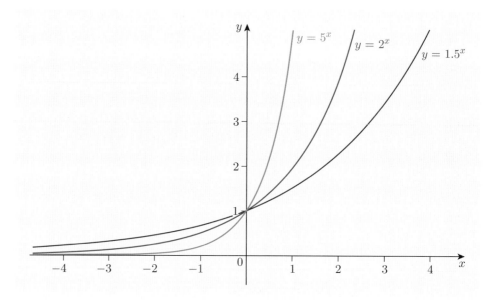

Figure 23 The graphs of three exponential functions

In the next activity you are asked to investigate the steepness of the graphs of exponential functions at the point $(0, 1)$.

 Graphplotter

---

Activity 19 *Investigating the gradient of the graph of $y = b^x$ at $(0, 1)$*

Use Graphplotter, with the 'One graph' tab selected. Choose the equation $y = ab^x + c$ from the drop-down list, if it is not already selected.

(a) Set $a = 1$ and $c = 0$, and keep them set to these values, since this activity is about equations of the form $y = b^x$. Set $b = 2$, to begin with.

(b) Zoom in on the point $(0, 1)$, by setting x min and x max to be -0.01 and 0.01, respectively, and y min and y max to be 0.99 and 1.01, respectively. At this level of detail the graph looks like a straight line, so you can get a good idea of how steep it is.

(c) Now use the slider to change the value of b until the gradient of the graph appears to be exactly 1; that is, until the graph goes up by the same distance vertically as it goes along horizontally. What value of b seems to achieve this?

You're so irrational!

Yeah - and look who's talking!

In Activity 19 you should have found that the value of b that gives a gradient of 1 at $(0, 1)$ seems to be about 2.7. In fact, the precise value is a special number sometimes called **Euler's number**, whose first few digits are $2.718\,28\ldots$. Like π, Euler's number is irrational, so its digits have no repeating pattern and it cannot be written down exactly as a fraction or terminating decimal. It is usually denoted by the letter e.

So the exponential function with the rule $y = e^x$ has the special property that its gradient is exactly 1 at the point $(0, 1)$. If you choose to study mathematics at a level beyond MU123, then you will learn about other, related, properties of this particular exponential function.

This function is important both in applications of mathematics and in pure mathematics, and because of its importance it is sometimes referred to as *the* **exponential function**. Its rule is sometimes written as $y = \exp x$, instead of $y = e^x$. The value of e is available from your calculator keypad, just as for π, and you can also work out values of e^x by using a function button on your calculator, as you will see later in the unit.

At higher levels of mathematics, the two mathematical constants e and π crop up everywhere, in all sorts of contexts.

There is a document on the module website that shows you another context, related to exponential growth, in which the constant e arises naturally.

The use of the letter e for the number $2.718\,28\ldots$ was introduced by the Swiss mathematician Leonhard Euler (Figure 24). He first used it in a manuscript that he wrote in 1727 or 1728, which described some experiments involving the firing of a cannon. The first appearance of the notation e in a published work was in Euler's *Mechanica* (1736), a fundamental book on mechanics.

'Euler' is pronounced 'oiler'.

It is not known why Euler chose the letter 'e': it could just have been because it is the first vowel after 'a', which Euler was already using in his work. (It was probably not because 'e' is the first letter of 'exponential' or 'Euler'.) Over the next two decades Euler went on to make various important discoveries about the number e.

Euler was a hugely prolific mathematician who made fundamental discoveries in many areas of mathematics, including number theory, calculus and, as mentioned above, mechanics. At present his collected works run to 73 volumes, with many volumes of his scientific correspondence and other manuscripts yet to appear. He was responsible for bringing into general use many pieces of mathematical notation that are still used today, including, as you saw in Unit 8, the notation π for the ratio of the circumference of a circle to its diameter.

Figure 24 Leonhard Euler (1707–1783)

In this section you have explored the shapes of the graphs of equations of the form $y = ab^x$, where a and b are constants with b positive. You have also met the number e, otherwise known as Euler's number, which has value $2.718\,28\ldots$.

4 Logarithms

In Activity 11 on page 133 you were asked to find roughly how many years after 16 August 1977 it would take for Elvis impersonators to account for the entire population of the world, assuming that there were 170 Elvis impersonators on that date, their number grows by 23% per year, and the population of the world remains constant at 7 billion. Under these assumptions, the number of Elvis impersonators after t years is

$$170 \times 1.23^t,$$

so the time t in years that it would take for everyone in the world to be an

Elvis impersonator is the solution of the equation

$$170 \times 1.23^t = 7\,000\,000\,000.$$

Equations like this, in which the unknown is in an exponent, are known as **exponential equations**. It is often useful to solve exponential equations when you are working with exponential models.

You were asked in Activity 11 to find an approximate solution of the equation above by using trial and improvement, and you also saw in Subsection 2.1 that another way to find approximate solutions to equations like this is to use graphs. However, there is a quicker method for solving exponential equations. It involves the use of *logarithms*, which you will learn about in this section. Logarithms are often called *logs* for short.

Logarithms are useful not only for solving equations, but also in many other contexts, such as in *logarithmic scales*, as you will see. It is important to have a good understanding of logarithms if you plan to take further mathematics modules.

4.1 A brief history of logarithms

Figure 25 John Napier (1550–1617)

The invention of logarithms is attributed to the sixteenth-century Scottish mathematician John Napier (Figure 25). One of the major hindrances to the mathematical work needed to create astronomical and navigational tables at that time was the difficulty of multiplying and dividing large numbers. Napier bemoaned the 'tedious expense of time' involved in these calculations and the fact that they were 'subject to many slippery errors'. So he tried to find a way of making the calculations easier.

Napier's breakthrough came about by studying the properties of numbers raised to a power. To take a simple example, he considered what happened when he multiplied, say, 2^3 and 2^5. Using the rule that you saw in Unit 3 for multiplying numbers in index form, $a^m \times a^n = a^{m+n}$, he obtained

$$2^3 \times 2^5 = 2^{3+5} = 2^8.$$

He observed that what started off as the problem of *multiplying* two numbers, 2^3 and 2^5, had been reduced to the much simpler problem of *adding* two numbers, 3 and 5. The key to this trick was that the numbers to be multiplied were expressed as powers of the same *base* – in this case the base is 2.

Recall from Unit 3 that the number b in an expression of the form b^x is called the *base* or *base number*. The number x is called the *power*, *index* or *exponent*.

Will somebody please, please, just invent a pocket calculator?

This idea can be applied to any multiplication. A particular number must be chosen as the base – any positive number except 1 can be used, but the obvious choice is the number 10. So, in order to multiply, say, 287 and 37, you would rewrite each of these numbers as ten to some power (approximately), and proceed like this:

$$287 \times 37 \approx 10^{2.4579} \times 10^{1.5682}$$
$$= 10^{2.4579+1.5682}$$
$$= 10^{4.0261}$$
$$\approx 10\,619.$$

This makes the multiplication easier, because it is done by doing an addition instead. But there remains the problem of finding the correct powers of ten for the numbers to be multiplied, and of turning the power of ten obtained as the answer back into an ordinary number.

This problem was solved in the early seventeenth century by drawing up sets of tables to be used whenever a calculation like this was to be performed. The tables gave the power of ten corresponding to each number that might need to be multiplied – these are called the **logarithms** of the numbers. The tables could also be used to find the ordinary number corresponding to each power, which are called the **antilogarithms** of the powers. Figure 26 shows an extract from an eighteenth-century book of such tables (the title page of this book was shown in Unit 12, on page 63), which shows that the logarithm of 37 is 1.568 2017, to seven decimal places. In other words,

$$37 \approx 10^{1.568\,2017}.$$

So, to multiply any two numbers, the procedure would be to use the tables to find the corresponding logarithms, add these logarithms together, and then use the tables again to find the antilogarithm of the result.

The precision of the answer obtained by using the logarithm method depends on the precision of the logarithms used. The seven decimal places in the old table in Figure 26 were sufficient for most practical purposes.

The logarithm method can be used for division as well as multiplication. To divide one number by another, you *subtract* their logarithms. For example,

$$287 \div 37 \approx 10^{2.4579} \div 10^{1.5682}$$
$$= 10^{2.4579-1.5682}$$
$$= 10^{0.8897}$$
$$\approx 7.757.$$

(This calculation uses the rule for dividing numbers in index form that you met in Unit 3: $a^m/a^n = a^{m-n}$.)

30	1.4771213	80	1.9030900	130	39434
31	1.4913617	81	1.9084850	131	72713
32	1.5051500	82	1.9138139	132	1205739
33	1.5185139	83	1.9190781	133	38516
34	1.5314789	84	1.9242793	134	71048
35	1.5440680	85	1.9294189	135	1303338
36	1.5563025	86	1.9344985	136	35389
37	1.5682017	87	1.9395193	137	67206
38	1.5797836	88	1.9444827	138	98791
39	1.5910646	89	1.9493900	139	1430148
40	1.6020600	90	1.9542425	140	6128
41	1.6127839	91	1.9590414	141	92191
42	1.6232493	92	1.9637878	142	1522883
43	1.6334685	93	1.9684829	143	5335

Figure 26 An extract from a book of logarithm tables published in 1717

The historical procedure described here was used to multiply numbers with more significant figures than 287 and 37. (The numbers 287 and 37 can be multiplied fairly quickly by using long multiplication, but are used here to illustrate the ideas.)

John Napier came from a distinguished Scottish family and held the title of the eighth Laird of Merchiston. He was educated at the University of St Andrews, which he entered in 1563 at the age of 13, and he also studied elsewhere in Europe. He spent most of his time running his estates in Scotland and working on theology – he was a fervent Protestant. Mathematics was only a hobby for him.

Napier's first work on logarithms was his *Mirifici logarithmorum canonis descriptio*, which was published in Latin in 1614. Part of this work consisted of tables listing the logarithms of the sines of angles, which could be used to simplify the work of ships' navigators. The East India Company, an English company that pursued trade with Eastern lands, had the *Descriptio* translated into English for use by its seafarers.

For several hundred years after Napier's invention, logarithm tables and slide rules (Figure 27), which exploit the same principle, were essential aids to calculation. They were finally swept away only with the arrival of cheap pocket calculators in the late 1970s. Logarithms themselves still have many other uses, as you will see in this section. Subsection 4.2 will help you to become familiar with the idea of logarithms and how to find them, and in the later subsections and the next section you will learn about the various ways in which they are useful.

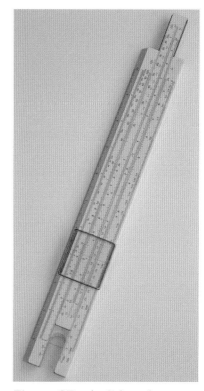

Figure 27 A slide rule

The invention of logarithms made things much easier for astronomers, whose work in calculating the orbits of planets involved a great deal of arithmetic. Two hundred years after their invention, the French scientist Pierre-Simon Laplace (1749–1827) said that logarithms 'by shortening the labours, doubled the life of the astronomer'.

4.2 Logarithms to base 10

In the previous subsection you met the idea that the logarithm of a number is the power to which 10 must be raised to give the number. For example, you saw that the logarithm of 37 is approximately 1.5682, because

$$10^{1.5682} \approx 37.$$

Similarly, the logarithm of 100 is exactly 2, because

$$10^2 = 100.$$

Napier coined the word 'logarithm' from the Greek words *logos* ('proportion, ratio') and *arithmos* ('number'). The 'arithm' part of the word comes from the same root as the start of 'arithmetic'.

Logarithms like these are more accurately called **logarithms to base 10**, because their values depend on the fact that the number 10 has been chosen as the base. You will see examples of logarithms with other bases later in the section, but in this subsection you will concentrate on logarithms to base 10, which are also known as **common logarithms**.

Figure 28 shows how the statement that the logarithm to base 10 of 100 is 2 is written in mathematical notation.

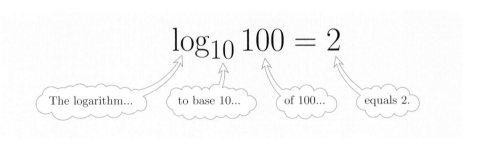

Figure 28   Notation for logarithms

So the two statements

$$10^2 = 100 \quad \text{and} \quad \log_{10} 100 = 2$$

are equivalent to each other – they mean the same thing.

You can use your calculator to find logarithms to base 10, and you will have a chance to practise this shortly. First, however, to make sure that you have a good understanding of the relationship between numbers and their logarithms, let's look at some examples of logarithms to base 10 that you can find without using your calculator.

You have already seen that the logarithm to base 10 of 100 is 2, since the power to which 10 must be raised to give 100 is 2. In general, if you can express a number as a power of 10, then you can write down its logarithm immediately, since it is just the power. For example, you can write 10 000 as 10^4, so the logarithm to base 10 of 10 000 is 4. That is,

$$\log_{10} 10\,000 = 4.$$

You can find the logarithms of any of the numbers 10, 100, 1000, 10 000, and so on, in this way, without using your calculator.

You can also express the numbers 0.1, 0.001, 0.0001, and so on, as powers
of 10, and hence write down their logarithms, without using your
calculator. For example, the number 0.01 has its 1 in the hundredths
place, so

$$0.01 = \frac{1}{100} = \frac{1}{10^2} = 10^{-2}.$$

Hence the logarithm to base 10 of 0.01 is -2. That is,

$$\log_{10} 0.01 = -2.$$

The last step in the
manipulation here follows from
the index law

$$a^{-n} = \frac{1}{a^n}.$$

Notice that if you know the logarithm of a number, then you can work out
the number simply by finding the appropriate power of 10. For example, if
you know that the logarithm of a number is -4, then the number is

$$10^{-4} = \frac{1}{10^4} = \frac{1}{10\,000} = 0.0001.$$

Here are some more examples.

Example 5   *Understanding logarithms*

Tutorial clip

Do the following without using your calculator.

(a) Find the logarithms, to base 10, of the following numbers.

   (i) A million   (ii) 1   (iii) 0.000 01

(b) Find the two consecutive integers between which the number $\log_{10} 568$
lies. Do the same for the number $\log_{10} 0.037$.

(c) The logarithms to base 10 of two numbers are 4 and -1. What are the
numbers?

Solution

(a) The logarithm to base 10 of a number is the power to which 10
must be raised to give the number. So start by expressing each of the
given numbers as a power of 10.

   (i) A million is 10^6, so $\log_{10}(1 \text{ million}) = 6$.

   (ii) $1 = 10^0$, so $\log_{10} 1 = 0$.

   (iii) $0.000\,01 = \dfrac{1}{100\,000} = \dfrac{1}{10^5} = 10^{-5}$, so $\log_{10} 0.000\,01 = -5$.

(b) Find two powers of 10, with integer exponents, between which the
number 568 lies.

The number 568 lies between 100 and 1000, that is, between 10^2
and 10^3. The logarithms to base 10 of 10^2 and 10^3 are 2 and 3,
respectively, so $\log_{10} 568$ lies between 2 and 3.

 Find two powers of 10, with integer exponents, between which the
number 0.037 lies.

The number 0.037 lies between 0.01 and 0.1, that is, between 10^{-2}
and 10^{-1}. The logarithms to base 10 of 10^{-2} and 10^{-1} are -2 and -1,
respectively, so $\log_{10} 0.037$ lies between -2 and -1.

(c) If the logarithm to base 10 of a number is 4, then the number is
$10^4 = 10\,000$.

Similarly, if the logarithm to base 10 of a number is -1, then the
number is $10^{-1} = 0.1$.

Here is a similar activity for you to try.

Activity 20 *Exploring logarithms*

Do the following without using your calculator.

(a) Find the following logarithms.

   (i) $\log_{10} 10$ (ii) $\log_{10} 1000$ (iii) $\log_{10} (1 \text{ billion})$

   (iv) $\log_{10} 0.001$

(b) Does the number zero have a logarithm to base 10?

(c) In each of part (c)(i) to (iv), find two consecutive integers between which the logarithm lies.

   (i) $\log_{10} 91$ (ii) $\log_{10} 2971$ (iii) $\log_{10} 8.8$ (iv) $\log_{10} 0.25$

(d) The logarithms to base 10 of two numbers are 5 and -2. What are the numbers?

You saw in Activity 20 that the number zero does not have a logarithm to base 10. In fact, only *positive* numbers have logarithms. For example, the number -1 doesn't have a logarithm to base 10, because there is no power to which 10 can be raised to give -1.

Notice, however, that logarithms *themselves* can be negative. For example, you saw in Example 5 that the logarithm to base 10 of 0.00001 is -5.

So, in summary, *only positive numbers have logarithms*, but *logarithms themselves can be any number*.

The box below summarises the definition of a logarithm to base 10.

Logarithms to base 10

The **logarithm to base 10** of a number x, denoted by $\log_{10} x$, is the power to which you have to raise 10 to get the answer x. So the two equations

$$x = 10^y \quad \text{and} \quad y = \log_{10} x$$

are equivalent.

Sometimes, when it is understood that a logarithm is a common logarithm, the subscript 10 is omitted from the logarithm notation. So, for example, we might write simply

$$\log 100 = 2,$$

rather than

$$\log_{10} 100 = 2.$$

Later in the unit you will see examples of equations involving logarithms that are true no matter what the base is. (The base must be the same for each logarithm in the equation.)

It is also common to omit the subscript when the notation is used in an equation involving logarithms that is true no matter what the base is.

You have seen that if a number is written as a power of 10, then you can write down its logarithm to base 10 immediately. If a number is not written as a power of 10, then it is not straightforward to find its logarithm to base 10, but you can use your calculator to obtain an approximate value. The next activity shows you how to do this.

Activity 21 *Logarithms on your calculator*

Work through Subsection 3.10 of the MU123 Guide.

In mathematics there are many pairs of operations that 'undo' or 'reverse the effect of' each other. For example, finding the cube of a number and finding the cube root of a number are like this. If you start with 5, say, and cube it, then you get 125; and if you then take the cube root, you get 5 again. Or you can apply the operations in the other order: for example, if you start with 8 and take the cube root then you get 2, and if you then cube this number you get 8 again.

Two operations that undo the effect of each other are called **inverse operations**.

Raising 10 to a number and finding the logarithm of a number to base 10 are inverse operations. For example, if you start with the number 5 and raise 10 to this number then you get $10^5 = 100\,000$; and if you then take the logarithm to base 10, you get 5 again. Or you can do the operations in the other order: for example, if you start with 100 and take the logarithm to base 10 then you get 2, and if you then raise 10 to this number, you get 100 again.

The inverse operation to finding the logarithm to base 10 of a number, which is raising 10 to a number, was called finding the *antilogarithm* in Subsection 4.1. This word is not commonly used nowadays, since the demise of logarithm tables!

You might like to try some more examples on your calculator: choose any (reasonably small) number and raise 10 to that number, then take the logarithm to base 10 of the result, and check that you get the number that you started with. Try applying the two operations in the other order, as well.

Raising 10 to a large power will give a number that is too big for your calculator to handle.

4.3 Logarithmic scales

Whenever you hear news of an earthquake reported in the media, its magnitude on the *Richter scale* is always mentioned. Table 4 shows the numbers of earthquakes between 2000 and 2008 measuring 5 or more on the Richter scale.

Table 4 The numbers of earthquakes by magnitude between 2000 and 2008 (data from United States Geological Survey Earthquake Hazards Program)

Year	5.0 to 5.9	6.0 to 6.9	7.0 to 7.9	8.0 to 9.9	Total 5.0 to 9.9
2003	1203	140	14	1	1358
2004	1515	141	14	2	1672
2005	1693	140	10	1	1844
2006	1712	142	9	2	1865
2007	1995	177	14	4	2190
2008	530	73	6	0	609

Source: http://earthquake.usgs.gov

Figure 29 *Seismographs* measure and record ground motion

The Richter scale measures the amount of seismic energy released by an earthquake. It is not a normal, 'linear' scale, but a **base 10 logarithmic scale**. What this means is that the size of an earthquake of magnitude 8, say, on the Richter scale should be thought of as 10^8, rather than simply the number 8. So, for example, an earthquake of magnitude 9 on the Richter scale is ten times more powerful than one of magnitude 8, because 10^9 is ten times larger than 10^8. Similarly, an earthquake of magnitude 6 on the Richter scale is a hundred times more powerful than one of magnitude 4, because 10^6 is a hundred times larger than 10^4. The magnitude of an earthquake on the Richter scale can be thought of as the logarithm to base 10 of the amount of energy released.

Logarithmic scales are useful for measuring quantities where the numbers vary from very small to extremely large, like the amount of seismic energy released by an earthquake. However, scales of this type need to be interpreted with care, as small differences on a logarithmic scale can represent very large differences in the quantities being measured.

Another well-known example of a base 10 logarithmic scale is the *decibel* (dB) scale, which is most commonly used for measuring the intensity of sound. This scale is slightly more complicated than the Richter scale, because the fundamental unit is not the decibel but the *bel* – a decibel is one tenth of a bel. A sound level of 9 bels is 10 times as strong as one of 8 bels.

> The intensity of an earthquake varies with the distance from its centre, so scales other than the Richter scale are used to describe the *local* intensity of earthquakes. These scales are often based on observations of damage to buildings – an example is the European Macroseismic Scale.

Activity 22 *Comparing values on logarithmic scales*

(a) An earthquake was recorded as having a magnitude of 6.6 on the Richter scale. A few minutes later, an aftershock was measured at 4.6. How did the amount of energy released by the two quakes compare?

(b) If the noise level in an industrial workplace goes up from 60 decibels (6 bels) to 70 decibels (7 bels), by what factor does the intensity of the sound increase?

4.4 Logarithms to other bases

Now let's consider logarithms to bases other than 10. Here is the general definition of a logarithm, to any base b.

Logarithms

The **logarithm to base** b of a number x, denoted by $\log_b x$, is the power to which you have to raise the base b to get the answer x. So the two equations

$$x = b^y \quad \text{and} \quad y = \log_b x$$

are equivalent.

(Remember that:

- the base b must be positive and not equal to 1;

- only positive numbers have logarithms, but logarithms themselves can be any number.)

> The number 1 cannot be the base of logarithms because raising 1 to a power always gives the value 1. The reason why only positive numbers have logarithms is explained for base 10 on page 152; a similar reason applies for any base.

As with logarithms to base 10, if you can express a number as a power of the base b, then you can immediately write down its logarithm to base b.

Example 6 *Understanding logarithms to base 2*

Find the logarithms to base 2 of the following numbers.

(a) 16   (b) $\frac{1}{8}$

Solution

💬 You need to find the powers to which you have to raise the base 2 to get the given numbers. So start by expressing each of the numbers as a power of 2. 💬

(a) $16 = 2^4$, so $\log_2 16 = 4$.

(b) $\frac{1}{8} = \frac{1}{2^3} = 2^{-3}$, so $\log_2 \left(\frac{1}{8} \right) = -3$.

The manipulation in part (b) uses the index law
$$a^{-n} = \frac{1}{a^n}.$$

Here is a similar activity for you to try.

Activity 23 *Exploring logarithms to base 2*

Find the logarithms to base 2 of the following numbers, without using your calculator.

(a) 8   (b) 32   (c) 2   (d) 1   (e) 0.5   (f) $\sqrt{2}$

You have seen that finding the logarithm of a number to base 10 and raising 10 to a number are inverse operations. The analogous fact holds for any base b: finding the logarithm of a number to base b and raising b to a number are inverse operations.

Euler's number e is often used as a base for logarithms in higher-level mathematics, because of the importance of the exponential function with rule $y = e^x$, and the fact that finding a logarithm to base e is the inverse operation to raising e to a number. Logarithms to base e turn out to be easier to work with in some ways than logarithms to any other base.

Logarithms to base e are called **natural logarithms**. The notation 'ln' is usually used in place of '$\log_e$', so, for example, the natural logarithm of 5 is usually written as

Logarithms to base e were first described as 'natural' logarithms in the seventeenth century, by the Danish mathematician Nicolaus Mercator (1620–1687).

    $\ln 5$

rather than $\log_e 5$. The box below summarises the definition of a natural logarithm, using this notation.

Natural logarithms

The **natural logarithm** of a number x, denoted by $\ln x$, is the power to which you have to raise the base e to get the answer x. So the two equations

    $x = e^y$ and $y = \ln x$

are equivalent.

In some disciplines the natural logarithm of x is denoted by $\log x$, rather than $\ln x$ or $\log_e x$. You saw earlier that $\log x$ is also often used to denote $\log_{10} x$, or alternatively the logarithm of x with no specific base (but the same base for each use of the notation), so if you see this notation used outside this module then it is worth checking its meaning.

As with logarithms to other bases, if a number is expressed as a power of e, then it is straightforward to write down its logarithm to base e, as illustrated in the next example.

The first published use of the notation ln for natural logarithm was in a book written by an American mathematician, Irving Stringham, which was published in 1893. He explained his choice, in a textbook published a little later, as follows: 'In place of ^{e}log we shall henceforth use the shorter symbol ln, made up of the initial letters of *logarithm* and of *natural* or *Napierian*.'

Example 7   *Understanding natural logarithms*

Find the natural logarithms of the following numbers.

(a) e^4 (b) $e^{-3.27}$ (c) e

Solution

The power to which e must be raised to give e^4 is 4, so the natural logarithm of e^4 is 4. This gives the answer to part (a), and the other two parts are similar.

(a) $\ln e^4 = 4$.

(b) $\ln(e^{-3.27}) = -3.27$.

(c) $e = e^1$, so $\ln e = 1$.

Activity 24   *Exploring natural logarithms*

(a) Find the natural logarithms of the following numbers, without using your calculator.

   (i) e^2 (ii) e^{-4} (iii) 1   (iv) $\dfrac{1}{e^2}$

(b) Given that $e^{5.37} = 214.86$ to two decimal places, write down the approximate value of $\ln 214.86$.

The next activity shows you how to use your calculator to find natural logarithms of numbers, and to find powers of e, which is the inverse operation.

Activity 25   *Natural logarithms and powers of e on your calculator*

Work through Subsection 3.11 of the MU123 Guide.

In the examples and activities in this section you have seen that

$$\log_{10} 1 = 0, \quad \log_2 1 = 0 \quad \text{and} \quad \ln 1 = 0.$$

In general, the logarithm of 1 to *any base* is 0. This is because if b is any base number, then $b^0 = 1$ and so the power to which b must be raised to give 1 is 0.

You have also seen that

$$\log_{10} 10 = 1, \quad \log_2 2 = 1 \quad \text{and} \quad \ln e = 1.$$

In general, for *any base* b, the logarithm of b to base b is 1. This is because $b^1 = b$ and so the power to which b must be raised to give b is 1.

These two facts are summarised below.

Logarithm of the number one and logarithm of the base

For any base b,

$$\log_b 1 = 0 \quad \text{and} \quad \log_b b = 1.$$

Benford's law

You might remember reading in Unit 3 that if you investigate the *first digits* of the numbers in a table of data, such as financial figures, then surprisingly the digits $1, 2, \ldots, 9$ do not occur equally often. Figure 30 shows the percentage occurrences of the nine digits.

It was mentioned in Unit 3 that there is a formula for the percentage occurrence of each digit, which is known as *Benford's law*. In fact this formula involves logarithms to base 10 and can be stated as

percentage occurrence of digit N

$= (\log_{10}(N+1) - \log_{10} N) \times 100\%.$

For example, this formula gives the percentage occurrence of the digit 2 as

$(\log_{10} 3 - \log_{10} 2) \times 100\% \approx 17.6\%,$

and the percentage occurrence of the digit 7 as

$(\log_{10} 8 - \log_{10} 7) \times 100\% \approx 5.8\%,$

so 2 occurs about three times as often as 7 as a first digit.

There are many other instances of logarithms cropping up in real life where you might least expect them!

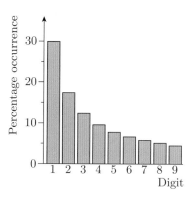

Figure 30 The percentage occurrences of $1, 2, \ldots, 9$ as the first digits of numbers in a table of data

In this section you have met the idea of logarithms. You have seen that taking a logarithm to base b is the inverse operation to raising the base b to a power. Any positive number except 1 can be used as the base of logarithms, but the two most commonly used bases are 10 and Euler's number e.

You have also learned about two measures that are based on logarithmic scales – the magnitude of an earthquake on the Richter scale, and the bel, which is a measure of sound intensity.

5 Working with logarithms

This section begins by introducing three rules that are useful when you are working with logarithms. Then you will learn how one of these rules can be used to help you to solve exponential equations, and you will find the answers to some problems by solving such equations. In the final subsection you will have a chance to explore the graphs of some functions of the form $y = \log_b x$.

5.1 Three logarithm laws

The three rules for logarithms that you will meet in this subsection depend on the following three index laws that you met in Unit 3.

Three index laws from Unit 3

$$a^m \times a^n = a^{m+n}, \qquad \frac{a^m}{a^n} = a^{m-n}, \qquad (a^m)^n = a^{mn}.$$

You will be introduced to the three rules for logarithms one at a time.

Rule for addition of logarithms

The first rule for logarithms is illustrated in the calculation below, which you saw in Subsection 4.1. The calculation works because of the first index law in the pink box on the previous page.

$$287 \times 37 \approx 10^{2.4579} \times 10^{1.5682}$$
$$= 10^{2.4579+1.5682}$$
$$= 10^{4.0261}$$
$$\approx 10\,619.$$

This calculation shows that you can multiply 287 and 37 by first finding their logarithms to base 10, which are approximately 2.4579 and 1.5682, respectively, then adding these logarithms to obtain 4.0261, and finally finding the number whose logarithm to base 10 is 4.0261, which is approximately 10 619. In other words, as you can see by looking at the calculation, if you add the logarithms to base 10 of 287 and 37, then you obtain the logarithm to base 10 of their product, 287×37. Or, in the usual notation,

$$\log_{10} 287 + \log_{10} 37 = \log_{10}(287 \times 37).$$

You can see that a similar statement will hold for any two positive numbers – it is the reason why the logarithm method for multiplying numbers works. And the base of the logarithms does not have to be 10.

So in general the following law holds, where x and y are any positive numbers, and the logarithms can be to any base.

The base must be the same for each logarithm, of course.

> ### Addition of logarithms
>
> $$\log x + \log y = \log(xy)$$

You can use algebra to prove this result formally, as follows. Suppose that the numbers x and y can be written as b^m and b^n, respectively. That is,

$$x = b^m \quad \text{and} \quad y = b^n.$$

Then

$$m = \log_b x \quad \text{and} \quad n = \log_b y.$$

The product xy can be written as

$$xy = b^m \times b^n = b^{m+n}.$$

This tells you that the power to which b must be raised to give xy is $m + n$. That is,

$$\log_b(xy) = m + n = \log_b x + \log_b y.$$

which is the logarithm law above.

Rule for subtraction of logarithms

The second rule for logarithms is illustrated in the calculation at the top of the next page, which you also saw in Subsection 4.1. This calculation works because of the second index law in the pink box on page 157.

$$287 \div 37 \approx 10^{2.4579} \div 10^{1.5682}$$
$$= 10^{2.4579-1.5682}$$
$$= 10^{0.8897}$$
$$\approx 7.757.$$

From this calculation you can see that if you subtract the logarithms to base 10 of 287 and 37, then you obtain the logarithm to base 10 of their quotient, $287 \div 37$. Or, in the usual notation,

$$\log_{10} 287 - \log_{10} 37 = \log_{10}\left(\frac{287}{37}\right).$$

Again, a similar equation will hold for any two positive numbers – it is the reason why the logarithm method for dividing numbers works, and again, the base of the logarithms does not have to be 10.

So in general the following law holds, where x and y are any positive numbers, and the logarithms can be to any base.

Subtraction of logarithms

$$\log x - \log y = \log\left(\frac{x}{y}\right)$$

You can formally prove this fact using an argument similar to that for the first logarithm law. You might like to try this in the next activity.

Activity 26 *Proving a logarithm law*

Prove that for any base b and any positive numbers x and y,

$$\log_b x - \log_b y = \log_b\left(\frac{x}{y}\right).$$

The next example shows you how you can apply the two logarithm laws that you have seen so far.

Example 8 *Combining logarithms*

Write each of the following expressions as a logarithm of a single number.

(a) $\log_{10} 4 + \log_{10} 5$ (b) $\ln 36 - \ln 9$ (c) $\ln 20 + \ln 3 - \ln 9$

Solution

Use the laws for addition and subtraction of logarithms.

(a) $\log_{10} 4 + \log_{10} 5 = \log_{10}(4 \times 5) = \log_{10} 20$

(b) $\ln 36 - \ln 9 = \ln\left(\frac{36}{9}\right) = \ln 4$

(c) $\ln 20 + \ln 3 - \ln 9 = \ln(20 \times 3) - \ln 9$
$$= \ln\left(\frac{20 \times 3}{9}\right)$$
$$= \ln\left(\frac{20}{3}\right)$$

Activity 27   *Combining logarithms*

Write each of the following expressions as a logarithm of a single number.

(a) $\log_{10} 3 + \log_{10} 4$ (b) $\ln 15 - \ln 3$

(c) $\log_{10} 2 + \log_{10} 3 + \log_{10} 5$ (d) $-\ln 4 + \ln 2$

Rule for a multiple of a logarithm

You have seen that, before the days of calculators and computers, logarithms made it easier to carry out multiplication and division calculations, because they allowed them to be turned into addition and subtraction calculations, respectively.

Logarithms could also be used to turn a calculation involving raising a number to a power into a multiplication calculation, as demonstrated by the calculation below. As with the earlier calculations, the initial step of finding the logarithm of 287 and the final step of finding the antilogarithm of 4.424 22 would have been carried out by using logarithm tables.

This third index law is $(a^m)^n = a^{mn}$.

This calculation works because of the third index law in the pink box on page 157.

$$287^{1.8} \approx \left(10^{2.4579}\right)^{1.8}$$
$$= 10^{2.4579 \times 1.8}$$
$$= 10^{4.424\,22}$$
$$\approx 26\,560.$$

From this calculation you can see that if the logarithm to base 10 of 287 is multiplied by 1.8 then the result is the logarithm to base 10 of $287^{1.8}$. Or, in the usual notation,

$$1.8 \times \log_{10} 287 = \log_{10} \left(287^{1.8}\right).$$

A similar equation will hold for any positive number replacing 287, and any number at all replacing 1.8. And, as before, the base of the logarithms does not have to be 10.

So in general the following law holds, where x is any positive number, n is any number at all (including any negative number) and the logarithms can be to any base.

Multiple of a logarithm

$$n \log x = \log \left(x^n\right)$$

You can use algebra to prove this result formally, as follows. Suppose that the number x can be written as b^m. That is,

$$x = b^m.$$

Then

$$m = \log_b x.$$

The power x^n can be written as

$$x^n = (b^m)^n = b^{mn}.$$

This tells you that the power to which b must be raised to give x^n is mn. That is,

$$\log_b(x^n) = mn = n\log_b x,$$

which is the logarithm law above.

The example below shows you some ways in which you can use the third logarithm law.

Example 9 *Combining more logarithms*

Write each of the following expressions as a logarithm of a single number.

(a) $2\log_{10} 3$ (b) $\ln 24 - 3\ln 2$

Solution

$\wp$ Use the logarithm law on page 160. In part (b), also use the logarithm law on page 159. $\wp$

(a) $2\log_{10} 3 = \log_{10}(3^2) = \log_{10} 9$

(b) $\ln 24 - 3\ln 2 = \ln 24 - \ln(2^3) = \ln\left(\dfrac{24}{2^3}\right) = \ln\left(\dfrac{24}{8}\right) = \ln 3$

Activity 28 *Combining more logarithms*

Write each of the following expressions as a logarithm of a single number.

(a) $3\log_{10} 3$ (b) $\ln 6 + 2\ln 5$ (c) $0.5\log_{10} 4$ (d) $\ln 27 - 2\ln 3$

Here is a summary of the three logarithm laws that you have seen in this section.

Three logarithm laws

$$\log x + \log y = \log(xy)$$

$$\log x - \log y = \log\left(\frac{x}{y}\right)$$

$$n\log x = \log(x^n)$$

As usual, these laws apply to all appropriate numbers. So n can be any number (in particular, it can be fractional and/or negative), but x and y must be positive, since only positive numbers have logarithms. These laws apply for logarithms to any base.

You might find the third of these three laws easier to remember if you notice how it is connected to the first law. The numbers x and y in the first law do not have to be different, of course. If they are the same, then you obtain

$$\log x + \log x = \log(x \times x),$$

that is,

$$2\log x = \log(x^2), \tag{4}$$

which is the third logarithm law with $n = 2$.

You can also add another $\log x$ to each side of equation (4), to give

$$2\log x + \log x = \log(x^2) + \log x.$$

Collecting the like terms on the left-hand side and using the first logarithm law again on the right-hand side gives

$$3 \log x = \log(x^3),$$

which is the third logarithm law with $n = 3$.

You can see that this pattern will continue, to give the third logarithm law for any positive whole number n. But remember that the law holds not just if n is a positive whole number, but for *any* number n.

5.2 Solving exponential equations by taking logs

As you saw at the beginning of Section 4, an *exponential* equation is an equation in which the unknown is in an exponent, such as

$$170 \times 1.23^t = 7\,000\,000\,000.$$

You may remember that this particular equation arose in the context of finding the number of years that it would take for the entire population of the world to be Elvis impersonators.

In the absence of a better method, so far you have solved equations of this sort by using trial and improvement or graphs. You are now ready to learn how to use logarithms to solve exponential equations.

The method involves using the third logarithm law from the previous subsection. For this purpose it is best to think of the law with its left- and right-hand sides swapped:

$$\log(x^n) = n \log x.$$

The next example shows how you can use this logarithm law to help you to solve exponential equations.

Example 10 *Solving an exponential equation by taking logs*

Solve the equation $0.7^x = 0.2$, giving the solution to three significant figures.

Solution

The equation is

$$0.7^x = 0.2.$$

  Take the logarithm to base 10 of both sides.

$$\log_{10}(0.7^x) = \log_{10} 0.2$$

  Use the fact that $\log(x^n) = n \log x$.

$$x \log_{10} 0.7 = \log_{10} 0.2$$

  Divide both sides by the coefficient of the unknown.

$$x = \frac{\log_{10} 0.2}{\log_{10} 0.7}$$

  Use your calculator to evaluate the answer.

$$x = 4.51 \text{ (to 3 s.f.).}$$

The solution is approximately $x = 4.51$.

(Check: When $x = 4.51$, LHS $= 0.7^{4.51} = 0.200\,16\ldots \approx 0.2 =$ RHS.)

So the basic procedure for solving an exponential equation is to take the logarithm of both sides of the equation – this is the 'taking logs' mentioned in the title of this subsection – and then apply the logarithm law mentioned on the opposite page to turn the awkward exponent into a straightforward coefficient. You can then solve the equation in the usual way.

You can use logarithms to any base in this procedure, as long as you are consistent. However, you will usually need to evaluate these logarithms, so it is best to use either logarithms to base 10 or natural logarithms, as these are easily available from your calculator.

Activity 29   *Solving an exponential equation by taking logs*

Solve the equation $1.4^x = 550$, giving the solution to three significant figures.

The method of taking logs is easiest to apply when one side of the equation consists only of a number raised to an exponent, where this exponent contains the unknown. So if you have to solve an exponential equation that is not in this form, then it is usually best to rearrange it into this form before you take logs.

This is demonstrated in the next example, which also illustrates the kind of problem that you can answer by solving exponential equations.

Example 11   *Solving another exponential equation*

 Tutorial clip

A population of insects currently numbers 200. If the size of the population increases by 10% each week, how long will it take to reach 400?

Solution

The starting number is 200 and the scale factor is 1.1, so the size of the population is modelled by the equation

$$P = 200 \times 1.1^t,$$

You saw how to obtain formulas like the one here in Section 1.

where t is the number of weeks and P is the size of the population.

So the time t weeks for the population to reach 400 is given by the equation

$$200 \times 1.1^t = 400.$$

This equation can be solved as follows.

First divide both sides by 200 to obtain 1.1^t by itself on one side.

$$1.1^t = 2$$

Now take logs, and solve the equation using the method that you have seen.

$$\log_{10}(1.1^t) = \log_{10} 2$$
$$t \log_{10} 1.1 = \log_{10} 2$$
$$t = \frac{\log_{10} 2}{\log_{10} 1.1}$$
$$t = 7.27 \text{ (to 2 d.p.)}$$

So the insect population will take about $7\frac{1}{4}$ weeks to reach 400.

(Check: When $t = 7.27$, $P = 200 \times 1.1^{7.27} = 399.90\ldots \approx 400$.)

Before you go on to solve similar equations yourself, there is something worth observing about Example 11. If the starting population of insects had been 300, say, and the question had asked you to find the time taken for it to reach double this number, which is 600, then the answer would have been the same. This is because the answer would be found by solving the equation

$$300 \times 1.1^t = 600,$$

and this simplifies to

$$1.1^t = 2,$$

which is the same equation as in the example. In fact, you can see that whatever the starting population is, the time taken for it to double would be the same. So the time taken for the population to double does not depend on the starting population, but depends only on the scale factor. You will learn more about this observation in the next subsection.

You can practise solving exponential equations by taking logs in the next activity.

Activity 30 *Solving the Elvis impersonator problem*

Solve the equation

$$170 \times 1.23^t = 7\,000\,000\,000$$

by taking logs, giving your answer to three significant figures.

(The solution of this equation is the time in years that it would take for Elvis impersonators to account for the entire population of the world, assuming that their number starts at 170 and grows by 23% per year, and that the population of the world remains constant at 7 billion.)

The method of taking logs can also be used for problems involving *discrete* exponential change. For example, in Subsection 2.1 you looked at the case of an athlete who plans a new training schedule in which the distance in kilometres that she will run in week n is

$$20 \times 1.1^n.$$

The problem was to find the week of the schedule in which the athlete is first due to run more than 65 km. In other words, you have to find the smallest integer value of n for which

$$20 \times 1.1^n > 65.$$

This problem was solved by trial and improvement in Example 2 on page 132. A quicker way to solve it is to use the method of taking logs to find the solution of the equation

$$20 \times 1.1^n = 65;$$

then the required value of n is the smallest whole number greater than this solution. You might like to try this – you can check your answer against the answer found in Example 2.

In higher-level mathematics modules many exponential equations involve the base e.

If you have to solve an exponential equation in which the base is e, then it is usually helpful to take *natural logarithms* of both sides, rather than logarithms to base 10. This often allows you to obtain an exact answer in terms of natural logarithms, which you can then evaluate if necessary. This is illustrated in the next example.

In this example the exponent is not simply the unknown, x, but an expression involving the unknown, namely $2x$. Taking logs is useful in cases like this too, whatever the base is.

Example 12   *Solving an exponential equation in which the base is e*

Find the exact solution of the equation $e^{2x} = 3$, then evaluate it to three significant figures.

Solution

The equation is

$e^{2x} = 3.$

The base is e, so take natural logarithms.

$\ln(e^{2x}) = \ln 3$

Use the fact that taking the natural logarithm of a number is the inverse operation to raising e to a number.

$2x = \ln 3$

Now rearrange the equation in the usual way.

$x = \frac{1}{2} \ln 3$

Evaluate the answer if required.

$x = 0.549$ (to 3 s.f.)

(Check: When $x = 0.549$, LHS $= e^{2 \times 0.549} = 2.998 \ldots \approx 3 = $ RHS.)

> Another way to obtain the third equation in the solution here is to notice that the first equation tells you that you can obtain 3 by raising the base e to the power $2x$; in other words, the natural logarithm of 3 is $2x$.

Activity 31   *Solving exponential equations in which the base is e*

Find the exact solutions of the following equations, then evaluate them to three significant figures.

(a) $e^t = 8$ (b) $e^{x-1} = 5$

The useful fact used in Example 12 and Activity 31 was as follows. Suppose that you take a number x and first raise the base e to that number, then take the natural logarithm of the result. Since the two operations are inverses of each other, the final result will just be x, which gives the following identity:

$\ln(e^x) = x.$

> Remember that an *identity* is an equation that is true for all appropriate values of its variable or variables.

You can also apply the operations in the other order. If you take a number x and first take the natural logarithm of that number, then raise the base e to the result, then again the final result will just be x, which gives the following second useful identity:

$e^{\ln x} = x.$

> Similar facts to those in these two pink boxes hold for bases other than e.

5.3   Doubling and halving times

Example 11 in the previous subsection was about a population of insects that increased by 10% each week, and it was pointed out that the time that it would take for the population to double does not depend on the number of insects at the start.

In fact, not only is this true, but you could look at the number of insects *at any point in time after the starting time,* and the time that it would take for the population to double *from its value at that point* would be the same as the time taken for the population at the start to double.

This is a consequence of the property of continuous exponential change that you met in Subsection 2.2. You saw there that if a quantity changes by the scale factor b every week, for example, then over any time interval of length i weeks, the quantity changes by the scale factor b^i.

The population of insects changes by the scale factor 1.1 every week, so, for example, over any time interval of length 3 weeks, it changes by the scale factor

$$1.1^3 \approx 1.33,$$

and similarly over any time interval of length 10 weeks, say, it changes by the scale factor

$$1.1^{10} \approx 2.59,$$

and so on. You can see that there must be a particular length of time in which the population changes by the scale factor 2 – that is, it *doubles* – and that this length of time, in weeks, will be the number i that satisfies the equation

$$1.1^i \approx 2.$$

This equation is the one that was solved in Example 11. It was solved by taking logs, and its solution was found to be about 7.27. So whenever you record the size of the population of insects, the population will have doubled about 7.27 weeks later.

You can see that you could apply the same argument to any example involving continuous exponential growth. So, for any quantity that is subject to continuous exponential growth over time, there will be a particular length of time in which its size always doubles. This length of time is called its **doubling time**.

The doubling time can be worked out in a similar way to the insect example. For example, if the quantity increases by the scale factor 1.8 each week, then the doubling time, in weeks, is the number i that satisfies the equation $1.8^i = 2$. Similarly, if the quantity increases by the scale factor 1.05 each year, then the doubling time, in years, is the number i that satisfies the equation $1.05^i = 2$. As you know, you can solve equations like these by taking logs.

Activity 32   *Finding a doubling time*

If the number of Elvis impersonators is increasing by 23% per year, what is its doubling time? Give your answer in years to two significant figures.

You might have heard of *Moore's law*, which suggests that the number of transistors on a typical microprocessor (computer chip) increases exponentially with time, and doubles approximately every two years. The number of transistors on a microprocessor is an important quantity, because it strongly influences the performance of the electronic device containing the microprocessor – for example, it affects the processing speed of a computer. Microprocessor manufacturers have largely kept to the rate of increase in Moore's law, or faster, since Gordon Moore first suggested this law in 1965, at least up until the time of writing of MU123. However, it will probably not be sustainable for much longer, because of physical limits in manufacturing processes.

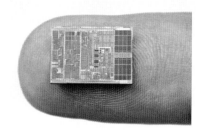

Figure 31 A microprocessor

A quantity that is subject to continuous exponential decay, rather than growth, will not have a doubling time, of course, but it will have a **halving time**.

For example, consider again the car discussed on page 135, whose value immediately after purchase is £20 000 and which depreciates at a rate of 20% per year. The value of the car depreciates by the scale factor 0.8 each year, so, for example, every two years it depreciates by the scale factor

$$0.8^2 = 0.64,$$

and every 3.5 years it depreciates by the scale factor

$$0.8^{3.5} \approx 0.46,$$

and so on. There will be a particular length of time in which the value of the car depreciates by the scale factor $\frac{1}{2}$ – that is, it halves – and this length of time, in years, will be the number i that satisfies the equation

$$0.8^i = \tfrac{1}{2}.$$

In other words, this number i is the halving time, in years, of the value of the car. The equation can be solved by taking logs, as follows.

$$\log_{10}\left(0.8^i\right) = \log_{10} 0.5$$
$$i \log_{10} 0.8 = \log_{10} 0.5$$
$$i = \frac{\log_{10} 0.5}{\log_{10} 0.8} \approx 3.1$$

So the value of the car halves every 3.1 years, approximately.

Activity 33 *Finding a halving time*

A population of elephants is thought to be declining at the rate of 4% per year. Find the scale factor by which the population decreases every year, and hence find its halving time, to the nearest year.

The halving time of a quantity that decays exponentially is often called its **half-life**. Both doubling times and halving times (half-lives) are useful as descriptions of the speed of exponential growth or decay. For example, doctors can use information about the typical half-lives of prescription drugs in patients' bloodstreams to help them to make decisions about the frequency of doses.

The ideas about doubling time and halving time that you have met in this subsection are summarised below.

> ### Doubling time and halving time (half-life)
>
> Suppose that a quantity is subject to continuous exponential change by the scale factor b every year.
>
> If the quantity grows (that is, if $b > 1$), then its doubling time in years is the solution i of the equation
>
> $$b^i = 2.$$
>
> If the quantity decays (that is, if $0 < b < 1$), then its halving time (half-life) in years is the solution i of the equation
>
> $$b^i = \tfrac{1}{2}.$$
>
> (If the quantity changes by the scale factor b every *week*, then the solution i of the equation is the halving time in *weeks*, and similarly for any other units of time, such as days or minutes.)

The half-lives of radioactive isotopes range from tiny fractions of a second to billions of years. Knowledge of the half-lives of some radioactive isotopes can be used to find out how old objects are. For example, the isotope carbon-14 has a half-life of 5730 years, and measurements of carbon-14 are used in carbon dating. This process can determine the approximate age of organic material, such as plant and animal remains, up to several tens of thousands of years old.

You may have heard the term half-life used in connection with radioactivity. Many chemical elements have several different forms, called *isotopes*, which differ in the number of a particular type of subatomic particle, called a *neutron*, in their atoms. Some chemical isotopes are radioactive, which means that over time they decay atom by atom into isotopes of a different element, emitting radiation as they do so.

Scientists have found that when a sample of a radioactive isotope decays, the amount of the original radioactive isotope remaining can be modelled by an exponential decay curve. The speed of the decay is usually described by giving the half-life. So, for example, if you are told that the half-life of a radioactive isotope is 100 years, then this means that the amount of the radioactive isotope halves every 100 years.

If a radioactive isotope decays into a non-radioactive isotope of another element, then the level of radioactivity drops in proportion to the amount of the radioactive isotope, so the level of radioactivity can also be modelled by an exponential decay curve, with the same halving time. This is the topic of the next activity.

Activity 34   *Finding a half-life*

A *becquerel* is one radioactive disintegration per second. This unit of measurement is named after the French physicist Henri Becquerel (1852–1908), who discovered radioactivity in 1896. He was awarded the 1903 Nobel prize for physics, along with Marie Curie and Pierre Curie, who found additional radioactive elements.

The level of radioactivity of a piece of material containing a single radioactive isotope was initially 40 becquerels. One day later the level had fallen to 38 becquerels. Assume that the radioactive isotope decays into a non-radioactive substance.

(a) Find the scale factor by which the radioactivity decreases each day.

(b) Hence find the half-life of the radioactive isotope, in days to one decimal place.

5.4 Graphs of logarithmic functions

As you know, the operations of raising a base b to a number and taking the logarithm to the same base b of a number are inverse operations. Another way to express this is to say that the functions with rules

$$y = b^x \quad \text{and} \quad y = \log_b x \tag{5}$$

are *inverse functions*. In general, **inverse functions** are functions whose rules undo the effects of each other.

In the final activity of this section you are asked to use Graphplotter to plot the graphs of some pairs of inverse functions of form (5). You should be able to gain a few useful insights, not just about these particular graphs but also about the connection between the graphs of any two inverse functions.

A function with a rule of the form $y = \log_b x$ is called a **logarithmic function**.

Activity 35 *Investigating graphs of equations of the form $y = \log_b x$ and $y = b^x$*

 Graphplotter

---

Use Graphplotter, with the 'Two graphs' tab selected. Click the 'Autoscale' button to ensure that the axis scales are at their default values. Make sure that the 'y-intercept' option is switched off – it is not needed in this activity.

(a) Choose the equation

$$y = ab^x + c$$

from the left-hand drop-down list, and make sure that $a = 1$ and $c = 0$, since this activity is about the graphs of equations of the form $y = b^x$. Then choose the equation

$$y = a \log_b(cx) + d$$

from the right-hand drop-down list, and make sure that $a = 1$, $c = 1$ and $d = 0$, since this activity is also about the graphs of equations of the form $y = \log_b x$.

Keep all these constants set to these values throughout the activity. You will need to change only the value of the base b for each graph.

(b) Set $b = 10$ for both equations to obtain the graphs of the equations

$$y = 10^x \quad \text{and} \quad y = \log_{10} x.$$

Make a note of how the two graphs seem to be related.

(c) Repeat part (b) for the equations

$$y = 2^x \quad \text{and} \quad y = \log_2 x.$$

(d) Repeat part (b) for the equations

$$y = e^x \quad \text{and} \quad y = \ln x.$$

You will see that there are checkboxes to set $b = e$.

(e) Repeat part (b) for the equations

$$y = 0.5^x \quad \text{and} \quad y = \log_{0.5} x.$$

In each part of Activity 35, you should have found that the two graphs are mirror images of each other, reflected in the line $y = x$. For example, Figure 32 (overleaf) shows the graphs of $y = 2^x$ and $y = \log_2 x$, with the line $y = x$ shown in red dashes.

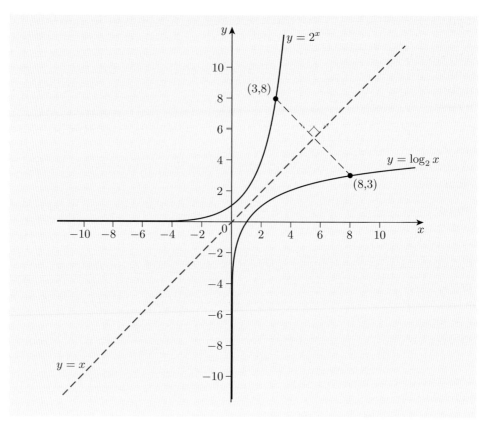

Figure 32   The graphs of the equations $y = 2^x$ and $y = \log_2 x$ are reflections of each other in the line $y = x$

To see why this symmetry occurs, consider a particular point on the graph of $y = 2^x$. For example, the point $(3, 8)$ lies on this graph, because inputting 3 to the rule $y = 2^x$ gives the output 8. Since the function with rule $y = \log_2 x$ is the inverse of the function with rule $y = 2^x$, inputting 8 to *this* function gives the output 3, and so the point $(8, 3)$, obtained by swapping the coordinates of the first point, lies on *its* graph. The two points are the reflections of each other in the line $y = x$, as shown in Figure 32.

In general, if you swap the coordinates of any point on the graph of $y = 2^x$, then you obtain the coordinates of a point on the graph of $y = \log_2 x$, and vice versa. And when you swap the coordinates of a point, the resulting point is always the reflection of the first point in the line $y = x$. This explains why the two graphs are reflections of each other in this line.

You can see that the same argument will apply to any pair of functions of the form $y = b^x$ and $y = \log_b x$, for any base b, and indeed it will apply to any pair of inverse functions. So we have the following fact.

Graphs of inverse functions

The graphs of a pair of inverse functions are reflections of each other in the line $y = x$.

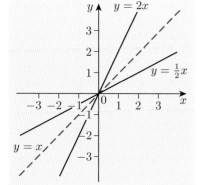

Figure 33   The lines $y = 2x$ and $y = \frac{1}{2}x$ are reflections of each other in the line $y = x$

For example, Figure 33 shows the graphs of the equations $y = 2x$ and $y = \frac{1}{2}x$. These follow the rules of inverse functions, since halving a number reverses the effect of doubling it, and vice versa. The line $y = x$ has been drawn in red dashes, and you can see that each of the graphs is a reflection of the other in this line.

If you know some features of the graph of a particular function, then you can use the property in the pink box on the opposite page to deduce some corresponding features of the graph of its inverse function. In particular, knowing what the graph of an exponential function looks like allows you to deduce some properties of the graph of the logarithmic function that is its inverse.

For example, you know that the graph of an equation of the form $y = b^x$ has the x-axis as an asymptote, unless $b = 1$. It follows that the graph of an equation of the form $y = \log_b x$ has the y-axis as an asymptote. Figure 32 illustrates this for the base $b = 2$.

Similarly, you know that the graph of $y = b^x$ has y-intercept 1. It follows that the graph of $y = \log_b x$ has x-intercept 1. Again, this is illustrated for $b = 2$ in Figure 32.

Also, you know that if $b > 1$, then the graph of $y = b^x$ increases, and increases more and more quickly. If you think about it (drawing a diagram helps), then you will see that this means that if $b > 1$, then the graph of $y = \log_b x$ increases, but increases more and more slowly. Again, you can see this illustrated for the base $b = 2$ in Figure 32.

In this section you have met some rules that you can use when you are working with logarithms. You have also learned how to solve exponential equations by taking logs. In the final subsection you saw that, for any base b, the graphs of the equations $y = b^x$ and $y = \log_b x$ are reflections of each other in the line $y = x$, and that this property applies to all pairs of inverse functions.

Learning checklist

After studying this unit, you should be able to:

- understand what is meant by exponential change
- recognise some standard examples of exponential growth and decay, such as repeated doubling or halving, compound interest and radioactive decay
- find and use formulas for exponential growth and decay
- use trial and improvement to solve problems
- understand the relationship between the scale factor by which a quantity changes over a particular length of time (or over one step) and the scale factor by which it changes over a different length of time (or different number of steps)
- know and understand the shapes of the graphs of equations of the form $y = b^x$ and $y = ab^x$
- understand logarithms to any base (in particular to base 10 and base e) and use appropriate notation
- use logarithm laws to manipulate expressions involving logarithms
- solve exponential equations by taking logs
- calculate doubling or halving times for quantities that are subject to continuous exponential growth or decay
- understand that exponential and logarithmic functions form pairs of inverse functions.

Solutions and comments on Activities

Activity 1

You might be surprised by the true answer for the height of the pile of paper. You can work it out, roughly, as follows. The thickness of a piece of paper is about one tenth of a millimetre, or about 0.0001 metres, so the height of the initial pile of one sheet of paper is 0.0001 metres. After each step of the process, the height of the paper pile doubles. So the heights, in metres, of the successive piles of paper are as follows:

the initial height is 0.0001;

after 1 step, the height is

0.0001×2;

after 2 steps, the height is

$0.0001 \times 2 \times 2 = 0.0001 \times 2^2$;

after 3 steps, the height is

$0.0001 \times 2 \times 2 \times 2 = 0.0001 \times 2^3$;

and so on. In general, after n steps the height in metres of the paper pile is

0.0001×2^n.

So after 50 steps the height is

0.0001×2^{50} m.

The number 2^{50}, which is the number of pieces of paper, is approximately 1.13×10^{15} in scientific notation, or $1\,130\,000\,000\,000\,000$ in ordinary notation. So the height of the pile is roughly

$$0.0001 \times 1.13 \times 10^{15}\,\text{m} = 10^{-4} \times 1.13 \times 10^{15}\,\text{m}$$
$$= 1.13 \times 10^{11}\,\text{m}$$
$$= 1.13 \times 10^8\,\text{km},$$

which is 113 million kilometres.

The average distance to the moon is about $384\,000$ km. So, if you could achieve the number of tears of a single piece of paper suggested in this activity, which in practice would, of course, be impossible, then the resulting pile of paper would correspond to roughly 150 trips to the moon and back!

Activity 2

The correct answer is that the pond was half covered after 29 days. If you are unsure why, consider the following statement.

If the area covered by the lily pads was twice as large on Thursday as it was on Wednesday, then it must have been half as large on Wednesday as it was on Thursday.

This demonstrates why the area covered by the lily pads was half of the size of the pond on the penultimate day (day 29): one day later, the area covered had doubled to fill the pond.

(A common wrong answer to this question is that it would take 15 days for the lily pads to cover half of the pond. This would be the correct answer if the area covered by the lily pads were increasing linearly – that is, by a fixed amount each day – and if the lily pads did not cover any of the pond at the start of the 30 days.)

Activity 3

(a) The stallholder's selling price is 165% of his buying price. So he must multiply the buying price by the scale factor $\frac{165}{100} = 1.65$.

So the selling price for a purse is

$£4.25 \times 1.65 \approx £7.01$.

(In practice, the stallholder may round the price to £7 or even to £6.99.)

(b) The stallholder's 30% discount means that he is selling at 70% of his usual price. So he must multiply the usual price by the scale factor $\frac{70}{100} = 0.7$.

The discounted price for a shirt is

$£7 \times 0.7 = £4.90$.

Activity 4

(a) (i) The scale factor for a 10% increase is 1.1.

(ii) The scale factor for a 3% increase is 1.03.

(iii) The scale factor for a 0.5% increase is 1.005.

(iv) The scale factor for a 15% decrease is 0.85.

(v) The scale factor for a 2% decrease is 0.98.

(vi) The scale factor for a 1.5% decrease is 0.985.

(b) (i) A scale factor of 1.08 gives a 8% increase.

(ii) A scale factor of 0.91 gives a 9% decrease.

(iii) A scale factor of 1.072 gives a 7.2% increase.

Activity 5

(a) (i) After 1 year, the investment will be worth

$£1800 \times 1.045 = £1881$.

(ii) After 3 years, the investment will be worth

$£1800 \times 1.045 \times 1.045 \times 1.045 = £2054.10$

(to the nearest penny).

(iii) After 10 years, the investment will be worth

$£1800 \times 1.045^{10} = £2795.34$

(to the nearest penny).

(b) (i) After 1 year, the interest earned is

$£1881 - £1800 = £81$.

(ii) After 3 years, the interest earned is
$$£2054.10 - £1800 = £254.10$$
(to the nearest penny).

(iii) After 10 years, the interest earned is
$$£2795.34 - £1800 = £995.34$$
(to the nearest penny).

(c) A formula for the value $£V$ of the investment after n years is
$$V = 1800 \times 1.045^n.$$
A formula for the amount $£W$ of interest earned after n years is
$$W = 1800 \times 1.045^n - 1800.$$
This formula can be simplified slightly, by taking out the common factor 1800:
$$W = 1800(1.045^n - 1).$$

Activity 6

(a) The value, in $£$, of the investment in 18 years' time will be
$$M \times 1.05^{18}.$$

(b) Hence M must satisfy the equation
$$M \times 1.05^{18} = 1000.$$
This gives
$$M = \frac{1000}{1.05^{18}}.$$
Evaluating this expression on a calculator gives
$$M = 415.52 \text{ (to 2 d.p.).}$$
Hence you must invest £415.52.

Activity 7

(a) The concentration decreases by 14% each hour. Since $100\% - 14\% = 86\%$, it decreases by the scale factor 0.86 each hour.

Also, the peak concentration is 90 ng/ml, so the concentration of the drug in the patient's bloodstream is given by the formula
$$C = 90 \times 0.86^t,$$
where t is the time in hours since the concentration peaked, and C is the concentration in ng/ml.

(b) **(i)** The concentration after 4 hours is
$$90 \times 0.86^4 \text{ ng/ml}$$
$$= 49.230\ldots \text{ng/ml}$$
$$= 50 \text{ ng/ml (to the nearest 5 ng/ml).}$$

(ii) The concentration after 30 minutes (0.5 hours) is
$$90 \times 0.86^{0.5} \text{ ng/ml}$$
$$= 83.462\ldots \text{ng/ml}$$
$$= 85 \text{ ng/ml (to the nearest 5 ng/ml).}$$

(c) The peak concentration occurs 40 minutes after the drug was administered. This means that two hours after the drug was administered is the same as 1 hour and 20 minutes after the concentration peaked. Now 1 hour and 20 minutes is equal to $1\frac{1}{3}$ hours; that is, $\frac{4}{3}$ hours. So the concentration at this time is
$$90 \times 0.86^{4/3} \text{ ng/ml}$$
$$= 73.604\ldots \text{ng/ml}$$
$$= 75 \text{ ng/ml (to the nearest 5 ng/ml).}$$

Activity 8

(a) The peak concentration is $36\,\mu\text{g/ml}$ and the concentration after one hour is $27\,\mu\text{g/ml}$, so the scale factor is
$$\frac{27}{36} = 0.75.$$

(b) Using the answer to part (a), together with the value of the peak concentration, gives the formula
$$C = 36 \times 0.75^t.$$

(c) Since 1 hour and 15 minutes is the same as 1.25 hours, the expected concentration after this time is
$$36 \times 0.75^{1.25} \,\mu\text{g/ml}$$
$$= 25.126\ldots \mu\text{g/ml}$$
$$= 25\,\mu\text{g/ml (to the nearest }\mu\text{g/ml).}$$

Activity 9

(a) The three most recent data points (corresponding to the years 1990, 2000 and 2009) all lie above the regression curve.

(b) Possible explanations might include improved preventative medicine, medical treatments and nutrition, leading to reduced death rates.

Activity 10

(b) The Graphplotter graph is shown below.

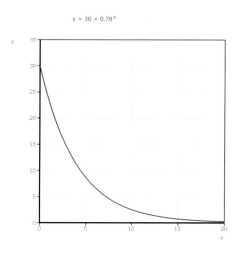

(c) By using the Trace facility you can find that the point on the graph with x-coordinate 4.4 has y-coordinate greater than 10, and the point on the graph with x-coordinate 4.5 has y-coordinate less than 10. Since both of these x-coordinates are 4.5 to the nearest 0.5, the point on the graph with y-coordinate 10 also has x-coordinate 4.5 to the nearest 0.5.

Hence the concentration falls to $10\,\mu\mathrm{g/ml}$ after about $4\frac{1}{2}$ hours.

Activity 11

(a) The scale factor by which the number of Elvis impersonators is increasing each year is 1.23. Hence the number of Elvis impersonators t years after 16 August 1977 is given by the formula

170×1.23^t.

(b) By the formula in part (a), the number of Elvis impersonators 30 years after 16 August 1977 is

$170 \times 1.23^{30} = 85000$ (to the nearest 1000).

(c) Your trial-and-improvement process might have been similar to that shown in the table below.

Guess for number of years	Number of Elvis impersonators	Evaluation
40	170×1.23^{40} $= 670\,893$	Much too small
80	170×1.23^{80} $= 2\,647\,633\,311$	Much closer but still too small
85	170×1.23^{85} $= 7\,453\,897\,111$	Just too big
84	170×1.23^{84} $= 6\,060\,078\,952$	Just too small

This calculation suggests that the entire population of the world will be Elvis impersonators roughly 84 to 85 years after his death. Since he died in 1977, the expected calendar year for this to happen is about 2061 or 2062.

Activity 12

(a) (i) The APR for an interest rate of 17.5%, charged annually, is 17.5%.

(ii) An interest rate of 8.5% each six months corresponds to a scale factor of 1.085 each six months. This gives a scale factor of

$1.085^2 = 1.177$ (to 3 d.p.)

per year, which gives an interest rate of 17.7% per year. That is, the APR is approximately 17.7%.

(iii) An interest rate of 1.4% each month corresponds to a scale factor of 1.014 each month. This gives a scale factor of

$1.014^{12} = 1.182$ (to 3 d.p.)

per year, which gives an interest rate of 18.2% per year. That is, the APR is approximately 18.2%.

(b) The interest rate in part (a)(i) would result in you paying the least interest.

Activity 13

The car depreciates at the rate of 16% per year, so its values change by the scale factor 0.84 each year.

(a) The value of the car one year after purchase was £15 450, so 0.25 years later its value was

£$15\,450 \times 0.84^{0.25} = £14\,790$ (to the nearest £10).

(b) The value of the car 2.75 years after purchase, which is 1.75 years after it had a value of £15 450, was

£$15\,450 \times 0.84^{1.75} = £11\,390$ (to the nearest £10).

(c) The value of the car at purchase was

£$15\,450 \times 0.84^{-1} = £18\,390$ (to the nearest £10).

Activity 14

(a) Each decade, the number of pigeons grows by a scale factor of 1.8.

(b) Each year, the number of pigeons grows by a scale factor of

$1.8^{1/10} = 1.0605\ldots = 1.061$ (to 4 s.f.).

(c) Each year, the number of pigeons grows by 6.1% (to 1 d.p.).

Activity 15

(a) The function with rule $y = 2x$ is linear, because this equation is of the form $y = mx + c$, with $m = 2$ and $c = 0$.

The function with rule $y = x^2$ is quadratic, because this equation is of the form $y = ax^2 + bx + c$, with $a = 1$ and $b = c = 0$.

The function with rule $y = 2^x$ is exponential, because this equation is of the form $y = b^x$, with $b = 2$.

(b) Here is the completed table.

x	0	1	2	3	4	5	6
$y = 2x$	0	2	4	6	8	10	12
$y = x^2$	0	1	4	9	16	25	36
$y = 2^x$	1	2	4	8	16	32	64

The largest increase is that of the exponential function $y = 2^x$. The smallest increase is that of the linear function $y = 2x$.

(You can get a better idea of the growth of the three functions by looking at their graphs plotted on the same axes, as shown below.

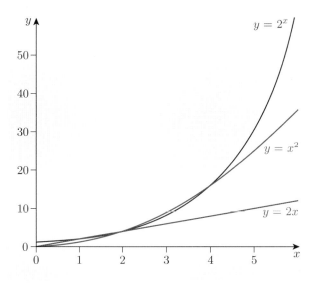

You can see that in the range $0 < x < 2$, there is not much difference in the growth rates of the three functions. In the range $2 < x < 4$, the linear function $y = 2x$ starts to lag behind the other two, and it continues to do so thereafter. For $x > 4$, the quadratic function $y = x^2$ starts to lag behind the exponential function $y = 2^x$.

For larger values of x, the differences become really dramatic. For example, when $x = 20$, the value of $2x$ is 40, the value of x^2 is 400, and the value of 2^x exceeds one million. Increase x to, say, 100 and the value of the exponential function $y = 2^x$ disappears into the stratosphere!)

Activity 16

(c) As expected, if $b > 1$ then the graph of $y = b^x$ is an exponential growth curve, while if $0 < b < 1$ then the graph is an exponential decay curve.

Setting b to exactly 1 gives a horizontal straight line with y-intercept 1. The reason for this is that if $b = 1$ then the equation $y = b^x$ becomes $y = 1^x$, which is the same as $y = 1$. This is not an exponential function.

Varying the value of b affects the steepness of the graph. In each of the ranges $0 < b < 1$ and $b > 1$, the closer the value of b is to 1, the flatter is the graph.

(d) The y-intercept is always 1, whatever the value of b.

This is because substituting $x = 0$ into the equation $y = b^x$ always gives $y = b^0 = 1$, no matter what the value of b is.

Activity 17

(b) As expected, since $b = 2$ (which is greater than 1), if a is positive then the shape of the graph is always an exponential growth curve. Varying the value of a affects the steepness of the graph: the larger the value of a, the steeper the graph.

If a is negative, then the shape of the graph is the reflection in the x-axis of an exponential growth curve. Varying a within negative values affects the steepness of the graph: the larger the magnitude of a, the steeper the graph.

Setting $a = 0$ gives the horizontal line $y = 0$.

Whether a is positive, negative or zero, the y-intercept is always a.

(The reason for this is given after the activity.)

(c) If a is positive, then, as expected, the shape of the graph is always an exponential growth curve, exponential decay curve or horizontal line, depending on whether $b > 1$, $0 < b < 1$ or $b = 1$.

As in part (b), varying a within positive values affects the steepness of the graph: the larger the value of a, the steeper the graph.

If a is negative, then the shape of the graph is the reflection in the x-axis of an exponential growth curve, exponential decay curve or horizontal line, depending on whether $b > 1$, $0 < b < 1$ or $b = 1$.

Varying a within negative values affects the steepness of the graph: the larger the magnitude of a, the steeper the graph.

Setting $a = 0$ gives the horizontal line $y = 0$.

In all cases, whether a is positive, negative or zero, and whatever the value of b, the y-intercept is a.

Activity 18

You should have chosen a positive value for a and a value between 0 and 1 (exclusive) for b. For example, you could have chosen $a = 3$ and $b = 0.5$, which gives the rule

$$y = 3 \times 0.5^x.$$

The graph of this equation is shown in Figure 22(b) on page 144.

(A common error is to assume that negative values for the constant a give exponential decay.)

Activity 19

(c) Setting b to about 2.7 seems to give a gradient of 1 at $(0, 1)$.

Activity 20

(a) (i) $10 = 10^1$, so $\log_{10} 10 = 1$.

(ii) $1000 = 10^3$, so $\log_{10} 1000 = 3$.

(iii) 1 billion $= 10^9$, so $\log_{10} (1 \text{ billion}) = 9$.

(iv) $0.001 = 10^{-3}$, so $\log_{10} 0.001 = -3$.

(b) It is not possible to find the logarithm to base 10 of zero. The reason is that there is no power to which 10 can be raised to give the answer zero.

(If you try to find the logarithm of zero on your calculator, you will get an error message.)

(c) (i) The number 91 lies between 10 and 100, that is, between 10^1 and 10^2. So $\log_{10} 91$ lies between 1 and 2.

(ii) The number 2971 lies between 1000 and 10 000, that is, between 10^3 and 10^4. So $\log_{10} 2971$ lies between 3 and 4.

(iii) The number 8.8 lies between 1 and 10, that is, between 10^0 and 10^1. So $\log_{10} 8.8$ lies between 0 and 1.

(iv) The number 0.25 lies between 0.1 and 1, that is, between 10^{-1} and 10^0. So $\log_{10} 0.25$ lies between -1 and 0.

(d) If the logarithm to base 10 of a number is 5, then the number is $10^5 = 100\,000$.

Similarly, if the logarithm to base 10 of a number is -2, then the number is $10^{-2} = 0.01$.

Activity 22

(a) The two shocks differ by 2 on the Richter scale, and $10^2 = 100$, so the energy released by the aftershock was one hundredth of the energy released by the original shock.

(b) The noise levels of 6 bels and 7 bels differ by 1, so the sound intensity increases by a factor of $10^1 = 10$.

Activity 23

(a) $8 = 2^3$, so $\log_2 8 = 3$.

(b) $32 = 2^5$, so $\log_2 32 = 5$.

(c) $2 = 2^1$, so $\log_2 2 = 1$.

(d) $1 = 2^0$, so $\log_2 1 = 0$.

(e) $0.5 = \frac{1}{2} = 2^{-1}$, so $\log_2 0.5 = -1$.

(f) $\sqrt{2} = 2^{0.5}$, so $\log_2 \sqrt{2} = 0.5$.

Activity 24

(a) (i) $\ln(e^2) = 2$

(ii) $\ln(e^{-4}) = -4$

(iii) $\ln 1 = \ln(e^0) = 0$

(iv) $\ln\left(\dfrac{1}{e^2}\right) = \ln(e^{-2}) = -2$

(b) $\ln 214.86 \approx \ln(e^{5.37}) = 5.37$

Activity 26

Suppose that the numbers x and y can be written as b^m and b^n, respectively. That is,

$$x = b^m \quad \text{and} \quad y = b^n.$$

Then

$$m = \log_b x \quad \text{and} \quad n = \log_b y.$$

The quotient x/y can be written as

$$\frac{x}{y} = \frac{b^m}{b^n} = b^{m-n}.$$

This tells you that

$$\log_b\left(\frac{x}{y}\right) = m - n = \log_b x - \log_b y.$$

Activity 27

(a) $\log_{10} 3 + \log_{10} 4 = \log_{10}(3 \times 4) = \log_{10} 12$

(b) $\ln 15 - \ln 3 = \ln\left(\dfrac{15}{3}\right) = \ln 5$

(c) $\log_{10} 2 + \log_{10} 3 + \log_{10} 5 = \log_{10}(2 \times 3 \times 5)$
$$= \log_{10} 30$$

(d) $-\ln 4 + \ln 2 = \ln 2 - \ln 4 = \ln\left(\dfrac{2}{4}\right) = \ln 0.5$

Activity 28

(a) $3\log_{10} 3 = \log_{10}(3^3) = \log_{10} 27$

(b) $\ln 6 + 2\ln 5 = \ln 6 + \ln(5^2)$
$$= \ln(6 \times 5^2)$$
$$= \ln 150$$

(c) $0.5\log_{10} 4 = \log_{10}(4^{0.5})$
$$= \log_{10}(\sqrt{4})$$
$$= \log_{10} 2$$

(d) $\ln 27 - 2\ln 3 = \ln 27 - \ln(3^2)$
$$= \ln\left(\frac{27}{3^2}\right)$$
$$= \ln\left(\frac{27}{9}\right)$$
$$= \ln 3$$

Activity 29

The equation is

$$1.4^x = 550.$$

Taking logs gives

$$\log_{10}(1.4^x) = \log_{10} 550$$
$$x \log_{10} 1.4 = \log_{10} 550$$
$$x = \frac{\log_{10} 550}{\log_{10} 1.4}$$
$$x = 18.753\ldots.$$

So the solution is $x = 18.8$ (to 3 s.f.).

(Check: When $x = 18.8$,

$$\text{LHS} = 1.4^{18.8} = 558.73\ldots \approx 550 = \text{RHS.})$$

Activity 30

The equation is

$$170 \times 1.23^t = 7\,000\,000\,000.$$

Dividing by 170 gives

$$1.23^t = \frac{7\,000\,000\,000}{170}.$$

Taking logs gives

$$\log_{10}(1.23^t) = \log_{10}\left(\frac{7\,000\,000\,000}{170}\right)$$
$$t \log_{10} 1.23 = \log_{10}\left(\frac{7\,000\,000\,000}{170}\right)$$
$$t = \log_{10}\left(\frac{7\,000\,000\,000}{170}\right) \div \log_{10} 1.23$$
$$t = 84.696\ldots.$$

So the solution is $t = 84.7$ (to 3 s.f.).

(Notice that this is consistent with the solution to Activity 11. That is, it will take 84 to 85 years for Elvis impersonators to account for the entire population of the world, under the assumptions stated in the question.)

Activity 31

(a) $e^t = 8$

$$\ln\left(e^t\right) = \ln 8$$
$$t = \ln 8$$

The solution is $t = 2.08$ (to 3 s.f.).

(Check: When $t = 2.08$,
$$\text{LHS} = e^{2.08} = 8.004\ldots \approx 8 = \text{RHS.})$$

(b) $e^{x-1} = 5$

$$\ln\left(e^{x-1}\right) = \ln 5$$
$$x - 1 = \ln 5$$
$$x = \ln 5 + 1$$

The solution is $x = 2.61$ (to 3 s.f.).

(Check: When $x = 2.61$,
$$\text{LHS} = e^{2.61-1} = e^{1.61} = 5.002\ldots \approx 5 = \text{RHS.})$$

(The expression $\ln 5 + 1$ needs to be evaluated with care. You first find the natural logarithm of 5, then add 1. The expression does not mean the same as $\ln(5 + 1)$.)

Activity 32

The number of Elvis impersonators increases by the scale factor 1.23 each year, so its doubling time in years is the solution i of the equation

$$1.23^i = 2.$$

Taking logs gives

$$\log_{10}(1.23^i) = \log_{10} 2$$
$$i \log_{10} 1.23 = \log_{10} 2$$
$$i = \frac{\log_{10} 2}{\log_{10} 1.23}$$
$$i = 3.3483\ldots = 3.3 \text{ (to 2 s.f.).}$$

So the doubling time for the number of Elvis impersonators is about 3.3 years.

Activity 33

The number of elephants decreases by the scale factor 0.96 each year.

So its halving time in years is the solution i of the equation

$$0.96^i = 0.5.$$

Taking logs gives

$$\log_{10}(0.96^i) = \log_{10} 0.5$$
$$i \log_{10} 0.96 = \log_{10} 0.5$$
$$i = \frac{\log_{10} 0.5}{\log_{10} 0.96}$$
$$i = 16.979\ldots = 17 \text{ (to the nearest whole number).}$$

So the halving time of the population is approximately 17 years.

Activity 34

(a) The initial level of radioactivity was 40 becquerels, and one day later it had fallen to 38 becquerels. Hence the scale factor is

$$\frac{38}{40} = 0.95.$$

(b) The half-life of the isotope, in days, is the solution i of the equation

$$0.95^i = \tfrac{1}{2}.$$

This equation can be solved by taking logs, as follows.

$$\log_{10}\left(0.95^i\right) = \log_{10} 0.5$$
$$i \log_{10} 0.95 = \log_{10} 0.5$$
$$i = \frac{\log_{10} 0.5}{\log_{10} 0.95} = 13.513\ldots = 13.5 \text{ (to 1 d.p.)}$$

So the half-life of the isotope is about 13.5 days.

Activity 35

(b)

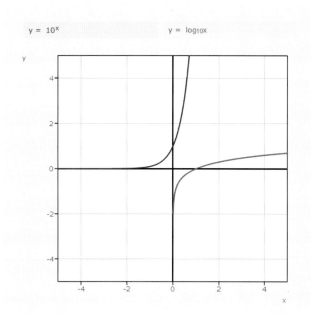

$y = 10^x$ $y = \log_{10} x$

The two graphs appear to be mirror images of each other, reflected in the line $y = x$.

(c)

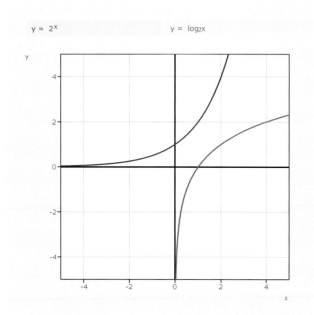

$y = 2^x$ $y = \log_2 x$

The two graphs appear to be related in the same way as in part (b).

(d)

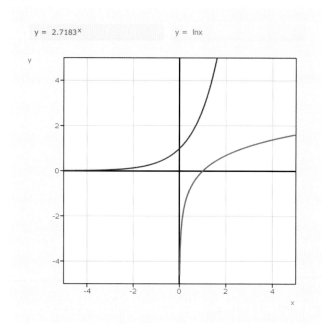

$y = 2.7183^x$ $y = \ln x$

Again, the two graphs appear to be related in the same way as in part (b).

(e)

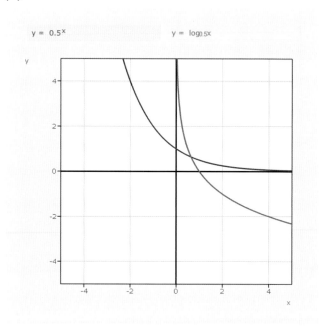

$y = 0.5^x$ $y = \log_{0.5} x$

Again, the two graphs appear to be related in the same way as in part (b).

Mathematics everywhere

Introduction

This final unit looks back at some of the main ideas that you have met in the module, and explores some new applications to illustrate that mathematics is indeed everywhere! The unit is divided into four sections, each corresponding to one of the main themes of the module.

Communicating clearly

Throughout the module you have been encouraged to explain your ideas clearly, and use graphs and diagrams appropriately. However, sometimes you have to engage with mathematical ideas that are not presented *to you* as clearly as they might have been. Section 1 considers how you can make sense of some of the numbers that you see in the media, particularly headlines about the risks of developing conditions such as cancer. This section also asks you to review your own progress in writing mathematically and highlights the importance of expressing ideas in a way that will be understood.

Extending your mathematical skills

Section 2 reviews some of the skills that you have developed in MU123, and shows you how these skills can be even more powerful when they are linked together and applied in new contexts. You'll see how the skills that you've developed in solving linear and quadratic equations can be adapted to enable you to solve simultaneous equations more complicated than those in Unit 7, and how your knowledge of trigonometry can be extended to enable you to solve some trigonometric equations.

Abstract mathematics

Figure 1 A geometric puzzle from Japan

A main theme of the module has been how mathematics can be used to describe abstract ideas and prove results. For example, in Units 5 and 9 you saw how algebra can be used to prove various results about numerical patterns and puzzles, and in Unit 8 you saw how some properties of shapes can be proved. Section 3 starts by looking at some Japanese puzzles from the eighteenth and nineteenth centuries (an example is shown in Figure 1) and then considers some general strategies for proving results involving number patterns. The final subsection illustrates how some quite abstract ideas, such as origami (the Japanese art of paper-folding), can have useful applications.

Using mathematics practically

Another main theme of the module has been how mathematical models are developed and used to solve problems in the real world. Examples include the route-planning model in Unit 2, the linear models for journeys in Units 6 and 7, the quadratic models describing the motion of projectiles in Unit 10, and the exponential models describing growth and decay in Unit 13. Section 4 shows you how you can use trigonometry to model the motion of a ferris wheel, and how to create a simple model to predict the height of the tide at different times on one particular day.

1 Communicating clearly

1.1 Interpreting information about risk

Thinking critically about numerical information that you see in the media is important if you want to make informed decisions.

For example, the following headline and short extract are from a newspaper article published in 2008.

Heavy mobile phone use a cancer risk

People who use a mobile phone for hours a day are 50 per cent more likely to develop mouth cancer than those who do not talk on them at all, new research has shown.

The Daily Telegraph, 18 February 2008

This is quite a frightening story – many people use mobile phones on a regular basis, 50% is a large increase and mouth cancer is a potentially fatal disease if it is not treated early. So if you have a mobile phone, should you use it less frequently, or even stop using it altogether?

Before you make a decision, it's worth looking at the article carefully, checking exactly what it is claiming, trying to establish whether the evidence supports the claim and seeing if any other research on the use of mobile phones has found similar results. The full newspaper article briefly summarised some of the main points from the research report, and also commented that other studies had not so far found a link between cancer and mobile phone use. Reading one newspaper article is unlikely to provide all the information that you might need to make a decision, but you may be able to glean sufficient detail to decide whether it is worth looking into the situation further.

In the extract, the idea of *how likely* something is to occur is mentioned. This is known as the **probability** or **chance** of the event occurring. If the event is something that you hope will not occur, then the chance that it occurs is often referred to as the **risk**. (All three of these terms mean essentially the same thing.) So before looking at the extract in detail, let's consider how probability can be measured. One way of assessing how likely an event is to occur is to find how frequently it has occurred in the past. This can be done by considering a large number of cases that *could* result in the event that you are interested in, and then counting how many of the cases *did* result in that event.

To illustrate this process, suppose that you are interested in the chance of getting a girl if you or your partner have a baby. To estimate the probability of this event, researchers have to consider a large number of births and then count how many result in a girl. The proportion of babies that are girls then gives an indication of how likely it is that a girl is born. The probability of having a girl may depend on many things, such as where the mother lives, her age, or even what she eats, so the researchers need to decide which cases they will consider.

For example, they might decide to look at women living in Britain. Researchers who have taken into account a large number of randomly chosen births in Britain have found that the chance of having a girl is about 49%. That's a chance of 49 in 100. So on average about 49 out of every 100 births in Britain are those of girls. This doesn't mean that if you

You have seen other media examples in Units 1 and 11.

Figure 2 It was estimated that there were 4.6 billion mobile phone subscribers worldwide by the end of 2009.

Girl, boy, girl, boy...

look at 100 births, then you'll find that *exactly* 49 are girls. It just means that, overall, the proportion of babies in Britain that are girls is 49%.

If the researchers had looked at a different group of births, for example in another country, then they might have got a different result.

Activity 1 *The chance of having a girl*

In one year, in a small hospital in a European country, 377 girls and 367 boys were born. What percentage of the births were girls? Can you suggest why this might *not* be an accurate estimate of the probability of having a girl in the country where the hospital is?

In a similar way, the chance of a person developing a disease can be estimated by considering how many people develop the disease over a particular period of time. For example, suppose that 2 people out of a town of 10 000 people develop a particular disease in a year. Then a rough estimate of the chance of developing the disease in this town in one year is 2 in 10 000, which is the same as 1 in 5000. If a different group of people from the town were considered, for example those people with a known risk factor such as not taking exercise, then the chance of developing the disease is likely to be different. The 1 in 5000 figure gives an overall indication of the risk, but it takes into account both people with the risk factors and people without them, so an individual with the risk factors may have a higher chance of developing the disease, and an individual without the risk factors may have a lower chance.

Probabilities can be expressed as fractions, decimals or percentages, or in the form of an 'x in y' chance. For example, a 1 in 10 chance can be expressed as a probability of $\frac{1}{10}$, 0.1 or 10%. Using percentages enables you to compare the chances of different events happening fairly easily. However, one disadvantage of giving probabilities as percentages is that it can be difficult to appreciate the probability of events that are fairly unlikely to happen. For example, suppose that there is a 0.05% chance of developing a disease over your lifetime. In order to appreciate how small this probability is, it is best to convert it to an 'x in y' chance. This can be done as follows:

$$0.05\% = \frac{0.05}{100} = \frac{5}{10\,000} = \frac{1}{2000}.$$

So the chance of developing the disease is 1 in 2000.

Activity 2 *Describing chance*

In October 2009, the US National Aeronautics and Space Administration (NASA) announced that the chance that the Apophis asteroid would collide with the Earth on 13 April 2036 had fallen. The new estimate for the risk was 0.0004%. Express this probability as an 'x in 1 million' chance.

What?! Fifty times more likely to be hit by an asteroid than I am to win the jackpot?

Now that you have seen how the probability of an event can be measured, let's return to the newspaper extract and examine the information that it gives. The extract says that people who use mobile phones for hours a day are 50% more likely to develop mouth cancer than those who do not use them at all. A useful question to ask when reading about percentages is

'Percentage of what?'. The extract doesn't tell you what the risk of developing mouth cancer actually is; it just tells you how much the risk is increased if you use your mobile phone a lot. This is not enough information to enable you to make an informed decision. If the risk is very small, then if it is increased by 50%, or even doubled or tripled, it will still be very small, and you might decide that it is not worth worrying about. The headline is dramatic, but it doesn't tell you anything about the chance of developing mouth cancer if you use a mobile phone, unless you know what the actual risk of developing the disease is.

Activity 3   *Reading critically*

Read the extract (on page 181) again carefully. What extra information do you think is needed before you can start to assess how likely it is that a person who uses a mobile phone will develop mouth cancer?

You have seen that an important question to sort out is: What is the actual risk of developing the type of cancer investigated in the research? Further on in the newspaper article, more details are given about the research that was carried out:

> ... a cancer specialist at Tel Aviv University, investigated the cases of nearly 500 people diagnosed with benign and malignant tumours of the salivary gland.

So the research was based not on people suffering from mouth cancer in general, but on a group of people who had tumours of the *salivary gland*. More specifically, as the article goes on to mention, it was based on people who had tumours of the *parotid* salivary gland (Figure 3), which is the largest of the three types of human salivary gland. Furthermore, not all the tumours were malignant.

Malignant tumours of the salivary gland are rare. According to information published on the Macmillan Cancer Support website in 2009, at that time there were about 550 new cases of salivary gland cancer each year in the UK. The population of the UK was about 61 million in 2009, so the probability of being diagnosed with the disease in any particular year was less than 1 in 100 000. (Notice that this probability is based on all the new cases diagnosed each year, and some of these people may be heavy mobile phone users. If you considered cases in which the person had never used a mobile phone, and if using a mobile phone genuinely increases the risk, then the probability might be lower.)

Now suppose that the chance of suffering from salivary gland cancer rises by 50% among heavy mobile phone users, as suggested in the newspaper article. Then, each year in the UK, you might expect about 1.5 new cases per 100 000 heavy mobile phone users. So in a group of 200 000 heavy mobile phone users, you might expect to see 3 new cases of salivary gland cancer each year, rather than the 2 new cases that you would expect in a general group of this size. This is still a small risk.

One way to think about this risk is that in the group of 200 000 heavy mobile phone users, each year you would expect two people to develop salivary gland cancer anyway, and one extra person to develop it as a result of their heavy mobile phone use. So, if the suggestion in the newspaper article is true, then as far as developing salivary gland cancer goes, heavy use of a mobile phone will make a difference to just one person out of 200 000 each year.

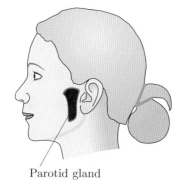

Parotid gland

Figure 3   The parotid salivary gland

The Macmillan website is at www.macmillan.org.uk.

The calculations on the previous page are, of course, very rough ones that do not take into account factors such as age – most people with salivary gland cancer are over the age of 55. Also, the risk referred to in the article may not have been the risk of developing the cancer in a year, but some other way of measuring the risk. For example, according to the US National Cancer Institute, the risk at birth of developing salivary gland cancer by the age of 80 is about 0.1%, or 1 in 1000. Nevertheless, the calculation does give a useful indication of the sort of risk level that you might expect if the claim in the newspaper article is true, and you use your mobile phone heavily.

NHS reports can be found at www.nhs.uk/news.

If you still had doubts about using a mobile phone (or if you were investigating claims about a disease that occurs more frequently), then it would be advisable to look at the original research paper to find out how the study was carried out and if the conclusions were reported accurately. Often when articles such as the mobile phone story are published, health organisations such as the UK National Health Service (NHS) release their own assessment of the research. In this case, an NHS report stated that:

> The '50% increased likelihood of developing mouth cancer' reported by the newspapers is mostly due to an increased risk of benign salivary gland tumours.

Benign tumours are those that do not spread or invade other organs, and they are not usually considered to be cancer. So the study did not in fact find that there was a 50% increase in the risk of developing a *malignant* tumour, which is what is normally meant by cancer.

The NHS report also noted that in the main part of the research, where regular mobile phone users (those who had made or received at least one call a week for six months) were compared with non-users, both groups were equally likely to have tumours. So although the newspaper article reported the finding of increased incidence of tumours among heavy mobile phone users, it did not report the less dramatic finding of no increased incidence among more typical mobile phone users. (However, as mentioned earlier, it did state that many other studies had found no increased risk of cancer due to mobile phone use.)

Even if a link is established between mobile phone use and salivary gland tumours, it is also important to consider whether there is a *causal* link or just a correlation, as you saw in Unit 6.

For example, suppose that smokers are more likely to use mobile phones than non-smokers, and suppose that smoking also causes salivary gland cancer. Then it is likely that there would be a higher number of cancer cases in the mobile phone users, but this may not be caused by their use of mobile phones.

So, overall the statistical facts behind the headline are not nearly so frightening as it might at first appear. Of course, there may be other health risks associated with using a mobile phone apart from the possibility of salivary gland cancer, and as further research is carried out, more convincing evidence of a link between cancer and mobile phone use may appear.

The next activity looks at a hypothetical scenario.

Activity 4   *Working out a risk*

A newspaper article claims that eating bananas regularly increases your chance of getting monkeypox sometime during your lifetime by 25%.

About 1 in 20 people who don't eat bananas get monkeypox in their lifetime.

(a) How many out of 1000 people who don't eat bananas are likely to get monkeypox sometime during their lifetime?

(b) Assume that the claim in the newspaper is true. If 1000 people eat bananas regularly, how many of these people might you expect to get monkeypox during their lifetime?

(c) If the claim in the newspaper is true, then, on average, for how many people out of 1000 does eating bananas regularly make a difference, as far as developing monkeypox goes?

Stories about risk occur frequently in the press, as they can make dramatic headlines. So if you read a headline like the one discussed in this subsection, then check the whole article (and other sources if necessary) to find out:

- exactly which disease is being discussed and which group of people is supposed to be at risk

- whether any information is given on the *actual* risk as well as the increase in the risk

- if other reports on the research are available or similar studies have been undertaken elsewhere.

In this subsection, you have seen how numerical information in a headline may give a misleading impression. This highlights the importance of reading (and writing!) articles carefully so that the ideas are understood.

1.2 Interpreting graphs and charts

In the previous subsection you saw the importance of reading media articles critically. Such articles often contain graphs or charts, as these can convey some types of numerical information more clearly and concisely than text. However, just as with text, the impression that you get when you look at a graph or chart can sometimes be misleading, and so it is important to interpret these items critically as well.

Consider the data in Table 1, which shows the estimated global number of fixed main telephone lines and mobile phone subscribers in each of the years from 1997 to 2007.

Table 1 Global growth in telephone communications (1997–2007)

Phone type (millions)	1997	1998	1999	2000	2001	2002	2003	2004	2005	2006	2007
Main telephone lines	792	838	904	975	1034	1083	1135	1204	1262	1263	1278
Mobile phone subscribers	215	318	490	738	961	1157	1417	1763	2219	2757	3305

Source: International Telecommunications Union, 2009

The table gives a lot of detailed information, but it is difficult to see how the numbers of telephone lines and mobile phone subscribers have grown over this period, or how the numbers compare. A graph or chart is more useful for communicating these aspects of the data.

See Maths Help, Module 5 for information on using and interpreting different kinds of graphs and charts.

Figure 4 (overleaf) shows a graph, a bar chart and another type of statistical chart, each of which is a helpful and appropriate representation of some or all of the data in Table 1.

Unlike the bar charts in Unit 11, the bar chart in Figure 4(b) has *two* bars for each year represented – one bar represents the number of main telephone lines, and the other represents the number of mobile phone subscribers. A bar chart in which there are two or more bars for each data item is called a **comparative bar chart**.

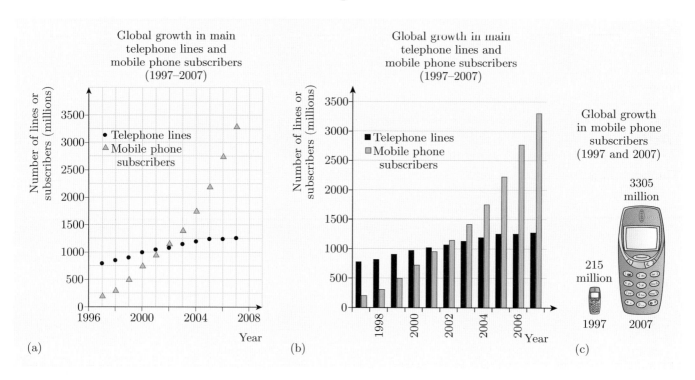

Figure 4 Three representations of data from Table 1

Notice that although the graph and bar chart in Figure 4(a) and (b) represent exactly the same data, and each does so in a way that is not misleading, they still give slightly different impressions.

The graph in Figure 4(a) makes it easy to compare the growth trends of the mobile phone data and fixed main telephone line data. To highlight the trends further, the points could be joined, or modelled by straight lines or curves, as appropriate. For example, a regression line could be fitted to the telephone line data.

On the other hand, the bar chart in Figure 4(b) makes it easy to see the *difference* between the number of telephone lines and the number of mobile subscribers in *each year* represented – these year-by-year differences are not so clear in the graph in Figure 4(a). The bar chart in Figure 4(b) also shows the long-term trends, although these are slightly more difficult to see than in the graph.

The chart in Figure 4(c) is much simpler than the graph and bar chart in Figure 4(a) and (b). It represents only the mobile phone data, not the telephone line data as well, and it depicts only the change in the number of mobile phone subscribers from 1997 to 2007, ignoring the intervening years. It uses two pictures of the front of a mobile phone and gives a visual impression that the number of subscribers in 2007 is about fifteen times larger than the number of subscribers in 1997, because approximately 15 copies of the 1997 picture would fit into the 2007 picture.

You saw another situation in which areas are used to represent numbers in Unit 11: in a histogram with unequal interval widths, the area of each bar is proportional to the number that it represents.

This chart is an example of a **pictogram**. The word *pictogram* describes any chart that conveys numerical information by means of pictures. Pictograms like the one in Figure 4(c) are commonly used in news media as a way of simplifying numerical information as much as possible – the pictures represent the topic, and their relative sizes represent the numbers. In another common type of pictogram, the charts are similar to bar charts, but with the data bars made up of pictures rather than being simple rectangles. All types of pictogram can be useful for conveying statistical information quickly and clearly, especially to audiences unfamiliar with graphs and charts.

In the next activity you are asked to look at two graphs and a pictogram that also represent data from Table 1, but create different, misleading impressions.

Activity 5 *Looking at statistical charts critically*

The graphs and pictogram below represent data from Table 1.

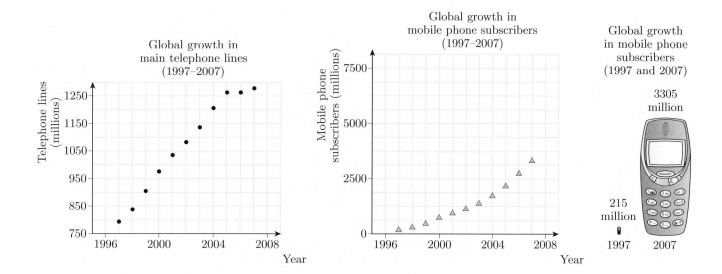

(a) If you were to glance at the two graphs on the left together, what misleading impression might they give you about how the growth in the number of mobile phone subscribers compares to the growth in the number of fixed main telephone lines? What causes this misleading impression?

(b) In the pictogram on the right, the picture that represents the number of mobile phone subscribers in 2007 is scaled up by a scale factor of 15 from the corresponding 1997 picture, to represent the fact that there were approximately 15 times more mobile phone subscribers in 2007 than in 1997. Why is this pictogram not an appropriate way to represent this fact?

A feature of the first graph in Activity 5 that is particularly worth noticing is that the vertical scale does not start at zero. This type of scale can give you the impression that the change in a quantity is much more significant than it actually is.

Activity 5 illustrates that when you are trying to interpret graphs and charts that have been produced by someone else, it is important to think about whether the data have been represented fairly, or whether the author might have represented them in an inappropriate way, perhaps to try to back up a point that he or she is making. You should also consider whether the data are from a reliable source and whether the author has ignored any important aspects of the data.

When you present your own mathematics, either in text or in graphs and diagrams, bear in mind that your readers might be critically assessing your work in a similar way to the examples in this section! So try to express your ideas clearly and concisely, using graphs and diagrams appropriately. Use sound logical arguments, and make sure that any use of statistical data is not misleading. You have been developing your skills in these areas throughout MU123.

In the final activity in this section you are asked to look back over your assignments, to see if there are any points that you need to consider as you tackle your final written assignment.

Activity 6 *Presenting your mathematics*

(a) Look back over your written assignments and your tutor's comments. What are the main points that you have learned about presenting your work?

(b) The final written assignment contains questions based on topics from throughout the module. If you have not already done so, download the assignment from the module website and look through the questions.

From your review in part (a), are there any points that you need to bear in mind when you tackle this assignment?

---

2 Extending your mathematical skills

During your study of MU123 you have developed a variety of skills for solving both abstract and practical mathematical problems. Many of these problems involve solving equations, that is, finding the values of the unknowns that satisfy the equations. This section concentrates on your equation-solving skills. You will see how the skills that you have already acquired can be extended to allow you to solve new problems, and you will learn some new skills for solving *trigonometric equations* – equations involving trigonometric functions. These skills will be needed if you plan to study more advanced mathematics modules.

2.1 Developing your equation-solving skills

Some of the equation-solving methods that you have met in MU123 are specific to particular kinds of equations. For example, you have seen how to solve quadratic equations by using the quadratic formula, and how to solve exponential equations by taking logarithms. Other methods can be used for different types of equations, or adapted for different types of equations, even though you might have met them in the context of a specific type of equation. Also, you can often combine more than one method to give you a way of solving a particular problem. You will see some examples of this in this section. Learning to adapt and combine your skills in this way is an important part of learning mathematics, as it extends the range of problems that you can deal with.

When you are choosing a method for solving an equation, or trying to adapt a method that you have seen in another context, one aspect that you have to bear in mind is whether you want an exact answer, or whether an approximate one will do. You have met various algebraic techniques that can give exact answers, such as 'doing the same thing to both sides', or using the quadratic formula. However, approximate answers are usually good enough for practical purposes, and you have also seen some techniques that give approximate answers, such as using graphs, and trial and improvement.

In this subsection you will see how you can extend both graphical and algebraic methods to new situations.

Adapting graphical methods

Suppose, for example, that you want to solve the quadratic equation

$$2x^2 + 2x = 9. \tag{1}$$

If approximate solutions are good enough, then you could use the graphical method that you saw in Unit 10 to find these. You rearrange the equation into the form

$$2x^2 + 2x - 9 = 0,$$

and then use Graphplotter to plot the graph of the associated quadratic function, $y = 2x^2 + 2x - 9$, as shown in Figure 5. The x-intercepts of the graph are the values of x for which $y = 0$, and hence are the solutions of the equation. You can find these accurately to a given number of decimal places by using a procedure given in Unit 10, which you will be reminded about shortly.

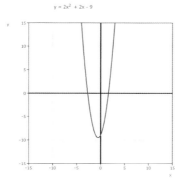

Figure 5 The graph of $y = 2x^2 + 2x - 9$

However, sometimes it is useful to solve an equation graphically by plotting, on the same axes, the two functions associated with the left- and right-hand sides of the equation, rather than by rearranging the equation and plotting a single function. For example, for equation (1) you would plot the graphs of the functions

$$y = 2x^2 + 2x \quad \text{and} \quad y = 9,$$

as shown in Figure 6. The x-coordinate of any point where the two graphs cross is a value of x for which the two y-values are the same – in other words, for which the left- and right-hand sides of equation (1) are equal. That is, it is a solution of the equation.

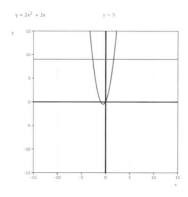

Figure 6 The graphs of $y = 2x^2 + 2x$ and $y = 9$

The usual reason why you would want to plot the two sides of an equation separately is that they represent particular quantities in the context that the equation comes from, so it is more meaningful to plot them than the single function given by the rearranged equation.

To use a Graphplotter graph of the two sides of an equation to find the solutions accurately to a given number of decimal places, you can adapt the procedure that you saw in Unit 10. Suppose that you want to use the graph in Figure 6 to find the solutions of equation (1) to two decimal places. You tick the Trace option, and zoom in on a crossing point until the x-coordinates of the trace points are shown to at least three decimal places (that is, to at least one more decimal place than the number that you eventually want). If you can find two trace points, one below the crossing point and one above, whose x-coordinates are the same when rounded to two decimal places, then the x-coordinate of the crossing point must also be the same when rounded to two decimal places.

For example, the two screenshots in Figure 7 show the left-hand crossing point in Figure 6. Figure 7(a) shows that there is a trace point below the crossing point with an x-coordinate of -2.676 to three decimal places, and Figure 7(b) shows that there is a trace point above the crossing point with an x-coordinate of -2.681 to three decimal places. Since both of these values are -2.68 to two decimal places, and the x-coordinate of the crossing point lies between these two values, it is also -2.68 to two decimal places. You can find in a similar way that the other crossing point in Figure 6 has x-coordinate 1.68. So the two solutions of equation (1) are -2.68 and 1.68, to two decimal places.

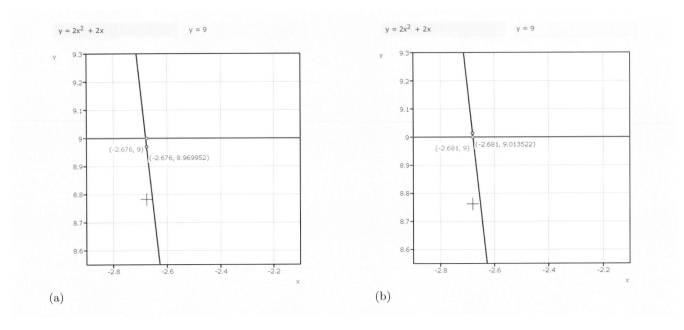

(a)   (b)

Figure 7   A crossing point of the graphs of $y = 2x^2 + 2x$ and $y = 9$, and trace points (a) below and (b) above the crossing point

You can use a similar method to find approximate values for the solutions of any equation. If you need to plot the graph of an equation whose form is not one of the standard ones in the Graphplotter drop-down list, then you can use 'Custom function', which is also available from the drop-down list. For example, to plot the graph of the equation $y = 4(x^3 - 2)$, choose Custom function and type

    4 * (x^3 - 2)

into the '$y =$' box. You can find more information about using Custom function on the Graphplotter Help page (press the orange 'Help' button at the top right of Graphplotter).

Graphplotter

Activity 7   *Solving an equation in different ways*

(a) Plot the two sides of the equation

$$(x - 3)(x + 2) = 2$$

on the same axes in Graphplotter. Then use the graphical method described on page 189 to solve the equation, giving your answers to two decimal places.

(b) Solve the same equation algebraically. Evaluate your answers to two decimal places and check that they match those in part (a).

In Unit 7 you saw that you can find an approximate solution of two simultaneous linear equations by drawing their graphs and reading off the x- and y-coordinates of the crossing point. The next activity illustrates that you can use the same method for any simultaneous equations in two unknowns, even if they are not linear. The x- and y-coordinates of the crossing point can both be found to a given number of decimal places by using the method discussed earlier in this subsection.

Activity 8 *Solving simultaneous equations graphically*

 Graphplotter

Consider the following simultaneous equations, in which one is linear and one is quadratic:

$$y = 2x + 3,$$
$$y = x^2 - 2x + 1.$$

(a) Use Graphplotter to plot the graphs of the two equations on the same axes, and to find the coordinates of their crossing points to two decimal places.

(b) Explain why these coordinates are the solutions of the simultaneous equations.

Adapting algebraic methods

You can also often adapt the algebraic methods that you have met for solving equations to allow you to deal with new situations. For example, you may be able to adapt the algebraic methods for solving simultaneous linear equations that you met in Unit 7 to allow you to solve simultaneous equations in which at least one equation is not linear. Suppose that you want to solve the following simultaneous equations algebraically:

$$y = 2 - 4x,$$
$$y = 2x^2 + x - 1.$$

A good strategy when faced with a new problem like this is to ask yourself: Have I seen anything with similarities to this before, and if so, can I use a similar approach here? In this case, you need to solve a linear equation and a quadratic equation simultaneously. In Unit 7 you met methods for solving simultaneous equations in which both equations are linear, and in Units 9 and 10 you saw some methods for solving quadratic equations, such as factorisation and the quadratic formula. So putting these ideas together could help you to solve simultaneous equations in which one equation is linear and the other is quadratic. This approach is used in the example below.

Example 1 *Solving non-linear simultaneous equations algebraically*

Use algebra to solve the following simultaneous equations:

$$y = 2 - 4x,$$
$$y = 2x^2 + x - 1.$$

Solution

💭 Try a method similar to one that you saw in Unit 7. 💭

The equations are

$$y = 2 - 4x, \tag{2}$$
$$y = 2x^2 + x - 1. \tag{3}$$

The right-hand sides must be equal to each other, which gives

$$2 - 4x = 2x^2 + x - 1.$$

💭 Simplify and solve this quadratic equation. 💭

Simplify: $\quad 0 = 2x^2 + 5x - 3$

Factorise: $\quad 0 = (2x - 1)(x + 3)$

So: $\quad 2x - 1 = 0$ or $x + 3 = 0$

So: $\quad x = \frac{1}{2}$ or $x = -3$

💭 Substitute into one of the original equations to find the values of y. 💭

Substituting $x = \frac{1}{2}$ into equation (2) gives

$$y = 2 - 4 \times \tfrac{1}{2} = 2 - 2 = 0.$$

Substituting $x = -3$ into the same equation gives

$$y = 2 - 4 \times (-3) = 2 + 12 = 14.$$

So the solutions are

$$x = \tfrac{1}{2}, \; y = 0 \quad \text{and} \quad x = -3, \; y = 14.$$

(Check: Substituting $x = \frac{1}{2}$, $y = 0$ into equation (3) gives

$$\text{RHS} = 2 \times \left(\tfrac{1}{2}\right)^2 + \tfrac{1}{2} - 1 = \tfrac{1}{2} + \tfrac{1}{2} - 1 = 0 = \text{LHS},$$

and substituting $x = -3$, $y = 14$ into the same equation gives

$$\text{RHS} = 2 \times (-3)^2 + (-3) - 1 = 18 - 3 - 1 = 14 = \text{LHS.})$$

Now let's just pause to think about what has been achieved here. A pair of simultaneous equations in which one equation is linear and one is quadratic was solved using algebra, by adapting and combining methods that you have seen for solving simultaneous linear equations and for solving single quadratic equations. There could be many other situations where you need to solve two simultaneous equations in which at least one equation is not linear, so this is an important step forward. Adapting and combining techniques with which you are already familiar has opened up a new set of problems that you can solve.

Activity 9 *Solving simultaneous equations algebraically*

For further practice, you might like to try solving the simultaneous equations in Activity 8 algebraically.

Use algebra to solve the following simultaneous equations:

$$y = x + 1,$$
$$y = x^2 + 2x - 5.$$

Using shortcuts

Another way in which you can develop your equation-solving skills is that, as you become more confident, you may be able to take shortcuts that reduce some of your working. You must be sure that you understand the reasoning behind such a shortcut, so that you are aware of the situations where the shortcut can be used and those where it cannot.

For instance, there is a shortcut that you can sometimes use when you are rearranging equations involving algebraic fractions. You saw earlier in the module that usually the first step in solving an equation involving algebraic fractions is to multiply both sides by an expression that is a multiple of all the denominators. This process clears the fractions, making the equation easier to solve.

For example, here is how you would solve the equation

$$\frac{4}{x-3} = \frac{3}{x-2}, \tag{4}$$

using the method that you have seen.

Assume that $x \neq 3$ and $x \neq 2$.

Multiplying by $(x-3)(x-2)$ gives

$$(x-3)(x-2)\frac{4}{(x-3)} = (x-3)(x-2)\frac{3}{(x-2)}.$$

Cancelling gives

$$4(x-2) = 3(x-3). \tag{5}$$

Hence

$$4x - 8 = 3x - 9$$

which gives $x = -1$.

This answer satisfies the initial assumptions $x \neq 3$ and $x \neq 2$, so the solution is $x = -1$.

You saw in Unit 9 that when you multiply an equation by an expression you must assume that the expression is non-zero. You should check that any solutions that you obtain at the end of your working satisfy your assumption.

Equation (4) is of a particular form for which there is a shortcut, known as **cross-multiplying**, that reduces some of the work in rearranging the equation. The shortcut applies to equations of the form

$$\frac{A}{B} = \frac{C}{D}, \tag{6}$$

where A, B, C and D are expressions. If you look back at equation (4), then you will see that it is of this form with $A = 4$, $B = x - 3$, $C = 3$ and $D = x - 2$.

Cross-multiplying allows you to remove the fractions in an equation of form (6) in one step instead of two. If you assume that the expressions on the denominators, B and D, are not equal to zero, and then multiply both sides of the equation by their product, BD, to clear the fractions, you obtain

$$BD \times \frac{A}{B} = BD \times \frac{C}{D}.$$

Cancelling gives

$$AD = BC.$$

You can think of this equation as being obtained from equation (6) by multiplying across the equals sign, like this:

$$\frac{A}{B} \diagdown\!\!\!\diagup \frac{C}{D} \quad \text{gives} \quad AD = BC.$$

This is the technique known as cross-multiplying.

For example, consider equation (4) again:

$$\frac{4}{x-3} = \frac{3}{x-2}.$$

To cross-multiply in this equation, you multiply across the equals sign like this:

$$\frac{4}{x-3} \diagdown\!\!\!\!\diagup \frac{3}{x-2}.$$

This gives

$$4(x-2) = 3(x-3),$$

which is equation (5), reached in a more straightforward way. You can solve the equation in the usual way from this stage. You still need to make the assumptions $x \neq 3$ and $x \neq 2$, of course, as cross-multiplying is just a shortened form of the usual method.

Activity 10 *Using cross-multiplication to solve equations*

Which two of the following three equations are in a suitable form for cross-multiplying? Solve the three equations.

(a) $\dfrac{x}{x+1} = \dfrac{2}{x+3}$ (b) $\dfrac{x}{x+1} = 2$ (c) $\dfrac{x}{x+1} = \dfrac{2}{x} + 3$

Remember that you should use shortcuts only in situations where you are confident that they apply. If you are not sure, then stick to a basic method, to avoid the possibility of errors.

2.2 Solving trigonometric equations

In Unit 12 you saw that when you use trigonometry to find an unknown angle θ in a triangle, the final step involves solving a trigonometric equation such as

$$\sin\theta = \tfrac{5}{6}, \quad \cos\theta = -0.87 \quad \text{or} \quad \tan\theta = 4.$$

In equations of this type involving $\sin\theta$ and $\cos\theta$, there is a solution only if the number on the right-hand side is between -1 and 1, inclusive.

Equations like these crop up frequently in trigonometry. You'll see them arise in three more situations in this unit, starting in the next subsection, where they occur when you calculate the angle that a straight line makes with the x-axis. Then in Section 4 you'll see equations of this sort when the motion of a ferris wheel and the height of a tide over a day are modelled.

As you know, you can obtain a solution of an equation like those above by using the $\sin^{-1}$, $\cos^{-1}$ or $\tan^{-1}$ function on your calculator. If you know that the angle θ that you are trying to find is *acute*, then the solution given by your calculator will be the angle that you want. In general, however, the solution given by your calculator is only one of many possible solutions.

Remember that an *acute* angle is one between $0°$ and $90°$, exclusive. Similarly, an *obtuse* angle is one between $90°$ and $180°$, exclusive.

For example, consider the equation

$$\sin\theta = \tfrac{5}{6}.$$

One solution of this equation is

$$\theta = \sin^{-1}\!\left(\tfrac{5}{6}\right) \approx 56°.$$

However, the graph in Figure 8 shows that there are other solutions. Each of the points marked with a black dot corresponds to a value of θ for which

$\sin\theta = \frac{5}{6}$. The dot between $0°$ and $90°$ corresponds to the solution on the opposite page, $\theta \approx 56°$, but you can see that there is another solution between $90°$ and $180°$, and since the graph of $y = \sin\theta$ repeats every $360°$, there are infinitely many solutions altogether.

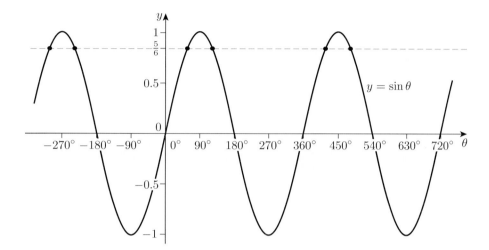

Figure 8   Some points on the graph of $y = \sin\theta$ that have y-coordinate $\frac{5}{6}$

When you need to solve a trigonometric equation like those on the opposite page, you often need solutions other than the one provided by your calculator. You saw an example of this in Unit 12. When you use the Sine Rule to find an angle θ of a triangle, you obtain an equation of the form

$$\sin\theta = \boxed{\text{a number}},$$

where the number on the right-hand side is positive, and less than or equal to 1. You can use the $\sin^{-1}$ function on your calculator to find one solution of the equation, but, except when $\theta = 90°$, there is always a second solution, which is $180°$ minus the first solution (as illustrated in Figure 8 for the equation $\sin\theta = \frac{5}{6}$). Both of the two solutions can occur as the angle θ of the triangle, and you need more information about the triangle in order to decide which is the correct angle.

You saw how to use the Sine Rule to find an angle of a triangle in Unit 12, Subsections 2.1 and 3.3.

So being able to find all the solutions of trigonometric equations is a useful skill. Once you know how to find all the solutions of an equation of this type, you can choose any particular solution that you might need for the situation that you're working with. For example, you might know that the angle that you are trying to find is between $90°$ and $180°$.

You can use Graphplotter to find approximate solutions of trigonometric equations, just as you can for any other type of equation, and you will be asked to use this method in Section 4.

However, as you have seen for other kinds of equations, it is also useful to have a non-graphical method for finding solutions. This often allows you to obtain solutions more quickly, it can enable you to obtain exact solutions rather than approximate ones, and it gives you a greater understanding of the mathematics.

So in this subsection you will learn a useful method for finding all the solutions of trigonometric equations like those at the beginning of this subsection.

The key to finding all the solutions of trigonometric equations is to understand how the sine, cosine and tangent of any angle are related to the sine, cosine and tangent of an acute angle. So let's look at that next.

Sines, cosines and tangents of related angles

The sine, cosine and tangent of a general angle were defined in Subsection 3.1 of Unit 12.

Think back to the way that the sine, cosine and tangent of a general angle were defined. Suppose that the angle is θ: remember that you think of it drawn on a pair of coordinate axes, as shown in Figure 9. It is measured from the positive direction of the x-axis, anticlockwise if θ is positive, and clockwise if θ is negative.

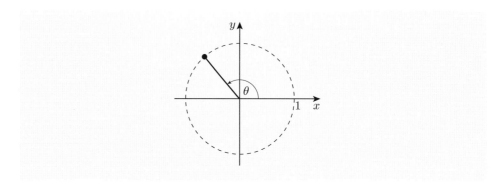

Figure 9   An angle θ drawn on a pair of coordinate axes

The angle θ corresponds to a point on the unit circle (the circle of radius 1 centred at the origin), and $\sin \theta$ and $\cos \theta$ are defined to be the y- and x-coordinates of this point, respectively. The value of $\tan \theta$ is defined by

$$\tan \theta = \frac{\sin \theta}{\cos \theta}.$$

For example, consider the angle $25°$. Figure 10 shows the point P on the unit circle that corresponds to $25°$.

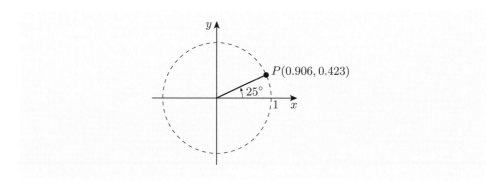

Figure 10   The point P corresponding to the angle $25°$

The y-coordinate of P is 0.423, to three decimal places, so

$$\sin 25° \approx 0.423.$$

The x-coordinate of P is 0.906, to three decimal places, so

$$\cos 25° \approx 0.906.$$

Using more precise values for $\cos 25°$ and $\sin 25°$ gives

$$\tan 25° = \frac{\sin 25°}{\cos 25°} = \frac{0.422\,61\ldots}{0.906\,30\ldots} \approx 0.466.$$

The angle $25°$, shown in Figure 10, is referred to as a *first-quadrant* angle, because the corresponding point P lies in the first quadrant. Similarly, any angle that corresponds to a point on the unit circle that lies in the second quadrant is called a *second-quadrant* angle, and so on. Figure 11 reminds you of how the quadrants are labelled. So, for example, any acute angle is a first-quadrant angle, and any obtuse angle is a second-quadrant angle.

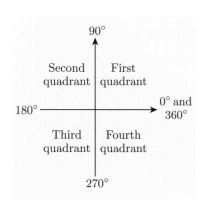

Figure 11   The four quadrants

Now consider what happens if you reflect the point P corresponding to $25°$ in the y-axis. The resulting point Q is shown in Figure 12. The angle corresponding to Q is a second-quadrant angle, namely $180° - 25° = 155°$. The x-coordinate of Q is the negative of the x-coordinate of P, and the y-coordinate of Q is the same as the y-coordinate of P.

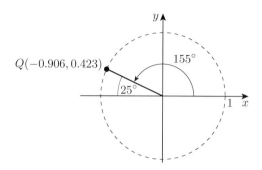

Figure 12   The point Q corresponding to the angle $155°$

The sine and cosine of $155°$ are given by the coordinates of Q. These coordinates give:

$$\sin 155° \approx 0.423, \quad \cos 155° \approx -0.906$$

and

$$\tan 155° = \frac{0.422\,61\ldots}{-0.906\,30\ldots} \approx -0.466.$$

So the sine, cosine and tangent of $155°$ are exactly the same as the sine, cosine and tangent of $25°$, except for some of the signs. The cosine and tangent of $155°$ are negative, whereas the cosine and tangent of $25°$ are positive. Another way to describe the relationship between the sines, cosines and tangents of these two angles is to say that they have the same *magnitudes*.

There are two other angles in the range $0°$ to $360°$ that also have the same sine, cosine and tangent as $25°$, except for some of the signs, as shown in Figure 13.

Remember that the *magnitude* of a number is the number without its negative sign, if it has one.

The first of these other angles is obtained by rotating the point P through a half-turn about the origin (or alternatively by reflecting the point Q in the x-axis). This gives the point R shown in Figure 13(a).

The second of the other angles is obtained by reflecting the point P in the x-axis (or alternatively by reflecting the point R in the y-axis). This gives the point S shown in Figure 13(b).

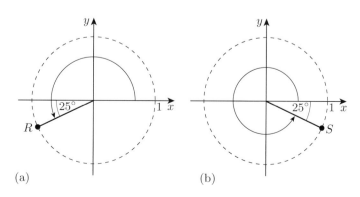

Figure 13   (a) The point R obtained by rotating P through a half-turn about the origin. (b) The point S obtained by reflecting P in the x-axis.

In the next activity you are asked to work out the angles corresponding to R and S, and find their sines, cosines and tangents.

Activity 11   *Finding the cosines, sines and tangents of angles related to $25°$*

(a) Work out the angles, measured anticlockwise from the positive x-axis as shown in Figure 13, corresponding to the points R and S.

(b) By considering how the coordinates of R and S are related to the coordinates of P (or Q), write down the coordinates of R and S, to three significant figures.

(c) Using your answers to part (b), find the sine, cosine and tangent of each of the two angles in part (a), to three significant figures. (For the tangents, you will need to use more precise values of the cosines and sines, to avoid rounding errors. You can find the numbers that you need on page 196.)

You have now seen that the four angles

$25°$,

$180° - 25° = 155°$,

$180° + 25° = 205°$,

$360° - 25° = 335°$

all have the same sine, cosine and tangent, except for the signs.

In general, you can see that, for any acute angle ϕ, the four angles

$$\phi, \quad 180° - \phi, \quad 180° + \phi \quad \text{and} \quad 360° - \phi$$

all have the same sine, cosine and tangent, except for the signs. These four related angles are shown in Figure 14.

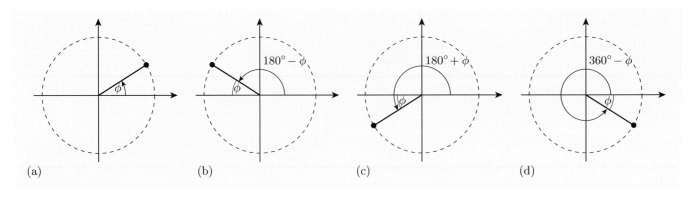

(a)   (b)   (c)   (d)

Figure 14   Four angles with the same sine, cosine and tangent, except for the signs

One of the four related angles lies in each of the four quadrants. The summary diagram in Figure 15 should help you to remember them.

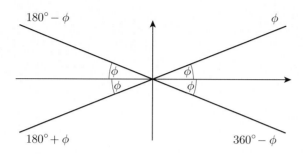

Figure 15   The related angles diagram

The signs of the sines, cosines and tangents are determined by the signs that the x- and y-coordinates take in the different quadrants, as follows.

- In the first quadrant, x and y are both positive, so sine, cosine and tangent are all positive.
- In the second quadrant, x is negative and y is positive, so sine is positive and cosine is negative, and hence tangent is negative.
- In the third quadrant, x and y are both negative, so sine and cosine are both negative, and hence tangent is positive.
- In the fourth quadrant, x is positive and y is negative, so sine is negative and cosine is positive, and hence tangent is negative.

The sign of the tangent is worked out from the signs of the sine and cosine by using the fact that
$$\tan\theta = \frac{\sin\theta}{\cos\theta},$$
for any angle θ.

There is a useful way to remember these signs, which is shown in Figure 16. The letters tell you which of sine, cosine and tangent are positive in which quadrants:

A stands for all,
S stands for sine,
T stands for tangent,
C stands for cosine.

To remember this diagram, you might like to think of the word CAST or the mnemonic phrase 'All Silly Tom Cats'.

Using the CAST diagram and the related angles diagram to solve trigonometric equations

You can use the information in the the CAST diagram and the related angles diagram to help you to solve simple trigonometric equations. The method is demonstrated in the example on the next page.

You usually also need to use your calculator. Whenever you use your calculator for trigonometry, remember to check that it is set to use the units for angles that you are working with – degrees or radians.

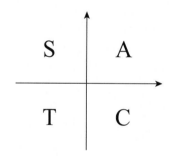

Figure 16   The CAST diagram

Subsections 3.7 and 3.9 of the MU123 Guide tell you how to set the calculator recommended for the module to degrees or radians.

Sometimes you might need to find the solutions of one of the seven 'special' trigonometric equations below.

$$\sin \theta = 1,$$
$$\cos \theta = 1,$$

$$\sin \theta = -1,$$
$$\cos \theta = -1,$$

$$\sin \theta = 0,$$
$$\cos \theta = 0,$$
$$\tan \theta = 0.$$

A good way to solve one of these equations is not to use the CAST diagram and the related angles diagram, but instead to just look at the graph of the sine, cosine or tangent function, as appropriate.

For example, you can see from the graph of the sine function (which is on page 94, and in the Handbook) that the only solution of the equation $\sin \theta = 1$ between $0°$ and $360°$ is $\theta = 90°$.

Example 2   *Solving trigonometric equations*

Find all the solutions between $0°$ and $360°$ of the following equations. Give your answers to the nearest degree.

(a) $\cos \theta = 0.8$ (b) $\tan \theta = -4$

Solution

(a) Use the CAST diagram to find the quadrants of the solutions.

The cosine of θ is positive, so θ is a first- or fourth-quadrant angle.

Use your calculator to find the first-quadrant angle.

One solution of the equation is

$$\theta = \cos^{-1}(0.8) = 37° \text{ (to the nearest degree).}$$

Use the related angles diagram to find the related fourth-quadrant angle.

The other solution is

$$\theta = 360° - 37° = 323° \text{ (to the nearest degree).}$$

(Check: A calculator gives

$$\cos 37° = 0.798\ldots \approx 0.8,$$
$$\cos 323° = 0.798\ldots \approx 0.8.)$$

(b) Use the CAST diagram to find the quadrants of the solutions.

The tangent of θ is negative, so θ is a second- or fourth-quadrant angle.

Use your calculator to find the related first-quadrant angle whose tangent has the same magnitude but is positive.

The related first-quadrant angle is

$$\tan^{-1}(4) = 76° \text{ (to the nearest degree).}$$

Use the related angles diagram to find the related second and fourth-quadrant angles.

The solutions are

$$\theta = 180° - 76° = 104° \text{ (to the nearest degree),}$$
$$\theta = 360° - 76° = 284° \text{ (to the nearest degree).}$$

(Check: A calculator gives

$$\tan 104° = -4.010\ldots \approx -4,$$
$$\tan 284° = -4.010\ldots \approx -4.)$$

Before you do the next activity, check that your calculator is set to use degrees rather than radians, if you haven't done so already.

Activity 12   *Solving trigonometric equations*

Find all the solutions between $0°$ and $360°$ of the following equations. Give your answers to the nearest degree.

(a) $\sin \theta = 0.2$ (b) $\cos \theta = -0.6$

Once you have found all the solutions of a trigonometric equation in the interval 0° to 360°, it is straightforward to find any other solutions that you want. The trigonometric functions repeat every 360°, so adding or subtracting a multiple of 360° to a solution gives another solution. For example, in Example 2(a) it was found that the solutions of the equation $\cos\theta = 0.8$ in the interval 0° to 360° are approximately 37° and 323°. So some other approximate solutions are, for example,

The tangent function repeats every 180°, but that means that it also repeats every 360°.

$$37° + 360° = 397°,$$
$$37° - 2 \times 360° = -683°,$$
$$323° - 360° = -37°.$$

2.3   Finding the angle of inclination of a line

In this subsection you'll look at another topic which illustrates that putting together ideas covered in different parts of the module can be helpful, and also involves the related angles and trigonometric equations that you learned about in the last subsection.

As you saw in Unit 6, one way to specify the slope of a straight line is to give its gradient.

Another way is to use the idea of angle, which was a topic in Unit 8. The **angle of inclination** of a line is its angle measured anticlockwise from the positive direction of the x-axis, when the line is drawn on a pair of axes *with equal scales*. In Figure 17, the angle of inclination of a straight line is marked as θ. An angle of inclination is always between 0° and 180°.

The gradient of a line ought to be related in some way to its angle of inclination, but how?

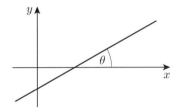

Figure 17   The angle of inclination of a straight line

To answer this question, first consider a line with a *positive* gradient – it has an *acute* angle of inclination θ, as shown in Figure 18(a).

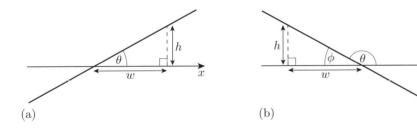

(a)   (b)

Figure 18   (a) A line with a positive gradient. (b) A line with a negative gradient.

A dashed line perpendicular to the x-axis has been added to the diagram in Figure 18(a), making a right-angled triangle with width w and height h. The gradient of the slant line is given by

$$\text{gradient} = \frac{\text{rise}}{\text{run}} = \frac{h}{w},$$

but you can also see that

$$\tan\theta = \frac{\text{opp}}{\text{adj}} = \frac{h}{w}.$$

So

$$\text{gradient} = \tan\theta.$$

This simple equation uses trigonometry to relate the ideas of gradient and angle of inclination.

In fact, the same equation also holds for lines with *negative* gradients. Such a line has an *obtuse* angle of inclination θ, as shown in Figure 18(b). In this diagram you can see that

$$\text{gradient} = \frac{\text{rise}}{\text{run}} = \frac{-h}{w} = -\frac{h}{w}.$$

The tangent of θ can be worked out from the tangent of the related acute angle ϕ. The diagram shows that

$$\tan\phi = \frac{\text{opp}}{\text{adj}} = \frac{h}{w}.$$

Also, since $\theta = 180° - \phi$, it follows from the related angles diagram that the two angles θ and ϕ have the same tangent values, except possibly for the signs. The angles ϕ and θ are acute and obtuse angles, respectively, so they are first- and second-quadrant angles, respectively, and hence it follows from the CAST diagram that their tangents are positive and negative, respectively. So

$$\tan\theta = -\tan\phi = -\frac{h}{w}.$$

So, again, gradient $= \tan\theta$. This useful relationship is summarised below.

Gradient and angle of inclination of a straight line

For any straight line with angle of inclination θ,

$$\text{gradient} = \tan\theta.$$

Remember that the angle of inclination is measured when the line is drawn on axes *with equal scales*.

Example 3   *Finding the equation of a line with a given angle of inclination*

Find the equation of the straight line shown below, which passes through the point $(0, -1)$ and whose angle of inclination is $30°$.

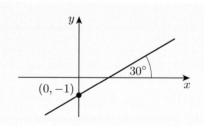

Table 2   Sines, cosines and tangents of special angles

θ	θ	$\sin\theta$	$\cos\theta$	$\tan\theta$
$0°$	0	0	1	0
$30°$	$\frac{\pi}{6}$	$\frac{1}{2}$	$\frac{\sqrt{3}}{2}$	$\frac{1}{\sqrt{3}}$
$45°$	$\frac{\pi}{4}$	$\frac{1}{\sqrt{2}}$	$\frac{1}{\sqrt{2}}$	1
$60°$	$\frac{\pi}{3}$	$\frac{\sqrt{3}}{2}$	$\frac{1}{2}$	$\sqrt{3}$
$90°$	$\frac{\pi}{2}$	1	0	$-$

The special angles table is also given in the Handbook.

Solution

The equation of the line is $y = mx + c$, where m is the gradient and c is the y-intercept.

The y-intercept is -1, since the line passes through the point $(0, -1)$.

💭 To find the gradient, use the fact that gradient $= \tan\theta$, where θ is the angle of inclination. You can find the tangent of $30°$ either by using your calculator or from the special angles table (Table 2). 💭

The gradient is $\tan 30° = \dfrac{1}{\sqrt{3}}$, so the equation of the line is

$$y = \frac{1}{\sqrt{3}}x - 1.$$

Now have a go at the following activity – it uses the same ideas but the other way round!

Activity 13   *Working with angles of inclination*

The diagram below shows the lines

$$y = x + 3 \quad \text{and} \quad y = x\sqrt{3} + 2,$$

drawn on axes with equal scales. The angles of inclination of these lines are α and β, respectively, and the acute angle between the lines is γ, as shown.

The second equation here can also be written as

$$y = \sqrt{3}x + 2.$$

However, to avoid the possibility of this being misread as

$$y = \sqrt{3x} + 2,$$

it is preferable to write it as shown.

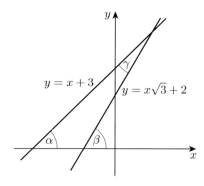

(a) Write down the gradient of each line.

(b) Use your answers to part (a) to calculate the angles α and β in degrees. You can use either your calculator or the table of special trigonometric values (Table 2).

(c) Hence work out the angle γ between the lines.

In the next activity you are asked to find the angle of inclination of a line whose gradient is negative. Since the gradient is negative, the angle of inclination is obtuse, and it is the solution θ of an equation of the form

$$\tan \theta = \text{(a negative number)}.$$

You can use the methods for solving trigonometric equations that you met in the last subsection to find this obtuse angle.

Activity 14   *Finding an angle of inclination when the gradient is negative*

Consider the straight line with equation

$$y = -2x + 1.$$

(a) Sketch the line on a graph, using equal scales on the axes.

(b) Suppose that the line has angle of inclination θ. Write down a trigonometric equation involving θ, and solve it to find the value of θ to the nearest degree. (Remember that an angle of inclination is between $0°$ and $180°$.)

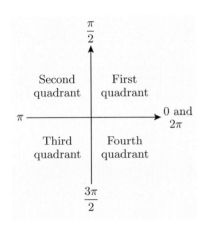

Figure 19 The quadrants

2.4 Solving trigonometric equations in radians

If you go on to higher-level mathematics modules, then you will often work with angles in radians rather than degrees. So in this subsection you will have a chance to practise solving trigonometric equations in radians. You can use exactly the same method as in Subsection 2.2, just with the angles converted to radians.

Remember that 2π radians is the same as $360°$, so the boundary values of the quadrants in radians are

$$0, \quad \frac{\pi}{2}, \quad \pi, \quad \frac{3\pi}{2} \quad \text{and} \quad 2\pi,$$

as shown in Figure 19.

Figure 20(a) repeats the CAST diagram from earlier, and Figure 20(b) shows the related angles diagram in radians.

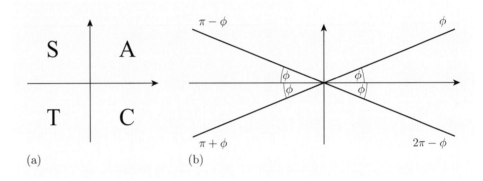

(a)   (b)

Figure 20 (a) The CAST diagram. (b) The related angles diagram in radians.

In the example below a trigonometric equation is solved in radians.

Example 4 *Solving a trigonometric equation in radians*

Find all the solutions between 0 and 2π of the equation

$$\sin\theta = -\frac{\sqrt{3}}{2},$$

giving exact answers in radians.

Solution

The equation is

$$\sin\theta = -\frac{\sqrt{3}}{2}.$$

🗨 Use the CAST diagram to find the quadrants of the solutions. 🗨

The sine of θ is negative, so θ is a third- or fourth-quadrant angle.

🗨 Find the related first-quadrant angle, either by using your calculator or by recognising that $\sqrt{3}/2$ appears as a sine value in the special angles table (Table 2 on page 202). 🗨

The related first-quadrant angle is

$$\sin^{-1}\left(\frac{\sqrt{3}}{2}\right) = \frac{\pi}{3}.$$

💬 Use the related angles diagram to find the solutions. 💬

The solutions are

$$\theta = \pi + \frac{\pi}{3} = \frac{4\pi}{3},$$

$$\theta = 2\pi - \frac{\pi}{3} = \frac{5\pi}{3}.$$

$\Bigg($Check: A calculator gives

$$\sin\left(\frac{4\pi}{3}\right) = -\frac{\sqrt{3}}{2}, \quad \sin\left(\frac{5\pi}{3}\right) = -\frac{\sqrt{3}}{2}.\Bigg)$$

Here is a similar activity for you to try. When you do it, don't solve the equations in degrees and then convert the solutions to radians. Instead, work with radians throughout, as in Example 4; this will be useful practice for doing mathematics at higher levels. Make sure that your calculator is set to use radians.

Activity 15   *Solving trigonometric equations in radians*

Find all the solutions between 0 and 2π radians of the following equations, giving your answers in radians. In parts (a) and (b) give exact answers, and in part (c) give answers to three significant figures.

(a) $\cos\theta = \dfrac{\sqrt{3}}{2}$ (b) $\tan\theta = -\sqrt{3}$ (c) $\cos\theta = 0.4$

Finally in this subsection, notice that you can use the CAST diagram and the related angles diagram, together with the table of special angles (Table 2 on page 202), to find the exact values of the sines, cosines and tangents of some more angles.

For example, the special angles table tells you that $\cos\left(\frac{\pi}{3}\right) = \frac{1}{2}$, so, by the related angles diagram, the cosine of each of the following angles is either $\frac{1}{2}$ or $-\frac{1}{2}$:

$$\pi - \frac{\pi}{3}, \quad \pi + \frac{\pi}{3}, \quad 2\pi - \frac{\pi}{3}.$$

These angles simplify to

$$\frac{2\pi}{3}, \quad \frac{4\pi}{3}, \quad \frac{5\pi}{3}.$$

They lie in the second, third and fourth quadrants, respectively, so, by the CAST diagram,

$$\cos\left(\frac{2\pi}{3}\right) = -\tfrac{1}{2}, \quad \cos\left(\frac{4\pi}{3}\right) = -\tfrac{1}{2}, \quad \cos\left(\frac{5\pi}{3}\right) = \tfrac{1}{2}.$$

You can use this method to find the exact value of the sine, cosine or tangent of any angle that is linked by the related angles diagram to one of the special angles.

2.5   Solving trigonometric equations by using sketch graphs

When you have to solve a trigonometric equation, an alternative to using the CAST diagram and the related angles diagram is to work with sketch graphs of the sine, cosine and tangent functions.

This method is not the same as the graphical method for solving equations that you used earlier in this unit – it does not involve using graphs to read off approximate solutions. Instead, it involves using sketch graphs to tell you the same information about related angles that you can obtain from the CAST diagram and the related angles diagram. So you do not need accurate graphs, but only sketches showing the basic shapes.

You might find the graphs of the sine, cosine and tangent functions easier to remember and use than the CAST diagram and the related angles diagram. If you cannot remember the shapes of these graphs, then you can look them up in the Handbook. You should work with graphs that have $0°$, $90°$, $180°$, $270°$ and $360°$ marked on the θ-axis (or the equivalents in radians), as these are the boundary values between the four quadrants.

The method is demonstrated in the example below, for angles in degrees. Remember that it is just an alternative to the method that you saw in Subsection 2.2 – if you find that you prefer the earlier method, then stick with that!

Tutorial clip

Example 5   *Using sketch graphs to solve trigonometric equations*

Find all the solutions between $0°$ and $360°$ of the following equations.

(a) $\sin\theta = \frac{1}{2}$ (b) $\cos\theta = -\frac{1}{2}$

Solution

(a) The equation is

$$\sin\theta = \tfrac{1}{2}.$$

🗨 Sketch the graph of $y = \sin\theta$ in the interval $0°$ to $360°$. Draw the horizontal line at $y = \frac{1}{2}$, and mark the crossing points. 🗨

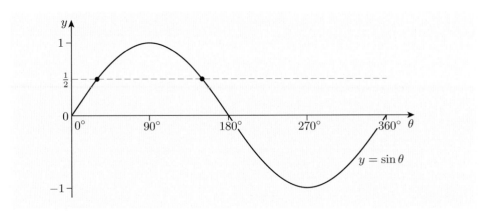

🗨 Find one solution, either by using your calculator or from the special angles table (Table 2 on page 202). 🗨

One solution is

$$\theta = \sin^{-1}\left(\tfrac{1}{2}\right) = 30°.$$

This solution is the θ-coordinate of the left-hand dot on the sketch graph. To find the other solution, which is the θ-coordinate of the right-hand dot, use the fact that the graph of $y = \sin\theta$ has mirror symmetry in the vertical line at $\theta = 90°$, as shown in the margin.

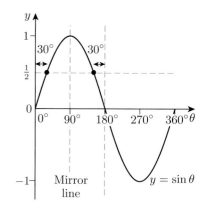

The second solution is as far below $180°$ as the first solution is above $0°$, so the second solution is

$$180° - 30° = 150°.$$

(Check: A calculator gives

$$\sin 30° = \tfrac{1}{2}, \quad \sin 150° = \tfrac{1}{2}.)$$

(b) The equation is

$$\cos\theta = -\tfrac{1}{2}.$$

Sketch the graph of $y = \cos\theta$ in the interval $0°$ to $360°$. Draw the horizontal line at $y = -\tfrac{1}{2}$, and mark the crossing points.

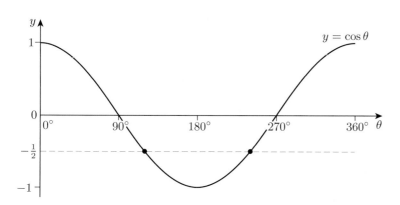

Use your calculator to find one solution.

One solution is

$$\theta = \cos^{-1}\left(-\tfrac{1}{2}\right) = 120°.$$

This solution corresponds to the left-hand dot on the sketch graph. To find the other solution, use the fact that the graph of $y = \cos\theta$ has mirror symmetry in the vertical line at $\theta = 180°$.

The second solution is as far above $180°$ as the first solution is below $180°$.

The first solution is $180° - 60°$, so the other solution is

$$180° + 60° = 240°.$$

(Check: A calculator gives

$$\cos 120° = -\tfrac{1}{2}, \quad \cos 240° = -\tfrac{1}{2}.)$$

Here is an activity in which you can practise using sketch graphs to help you to solve trigonometric equations. Remember that you need to draw only rough sketch graphs, as their purpose is just to give you information about the symmetry of where the solutions occur. Remember also to set your calculator to use degrees.

Activity 16 *Using sketch graphs to solve trigonometric equations*

Use sketch graphs to find all the solutions between $0°$ and $360°$ of the following equations. Give your answers to part (a) to the nearest degree, and exact answers to part (b).

(a) $\cos\theta = 0.7$ (b) $\tan\theta = 1$

As you have seen, when you use a sketch graph to solve a trigonometric equation of the type considered in this section, the first step after sketching the graph is to use your calculator (or the table of special angles) to find one solution of the equation. If the number on the right-hand side of the equation is negative, then the solution given by your calculator may not be in the range $0°$ to $360°$. In this situation, you can find a solution in the range $0°$ to $360°$ by adding $360°$.

You might like to practise using sketch graphs to solve trigonometric equations in radians rather than degrees. You could try to solve the equations in Activity 15 on page 205 by this method.

In this section, you have reviewed and extended your skills in solving equations, you have learned how to solve simple trigonometric equations, and you have also seen the importance of linking together different mathematical ideas in order to tackle more complicated problems.

3 Abstract mathematics

Mathematics is a fascinating subject in its own right, and it has been appreciated for its beauty for centuries and throughout many different cultures. An important part of mathematics is asking questions, for example about properties of numbers or geometric figures, investigating ideas that arise from these questions, then proposing conjectures, and finally proving that the conjectures are true. Although initially these abstract ideas often do not appear to have any practical use and are studied for their own interest, important applications are sometimes developed later. This section gives a flavour of some of these aspects of mathematics, as well as illustrating that mathematics is everywhere. The first subsection considers some mathematical puzzles from Japan; the second subsection is about some numerical results that can be shown to be true generally; and the final subsection takes a geometric look at paper-folding and its practical applications.

3.1 Japanese puzzles

In Japan, during the Edo period (1603–1868), mathematical ideas flourished in a magnificent way! Instead of mathematics being studied just by experts and in schools, it became available to many people through thousands of *sangaku puzzles*. These were beautiful wooden tablets that were hung as offerings in Shinto shrines and Buddhist temples throughout the country. An example is shown in Figure 21. Each sangaku contained theorems or problems with their answers, but often not the full explanations or solutions. So they became challenges for anyone who could

Sangaku is pronounced as 'san-gak'. The word means 'mathematical tablet'. The oldest surviving sangaku dates from 1683.

understand the language used and wanted to try them. Although many of the tablets were produced by the samurai (the military nobility), anyone could make one, and women and children produced sangaku problems and solutions too. Many of the sangaku described complicated geometric problems.

By this time, most of the samurai were no longer warriors, but government officials and courtiers.

Figure 21 A sangaku tablet featuring eleven geometric problems

The next activity is about a sangaku that was hung in the Kurasako Kannon temple in the Iwate Prefecture in the north of the main island, Honshu, in 1743.

Activity 17   *Solving a sangaku puzzle*

The question on the sangaku is as follows.

> There are 50 chickens and rabbits. The total number of feet is 122. How many chickens and how many rabbits are there?

(Source: Fukagawa, H. and Rothman, T. (2008) *Sacred mathematics*, Princeton, Princeton University Press.)

Note that here '50 chickens and rabbits' means 50 animals altogether; some are rabbits and some are chickens.

(a) Let the number of chickens be c and the number of rabbits be r. Write down an expression for the total number of chickens and rabbits, and an expression for the total number of feet, both in terms of c and r. Hence write down two simultaneous equations in c and r, and solve them to find c and r.

(b) Find another way of solving the puzzle that involves arithmetic, but not algebra.

Being able to solve a sangaku was quite an achievement, but a much better way to impress your fellow mathematicians, and to thank the gods for your mathematical prowess, was to create one. That meant thinking up your own mathematical question and then solving it – just like research mathematicians do today, but on a smaller scale.

Researchers in pure mathematics usually try to use mathematical reasoning to answer a whole family of questions at once, rather than a particular question.

Constructing your own questions can be an excellent way of deepening your understanding of a topic, because you have to think carefully about what restrictions might apply as well as providing a full solution.

One way to start thinking about new questions is to see whether a problem that you have already met can be extended, or ask yourself what would happen if you changed one aspect of the problem in some way. The next activity challenges you to do this, by using Activity 17 as a starting point.

Activity 18   *Creating your own puzzle*

The question in Activity 17 was based on two kinds of animal, one with two feet and the other with four feet.

(a) Consider the following question.

> There are 6 cats and dogs. The total number of feet is 24. How many cats are there?

Explain why there is no single answer to this question.

(b) Think of a scenario for a new question. For example, you could choose 5 insects (each with 6 legs) and 4 spiders (each with 8 legs).

Calculate how many animals and how many legs (or feet) there are for your example.

Then write down a question. For example: 'There are 9 insects and spiders. The total number of legs is 62. How many insects and how many spiders are there?'

If you like, post your question to the module forum and see if anyone can solve it!

(c) Write down two equations that describe your scenario, and solve them. Check that your answers are correct.

(d) Now try varying the problem. For example, instead of saying how many animals there are, you could say how many eyes there are, or you could vary the body parts from feet and legs, or you could vary the number of kinds of animal. Write down a new question and see if you can solve it.

Some of the most beautiful sangaku puzzles posed complicated geometric questions involving circles, triangles and squares. Often Pythagoras' Theorem was needed to solve them.

If you ever needed convincing that problems can be solved in different ways, then Pythagoras' Theorem is an excellent example, as there are hundreds of different proofs from all over the world. In Unit 8, you saw two of these; one proof (in the text) used similar triangles, and another (in the video) involved rearranging four triangles and calculating areas.

In the next activity, you are asked to construct another proof of Pythagoras' Theorem. This proof uses the same geometric construction as in the Unit 8 video, but then uses some of the algebra that you met in Unit 9 to prove the result, rather than a geometric argument.

Activity 19   *Proving Pythagoras' Theorem*

In this activity you are asked to prove Pythagoras' Theorem for a general right-angled triangle with shorter sides of lengths a and b, and hypotenuse of length c, as shown in Figure 22.

In the following diagram, four identical copies of this triangle are arranged to make a square, $WXYZ$, with sides of length $a + b$. By the symmetry of the situation, the four angles formed by the hypotenuses of the triangles are all equal, so the hypotenuses form a smaller square, $EFGH$, with sides of length c.

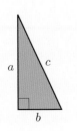

Figure 22   A right-angled triangle

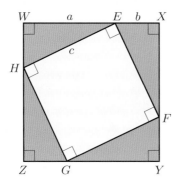

(a) Write down an expression for the area of the large square, $WXYZ$, in terms of a and b.

(b) Write down an expression for the area of triangle WEH, in terms of a and b.

(c) Deduce an expression in terms of a and b for the area of the smaller square, $EFGH$, and simplify it.

(d) Using your answer to part (c), deduce Pythagoras' Theorem.

In Activity 19, you saw that applying some of the algebra that you met in Unit 9 to the geometric construction given in Unit 8 led to a new way to prove Pythagoras' Theorem. Making connections between different mathematical ideas like this is a powerful way to solve problems, as you also saw in the last section.

3.2 Proving results

In Unit 1, you found by looking at some examples that if you add up the first n odd numbers, then the sum always seems to be n^2, and you saw how a geometric argument involving arrays of dots could be developed to prove that this result is true in general. This investigation illustrated some steps that are useful for investigating any number pattern or puzzle. These steps are:

1. Look at some numerical examples first.

2. Spot a pattern.

3. Make a conjecture.

4. Prove your conjecture.

You saw a similar approach with the think-of-a-number puzzles in Unit 5, and with some of the number patterns in Unit 9. Most of the conjectures were proved by using algebra.

The steps above are used in the next example, and again the conjecture is proved by using algebra.

Example 6   *Squaring an odd number*

Investigate what happens when an odd number is squared. Make a conjecture and then prove that your conjecture is true for any odd number.

Solution

💬 Try some numerical examples first. 💬

$1^2 = 1; \quad 3^2 = 9; \quad (-5)^2 = 25; \quad 9^2 = 81.$

💬 Spot a pattern. 💬

All these answers are odd.

💬 Make a conjecture. 💬

A conjecture is: 'The square of an odd number is always odd.'

💬 Prove your conjecture. 💬

Consider any odd number. Since it is not divisible by 2, it is equal to $2n + 1$, for some integer n.

The square of the odd number is $(2n + 1)^2 = 4n^2 + 4n + 1$.

Now $4n^2$ and $4n$ are both even numbers, because 4 is divisible by 2 and n is an integer. Hence $4n^2 + 4n$ is an even number. So the square of the odd number is one more than an even number, so it is an odd number.

This proves the conjecture that the square of an odd number is always odd.

Can you suggest a similar conjecture for the square of an even number?

The algebraic proof in the example above shows that the conjecture holds for *any* odd number, not just for the numerical examples that have been calculated.

Try a similar approach in the following activity.

Activity 20 *Conjecturing and proving*

Consider the following instructions.

- Take any two numbers that sum to 1.
- Square the larger and add the smaller.
- Square the smaller and add the larger.
- Compare the two results – which is larger?

(a) Try some numerical examples first, then make a conjecture.

(b) Let the larger number be x. Write down an expression for the smaller number in terms of x. Prove your conjecture using algebra.

This subsection has highlighted how algebra can be used to prove general results.

3.3 Geometry everywhere

You have already seen several applications of geometry, for example in architecture, surveying, design and navigation. However, there are many more applications of geometry and plenty of discoveries still to be made, and this subsection gives a glimpse of just a few of these.

In the first part of this subsection, you are invited to apply some of the geometric ideas that you have met already to origami – the Japanese art of paper-folding.

Folding squares into triangles

The next two activities pose a challenge: using only the geometric properties of squares and triangles, can you prove that the angles in a triangle made by folding a square in a particular way are certain sizes?

Each of the activities involves a square of paper, which you can make from a rectangular piece, such as A4, in the way shown in Figure 23.

The method for folding a square into a triangle in Activity 21 was designed by Kunihiko Kasahara, a Japanese origami expert who is interested in the relationship between mathematics and origami.

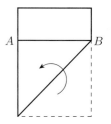

Figure 23 To make a square from a rectangle, fold the rectangle as shown and cut along the line AB.

Activity 21 *Folding a square into a triangle*

Take a square of paper and fold it carefully as shown in the diagrams below. In step 3, you should find that two of the folded-over edges lie in a straight line – this is because you have placed two right angles together. In step 4, you should find that when you fold along this straight line, the corner of the square that was at the top right folds down to lie exactly on the edge of the paper shape. You will see why this happens shortly!

The method used in Activity 21 is given in Franco, B. (1999) *Unfolding mathematics with unit origami*, Emeryville, Key Curriculum Press.

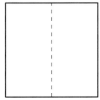 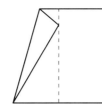  

| 1. Fold in half, crease and unfold | 2. Fold top left corner to centre line | 3. Fold bottom right corner to centre line | 4. Fold top right corner down |

(a) The diagram below shows the folded square after step 2. Suppose that the sides of the square have length 2 units. Write down the lengths of AB and BC. By using a trigonometric ratio, or otherwise, find $\angle ABC$.

The sides of the square have been chosen to have length 2 units, rather than 1 unit, to simplify the arithmetic. You saw a similar approach when the sine, cosine and tangent of special angles were found in Unit 12.

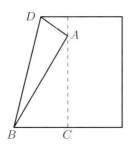

(b) The diagram overleaf shows the folded square after step 3. Use your answer to part (a) to find the angles α, β, γ and δ.

Hint: First find the angle α. To find β, notice that there are two layers of paper between the edges DB and EB, so, since an angle of a square is 90°, it follows that $2(\alpha + \beta) = 90°$.

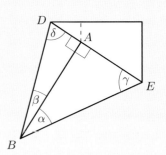

(c) Use the size of one of the angles that you found in part (b) to explain why, when you make the fold in step 4, the corner of the square that was at the top right lies exactly on the edge of the paper shape.

(d) Write down the sizes of the three angles of the final triangle.

You can use the triangle constructed in Activity 21 to measure angles of 45°, 60° and 75°, or any combination of these angles. In fact, you can use it to check your progress in the next activity.

Activity 22 *Folding a square into an equilateral triangle*

(a) What size are the angles in an equilateral triangle?

(b) Take a square of paper. Can you fold it into an equilateral triangle, without using a ruler or protractor? You might find it helpful to look back at Activity 21 to see how you constructed angles of different sizes.

Figure 24 An equilateral triangle larger than the one in the solution to Activity 22

Another interesting question is: Can you fold a square into a larger equilateral triangle than that given in the solution to Activity 22?

You can indeed do this – $\triangle ADE$ in Figure 24 is obtained by rotating $\triangle ABC$ anticlockwise about the bottom left-hand corner of the square and extending the lengths of its three sides, so it is larger than $\triangle ABC$. You might like to think about how you could fold the square into this larger triangle without using a protractor – it is possible!

Applications of geometry

From Activities 21 and 22, you can see that there is a lot of mathematics even in simple paper-folding. Research into the mathematics of origami has shown that there are four mathematical rules that apply to the fold pattern for any origami design. This has resulted in many complicated designs being developed.

Some origami designs have practical applications, especially in situations where it is important to fold items compactly before they are used. For example, in 1995 a large folding solar panel was packed compactly into the shape of a parallelogram and then expanded in space, on a Japanese satellite known as the Space Flyer Unit. The design was based on ideas by Japanese professor Koryo Miura at Tokyo University, who has also designed effective ways of folding maps.

More recently, in 2007, folding techniques were used by engineers at the University of California to develop a very thin optical device to replace the conventional lens in a digital camera, which could then be used in a mobile phone, for example. Another application of origami is in the design of car airbags, so that they can fit within a small space, yet be deployed quickly and effectively when needed.

You may have got the impression from the last few paragraphs that the only people who make new discoveries in geometry, or indeed in mathematics generally, are university academics! However, this isn't the case. In 1975, American housewife Marjorie Rice discovered four previously unknown tiling patterns using pentagons, which are shown in Figure 25. Although she had studied mathematics only at school, she had been inspired to try to find new tiling patterns after reading an article in the magazine *Scientific American*.

The article referred to here is Gardner, M. (1975) 'On tessellating the plane with convex polygon tiles', *Scientific American*, vol. 233, no. 1, pp. 112–17.

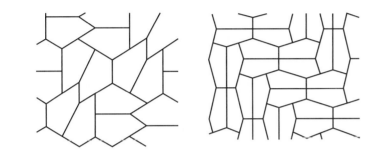

Figure 25   Four new pentagonal tilings discovered by Marjorie Rice

Occasionally new advances are made because someone has come up with a better attempt at solving a long-standing problem. In 1887, Lord Kelvin considered the problem of how to partition space into cells of equal volume in such a way that the area of surface between the cells is as small as possible. This problem has since become known as the *Kelvin problem*. Lord Kelvin suggested that the solution to the problem might be a structure based on a 14-sided polyhedron known as a *truncated octahedron*, as shown in Figure 26. No better structure was found for over a century, until in 1993 two Irish physicists, Denis Weaire and Robert Phelan, discovered a new structure with a smaller area of surface between the cells than in Lord Kelvin's structure. Weaire and Phelan's structure uses two different types of polyhedra, one with 14 sides and the other with 12 sides. It is now thought that Weaire and Phelan's structure is the best possible – in other words, that it is the solution to the Kelvin problem – but at the time of writing, this has not been proved.

There is some information about Lord Kelvin, William Thompson, in Unit 7, Subsection 1.1.

A **polyhedron** is a solid with flat faces.

The architects who designed the Water Cube (Figure 27), the building for the swimming pool used in the 2008 Beijing Olympics, were inspired by Weaire and Phelan's ideas. Despite its name, the building is actually a cuboid, not a cube!

Figure 26   Lord Kelvin's structure

Figure 27   The Water Cube in Beijing, built for the 2008 Olympics

Figure 28   A gömböc
(pronounced 'goemboets',
which is something like
'gumboots')

Another recent geometric discovery is the gömböc. This is a very particular type of solid object that was constructed in 2006 by the Hungarian scientists Gábor Domokos and Péter Várkonyi. The solid is made from a uniformly dense material, but it has the amazing property that whichever way you try to make it balance, it always self-rights itself to a standard position. There are different shapes of gömböc – one example is shown in Figure 28. Some turtle shells have similar properties to gömböcs, which may help the turtles to get back onto their feet when they are turned over!

Geometric discoveries are not just about structures and shapes – whole new geometries have been discovered too.

Some new geometries

In Unit 8 you learned that all of the results that are used in geometry, such as the fact that opposite angles of a parallelogram are equal, can be proved by starting with a small number of initial assumptions about elements of geometry, such as points and lines. The initial assumptions are usually called *axioms* or *postulates*. A suitable list of axioms is set out in Euclid's *Elements*, and the geometry that is developed from them is called *Euclidean geometry*. This is the familiar geometry that you have learned in MU123, and that is generally used in everyday applications.

Euclidean geometry can be two-dimensional – the geometry that you do in a plane – or it can be extended to three dimensions – the geometry that you do in three-dimensional space. (It can even be extended to more dimensions, but the resulting geometries do not apply to 'real-life' space.)

One of Euclid's axioms for two-dimensional geometry is known as the *parallel postulate*, and it is equivalent to the following statement:

> Given a line and a point that does not lie on the line, there is exactly one line through the given point that is parallel to the given line.

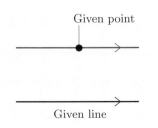

Given point

Given line

Figure 29   Euclid's parallel postulate

Figure 29 shows that this assumption appears to be true – given any line and point on a plane, where the point does not lie on the line, you can draw exactly one line through the given point that does not cross the given line.

In the nineteenth century, mathematicians discovered that it was possible to replace the parallel postulate with either of two different assumptions, with each of these two possibilities leading to a whole new type of geometry that made sense in itself but was very different from Euclidean geometry. As with Euclidean geometry, these new types of geometry can be two-dimensional or three-dimensional (or can be extended to more dimensions).

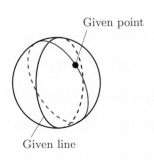

Given point

Given line

Figure 30   Elliptic geometry

In the two-dimensional version of one of these types of geometry, called *elliptic geometry*, the new assumption is that, given a line and a point that does not lie on the line, there are *no* lines through the given point that are parallel to the given line – in other words, *every* line through the given point crosses the given line. This type of geometry can be visualised by thinking of points as the points on a sphere, and lines as the circles of maximum diameter on the sphere – these are called *great circles*. (Another way to think of the great circles is that if you cut down through a great circle you cut the sphere in half.) The great circles are the 'paths of shortest distance' on the sphere, just as straight lines are the paths of shortest distance on a plane. Now if you draw a 'line' (great circle) on the sphere and choose a point not on this 'line', then any 'line' that you draw through the point will cross the original 'line', as illustrated in Figure 30. So there are no 'lines' that pass through the given point that are parallel to the given 'line'.

In the two-dimensional version of the other type of geometry, called *hyperbolic geometry*, the new assumption is that there are at least *two* lines that pass through any given point and are parallel to a given line. One way to visualise this type of geometry is by thinking of a type of surface called a *hyperbolic plane*, in a similar way to the sphere for elliptic geometry. You think of points as the points on the hyperbolic plane, and lines as the paths of shortest distance on the hyperbolic plane. Unfortunately a hyperbolic plane is itself less easy to visualise than a sphere, but one surprising way to gain some insights into this type of surface, and hence into hyperbolic geometry, is by crocheting part of such a surface!

Crochet is a handicraft similar to knitting that involves looping and intertwining yarn with a hooked needle. Figure 31 illustrates a crochet model for part of a hyperbolic plane, with four 'lines' sewn on it. Three of the 'lines' pass through the same point, and they are all parallel to the fourth 'line': they do not cross it because of the way that the surface curves.

Figure 31   Parallel lines on a hyperbolic plane

Some natural objects exhibit some of the properties of hyperbolic planes, and of other types of 'hyperbolic surfaces'. For example, Figure 32 shows the similarities between the edges of a marine flatworm and part of a hyperbolic surface.

(a)

(b)

Figure 32   A marine flatworm and part of a hyperbolic surface

Some crocheted hyperbolic surfaces look very similar to certain types of coral. In 2005, the science writer Margaret Wertheim started an arts project in the USA known as the 'Hyperbolic Crochet Coral Reef' that uses crocheted hyperbolic surfaces. She decided to crochet a giant coral reef to draw attention to the damage done to coral reefs by global warming. This stunning exhibition has now toured all over the world, introducing many people to both hyperbolic geometry and crochet, as well as highlighting the plight of coral reefs. Part of the crochet coral reef is shown in Figure 33, and on the module website there are some links to other websites where you can find out more about it.

A book entitled *Crocheting Adventures with Hyperbolic Planes*, by Dr Daina Taimina, won the Diagram prize for the world's oddest book title in 2010. The prize has been awarded annually by *The Bookseller* magazine since 1978.

Figure 33   Part of the crochet coral reef

So whether you are looking at paper-folding, airbags, crochet or coral reefs, mathematics really is everywhere!

4 Using mathematics practically

An important aspect of mathematics is using it to describe aspects of the world, and solve associated real-life problems. For small problems, you may be able to use an appropriate mathematical technique straightaway. However, as you have seen in the module, in many cases assumptions have to be made to simplify a situation before any mathematics can be applied. Then an appropriate mathematical model is used to describe the situation and obtain results. The results have to be interpreted and checked carefully to ensure that the mathematical model is appropriate. Sometimes, further modifications to the model are then required. This process is summarised in the modelling cycle shown in Figure 34.

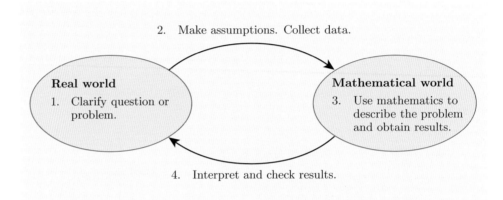

Figure 34   The mathematical modelling cycle

In Unit 2, you saw how this process was used in developing some route-planning software. You have also seen how a similar cycle can be used when carrying out a statistical investigation such as the ESP experiment in Unit 11.

In this section, you'll learn how trigonometric functions can be used in mathematical modelling. These functions are useful for modelling situations that are cyclical, such as circular motion, the heights of the tides or the amount of daylight on different days of the year.

The first subsection considers how the height of a gondola on a ferris wheel changes as the wheel rotates. A gondola on a ferris wheel is a viewing capsule suspended on an axle, which hangs down as the wheel rotates. You will see how a formula for the height of a gondola can be developed, using the trigonometry that you learned in Unit 12 and earlier in this unit. Since the assumptions needed for modelling this situation, and the interpretation of the mathematical results, are relatively straightforward, this subsection concentrates on the mathematical ideas rather than the modelling cycle. The formula developed belongs to a family of trigonometric functions that are related to the sine and cosine functions, and you will explore this family of functions in the next subsection, using Graphplotter. These functions are useful in several modelling situations, and in the final subsection you'll learn how you can apply them and the modelling cycle to predict the height of the tide in certain situations.

Angles are measured in radians rather than degrees throughout this section, as this is usual when trigonometric functions are used for modelling. Remember that a full turn (360°) is the same as 2π radians, so a half-turn (180°) is π radians, a quarter-turn (90°) is $\pi/2$ radians, and so on.

4.1 Modelling the motion of a ferris wheel

Large ferris wheels are popular attractions, as they give open views of the surrounding area as well as being fun to ride on. For example, Figure 35 shows the Big Wheel that was constructed in Centenary Square in Birmingham, UK, in November 2009. As the wheel slowly rotates, the gondolas travel up and then down, and extensive views of the city are visible from gondolas above a certain height.

In this subsection we'll consider the example of a ferris wheel that has a diameter of 60 metres, with the lowest point of the rim 2 metres above the ground. Once all the occupants of the gondolas have embarked, the wheel rotates continuously at a constant speed, taking 20 minutes to make a complete revolution. The best views are visible from gondolas whose points of attachment to the rim of the wheel are 20 metres or more above the ground.

Figure 35 The Big Wheel, Birmingham, UK

Now suppose that you want to know the times when the best views are visible during the 20-minute journey of a gondola from its lowest point and back again.

By looking at the geometry of the wheel, you can work out a formula for the height of the gondola (which you can take to mean the height of its point of attachment) at any time during its circular journey.

Let's begin by working out a formula for the height of the gondola in terms of the angle θ through which it has rotated from its lowest point. Once we've found this formula, we'll use it to find a formula for the height of the gondola in terms of the time since it was at its lowest point.

Figure 36 shows the situation when the gondola has rotated through an angle θ from its lowest point. The point P is the position of the point of attachment of the gondola, and h is its height above the ground in metres.

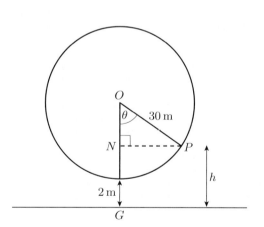

This diagram is not drawn to scale.

Figure 36 The height h of the point P after a rotation through an angle θ

The diagram shows the situation when the angle θ is acute, so h is equal to $OG - ON$.

The distance OG is the radius of the wheel plus the height of its lowest point above the ground. The radius of the wheel is 30 metres, since its diameter is 60 metres, and the lowest point is 2 metres above the ground. Hence

$$OG = 30 + 2 = 32.$$

The distance ON can be found by using a trigonometric ratio in the right-angled triangle OPN, as follows:

$$\cos\theta = \frac{\text{adj}}{\text{hyp}} = \frac{ON}{30},$$

so

$$ON = 30\cos\theta.$$

Hence, when θ is acute,

$$h = OG - ON = 32 - 30\cos\theta.$$

In fact, because of the way that the cosine of an angle is defined, this formula holds for any angle θ, whether it is acute or of any other size. In the next activity you are asked to check that it holds for obtuse angles.

Activity 23   Showing that the formula for h holds when θ is obtuse

The diagram below shows the situation when the angle θ is obtuse. The acute angle between OP and the upward vertical from O is labelled as ϕ.

This diagram is not drawn to scale.

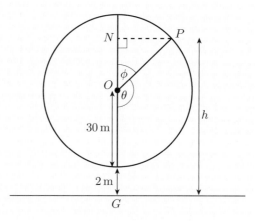

(a) Use this diagram to work out a formula for h in terms of ϕ.

(b) Notice that $\theta = \pi - \phi$. Use the facts about related angles that you learned in Subsection 2.2 to show that $\cos\theta = -\cos\phi$.

(Hint: Use an argument similar to the one that shows that $\tan\theta = -\tan\phi$ on page 202.)

(c) Hence show that the formula found in part (a) is equivalent to the formula $h = 32 - 30\cos\theta$ that was found for acute angles θ.

An argument similar to that in Activity 23, based on related angles, holds for an angle θ of any size.

So we now have a formula for h in terms of θ. However, what we really want is a formula for h in terms of the time t minutes since P was the lowest point on the wheel. Such a formula can be found by working out how θ is related to t.

The wheel rotates through 2π radians every 20 minutes. So in 1 minute it rotates through

$$\frac{2\pi}{20} = \frac{\pi}{10} = 0.314 \text{ radians (to 3 s.f.)},$$

and hence in t minutes it rotates through $0.314t$ radians.

So, t minutes after the point P was the lowest point on the wheel, it has rotated through an angle of $\theta = 0.314t$ radians, and therefore its height h metres is given by

$$h = 32 - 30\cos(0.314t).$$

This is the formula for h in terms of t that we wanted.

Now that you have this formula, you can find the times for which the best views are visible. These views are visible when the height is greater than or equal to 20 metres, so one way to find the times is to draw the graph of h against t and read off the values of t for which $h \geq 20$. In the next activity you are asked to use Graphplotter to do this.

 Graphplotter

Activity 24 *Finding the times during which the best views are visible*

Use Graphplotter, with the 'Two graphs' tab selected. On the Options page, ensure that 'Grid', 'Axes', 'Trace' and 'Radians' are all ticked. Choose the equations $y = a\cos(b(x - c)) + d$ and $y = mx + c$ from the two drop-down lists.

(a) Enter the appropriate values for the constants a, b, c and d, and then m and c, so that the graphs of the equations $y = 32 - 30\cos(0.314x)$ and $y = 20$ are plotted. Set the minimum and maximum values on the x-axis to 0 and 20, respectively, by entering these numbers into the x min and x max boxes at the bottom right of Graphplotter. Set the minimum and maximum values on the y-axis to suitable numbers.

(b) Hence find the times, after the gondola is at its lowest point, when the best views become visible and when they cease to be visible. Give your answers to the nearest minute.

An alternative way to find the times for which the best views are visible is to use the methods for solving trigonometric equations from Section 2 to find the values of t for which $h = 20$. That is, you have to find the solutions of the equation

$$32 - 30\cos(0.314t) = 20.$$

To do this, you can first rearrange the equation as follows:

$$12 - 30\cos(0.314t) = 0$$
$$30\cos(0.314t) = 12$$
$$\cos(0.314t) = 0.4.$$

Then you can use the methods for solving trigonometric equations to find the values of θ (in radians) between 0 and 2π for which $\cos\theta = 0.4$. In fact, you were asked to do this in Activity 15(c) on page 205 – the values are

$$\theta = 1.1592\ldots \quad \text{and} \quad \theta = 2\pi - 1.1592\ldots = 5.1239\ldots.$$

This means that the required values of t are given by

$$0.314t = 1.1592\ldots \quad \text{and} \quad 0.314t = 5.1239\ldots.$$

These equations give

$$t = \frac{1.1592\ldots}{0.314} = 3.6919\ldots = 4 \text{ (to the nearest whole number)}$$

and

$$t = \frac{5.1239\ldots}{0.314} = 16.3181\ldots = 16 \text{ (to the nearest whole number)}.$$

You need to find the values of θ between 0 and 2π because θ is the angle of rotation and you are interested in the times when the best views are visible during one rotation of the wheel. These times will correspond to angles of rotation between 0 and 2π.

So, as you should have found in the solution to Activity 24, the best views become visible approximately 4 minutes after the gondola was at its lowest point, and cease to be visible approximately 16 minutes after the gondola was at its lowest point.

In Activity 24 you were asked to plot the height of the gondola for one complete revolution of the ferris wheel. If you plot the height for a longer period of time, then you obtain a graph like the one in Figure 37.

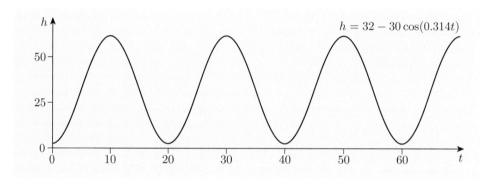

Figure 37   The height h metres of the gondola plotted against the time t minutes after it is at its lowest point

The graph in Figure 37 appears to have a shape similar to that of a sine or cosine curve, but it lies at a different position on the axes and it is stretched horizontally and vertically. A curve that can be obtained from the graph of the sine function by shifting, stretching or compressing it horizontally or vertically is called a **sinusoidal curve**, and a function whose graph is a sinusoidal curve is called a **sinusoidal function**.

4.2   Exploring sinusoidal functions

In this subsection you will explore the graphs of equations of the form

$$y = a \sin(b(x - c)) + d \quad \text{and} \quad y = a \cos(b(x - c)) + d,$$

where a, b, c and d are constants. Functions with rules of these forms where a and b are non-zero are called **general sine functions** and **general cosine functions**, respectively, and you will see that they are always sinusoidal functions. In the next activity, you'll see how the values of the constants a, b, c and d affect the shapes of the graphs of these equations.

The y-value of any sinusoidal function *oscillates* between a minimum value and a maximum value, and the shape of the graph is continually repeated. The length on the x-axis that it takes for the graph to repeat is called the **period** of the graph, as you saw in Unit 12. Any section of the graph covering this length on the x-axis is referred to as an **oscillation** or *cycle*, as illustrated in Figure 38.

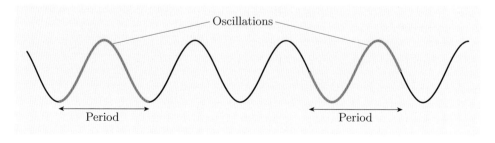

Figure 38   Oscillations of a sinusoidal function

Graphplotter

Activity 25 *Exploring the graphs of general sine and cosine functions*

Use Graphplotter, with the 'One graph' tab selected. On the Options page ensure that 'Grid', 'Axes' and 'Radians' are all ticked, and the other options are not ticked.

Choose the function $y = a\sin(b(x - c)) + d$ from the drop-down list. The default values of the constants are $a = 1$, $b = 1$, $c = 0$ and $d = 0$, so you should see the graph of $y = \sin x$.

Choosing the function also has the effect of setting the x-axis to the interval from -2π to 2π, which is about -6.3 to 6.3. Set $x\,\text{min} = 0$, so that the x-axis is set to the interval from 0 to 2π instead; then you will see one complete oscillation.

(a) Set $y\,\text{min}$ and $y\,\text{max}$ to -5 and 5, respectively. Use the slider to change the value of a, and note the effect on the graph. What do you notice about the value of a and the minimum and maximum values of y?

What happens if you change the value of a to its negative (for example, from 2 to -2)?

(b) Set $a = 1$, so you see the graph of $y = \sin x$ again. Then change the value of b to 2, 3 and 4 in turn. For each of these values, count how many complete oscillations there are in the interval from 0 to 2π.

Can you make a conjecture about the value of b and the number of oscillations in this interval, if b is a positive integer? Check your conjecture by trying another value of b. Does your conjecture hold for fractional values of b, such as 2.5?

What happens if b is negative? In particular, what happens if you change the value of b to its negative?

(c) Set $b = 1$, so you see the graph of $y = \sin x$ again. Also set $x\,\text{min} = -6.3$, so that the x-axis is set to the interval -2π to 2π again (approximately).

Use the slider to increase and decrease the value of c. Notice that the graph appears to move to the right if c is increased, and to the left if c is decreased.

To investigate the relationship between the graphs of $y = \sin x$ and $y = \sin(x - c)$, first tick the 'Trace' option and set $c = 0$. Then concentrate on the point on the curve that is at the origin when $c = 0$, and find the coordinates of the position that this point moves to when you choose a new value of c. Start by choosing small values for c, such as 0.1, 0.2, 0.3 and their negatives, typing the values into the box rather than using the slider.

What do you think is the relationship between the graphs of $y = \sin x$ and $y = \sin(x - c)$?

(d) Set $c = 0$, so you see the graph of $y = \sin x$ again. What do you think would be the effect on the graph of changing the value of d? Untick 'Trace' on the Options page and tick 'y-intercept' instead. Then use the slider to vary d, to see if your prediction is correct.

(e) Now select the equation $y = a\cos(b(x - c)) + d$ from the drop-down list. Vary the constants a, b, c and d in the same way as you did for the general sine function. How does the graph change?

When you have completed your investigation, read the comments on this activity at the end of the unit.

In Activity 25, you looked at the graphs of general sine and cosine functions, which have equations of the form

$$y = a\sin(b(x-c)) + d \quad \text{and} \quad y = a\cos(b(x-c)) + d. \tag{7}$$

The effects that you saw when you varied the values of a, b, c and d might have been familiar to you from your investigations of other functions, such as quadratic functions. For example, if you replace the variable x in the equation of any function by the expression $x - c$, where c is a constant, then the graph of the function moves right by distance c (the graph moves left if c is negative).

Similarly, if you replace x by bx, where b is a constant, then the graph is compressed or stretched in the x-direction. For a general sine or cosine function, this changes the number of oscillations within a given interval. You saw in the activity that if the constant b in either of equations (7) is positive, then the number of oscillations in the interval from 0 to 2π seems to be b, and if b is negative, then the number of oscillations seems to be the magnitude of b.

This finding can be stated concisely by using notation for the magnitude of a number. In general, the magnitude of any number x is denoted by $|x|$. So, for example, $|-5| = 5$ and $|2| = 2$. So the activity seemed to show that the number of oscillations in the interval from 0 to 2π is $|b|$.

Another way to think of this finding is in terms of the *period* of the graph, that is, the length along the x-axis that the graph takes to repeat. The period of a general sine or cosine graph can be worked out by dividing the length of a given interval on the horizontal axis by the number of oscillations in that interval. For example, in Figure 39 there are two oscillations in the interval from 0 to 2π, so the period of this graph is $2\pi/2 = \pi$. So another way of stating the finding about b is that the period of the graph seems to be $2\pi/|b|$. This finding is indeed true in general, as stated below.

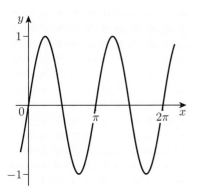

Figure 39 The graph of the equation $y = \sin(2x)$

The period of a general sine or cosine function

The period of $y = a\sin(b(x-c)) + d$ or $y = a\cos(b(x-c)) + d$ is $\dfrac{2\pi}{|b|}$.

To see why this result holds, first notice that the period of $y = a\sin(b(x-c)) + d$ or $y = a\cos(b(x-c)) + d$ is the same as the period of $y = \sin(bx)$, since either of the former graphs is obtained from the latter by shifting it horizontally and vertically, and/or stretching or compressing it vertically. (The cosine curve can be obtained from the sine curve by shifting it along the x-axis.)

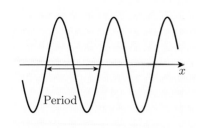

Figure 40 The graph of an equation of the form $y = \sin(bx)$

You can find the period of the graph of $y = \sin(bx)$ by considering where it crosses the x-axis. As illustrated in Figure 40, the period is twice the distance between any two consecutive x-intercepts. The x-intercepts are the solutions of the equation $\sin(bx) = 0$. Now $\sin\theta = 0$ whenever θ is a multiple of π (that is, 180°), so $\sin(bx) = 0$ whenever bx is a multiple of π. So one pair of consecutive x-intercepts is given by

$$bx = 0 \quad \text{and} \quad bx = \pi,$$

that is, $x = 0$ and $x = \pi/b$. The second of these x-intercepts could be either larger or smaller than the first, depending on whether b is positive or negative, but in either case the distance between the two x-intercepts is $\pi/|b|$, so the period is $2\pi/|b|$, as stated in the pink box.

To illustrate this result, consider the equation $y = \sin(3(x+1))$. The value of the constant b is 3, so the graph of this equation has period $2\pi/3$.

Activity 26 *Finding the periods of general sine and cosine functions*

Find the periods of the graphs of the following equations.

(a) $y = \sin 4x$ (b) $y = 3\sin 5x - 2$ (c) $y = \cos\dfrac{x}{2} - 1$

(d) $y = 2\cos(-x)$

Before going on, let's check that the formula for the period works for the ferris wheel example that you met earlier. The formula that was worked out for the height of a gondola was $h = 32 - 30\cos(0.314t)$. This equation is of the form $y = a\sin(b(x-c)) + d$, with $b = 0.314$ (and x and y replaced by t and h, respectively), so the period of the graph is

$$\frac{2\pi}{0.314} = 20.01 \text{ (to 2 d.p.)}.$$

The variable t is measured in minutes, so this means that the values for the height repeat every 20.01 minutes, approximately. This is as expected, because the model was based on the assumption that the time for a complete revolution of the wheel is 20 minutes. The slight discrepancy arises from the rounding that was done when the formula was worked out.

You have seen that general sine functions and general cosine functions give exactly the same family of graphs, namely the sinusoidal curves. Because of this, the remainder of this subsection will concentrate on general sine functions, that is, functions with rules of the form

$$y = a\sin(b(x-c)) + d. \tag{8}$$

Also, exactly the same family of graphs is obtained if the constants a and b in equation (8) are allowed to take only *positive* values, instead of either positive or negative values. This is because the effect obtained by changing the value of a or b to its negative can also be obtained by just shifting the graph horizontally, by changing the value of c. So, from now on, this subsection will concentrate on equations of form (8) where a and b are *positive*.

Each of the constants a, b, c and d in equation (8) relates to a key feature of the graph of the equation, as illustrated in Figure 41 below and explained in the box overleaf.

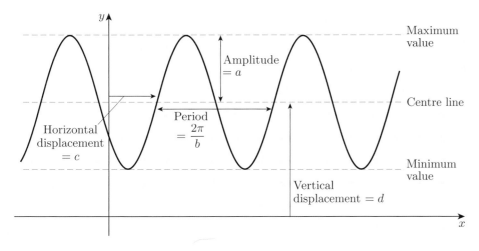

Figure 41 The graph of a general sine function

The graph of a general sine function

The graph of the equation

$$y = a\sin(b(x - c)) + d,$$

where a and b are positive, and c and d can take any values, has the following features.

- a is the **amplitude**: the distance between the centre line and the maximum (or minimum) value.
- b determines the *period*, which is equal to $2\pi/b$.
- c is the **horizontal displacement**: the amount that the graph of $y = a\sin(bx) + d$ is shifted to the right to obtain the graph of $y = a\sin(b(x - c)) + d$. (The shift is to the left if c is negative.)
- d is the **vertical displacement**: the amount that the centre line is shifted up from the x-axis. (The shift is down if d is negative.)

Also,

- the minimum value is $d - a$ (the vertical displacement minus the amplitude)
- the maximum value is $d + a$ (the vertical displacement plus the amplitude).

The following example illustrates how you can sketch the graph of a general sine function.

Example 7   *Sketching the graph of a general sine function*

Sketch the graph of the equation

$$y = 4\sin(2x - 1) + 1.5.$$

Solution

☁ Make sure that the equation is in the form of the general equation. ☁

Factorising part of the given equation gives

$$y = 4\sin(2(x - 0.5)) + 1.5.$$

☁ Find the values of a, b, c and d, and use them to find the features of the graph. ☁

Here $a = 4$, $b = 2$, $c = 0.5$ and $d = 1.5$. So

amplitude $= 4$,
period $= 2\pi/2 = \pi \approx 3.14$,
horizontal displacement $= 0.5$,
vertical displacement $= 1.5$,
minimum value $= 1.5 - 4 = -2.5$,
maximum value $= 1.5 + 4 = 5.5$.

💭 Choose suitable axis limits. The x-axis should include a few period lengths, so choose, say, -4 to 8. The y-axis should include the minimum and maximum values, so choose, say, -3 to 6.

Mark the centre line, minimum and maximum as dashed lines.

Mark the point on the centre line that is the distance of the horizontal displacement, which is 0.5, to the right of the y-axis (it would be to the left if the horizontal displacement were negative). Mark other points on the centre line at intervals of a period length, which is approximately 3.14. 💭

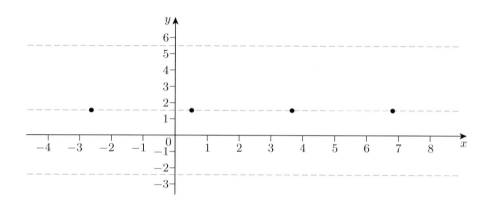

The points marked on the centre line have the following x-coordinates:

$0.5 - 3.14 = -2.64,$

$0.5,$

$0.5 + 3.14 = 3.64,$

$0.5 + 2 \times 3.14 = 6.78.$

💭 Draw an oscillation between each pair of marked points. The graph goes up and then down to the right of each marked point (since a and b are positive). 💭

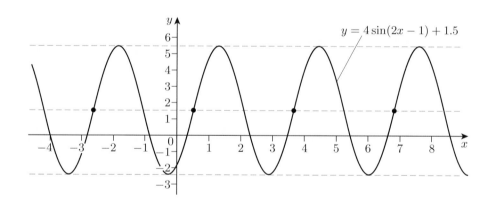

$y = 4\sin(2x - 1) + 1.5$

Here is a similar activity for you to try.

Activity 27   *Sketching the graphs of general sine functions*

Sketch the graphs of the following equations.

(a) $y = \sin 3x$ (b) $y = \sin(x + 2)$ (c) $y = 2\sin(x - 1.5) - 1$

Hint: In part (b), remember that $x + 2$ is the same as $x - (-2)$.

Figure 42 A harbour tide gauge

4.3 Modelling the tides

In the video for Unit 12, you saw how the height of the tide varies both throughout the day and throughout the year. The physical model developed to predict the tide heights didn't take account of factors such as weather conditions (which can affect tide heights), but nevertheless the model proved very useful for producing tide tables. Knowing the height of the tide at different times is important so that people on the coast or at sea can plan their activities safely. For example, when navigating a ship or boat into a harbour, it is important to check that the water is deep enough so that the vessel does not run aground. For small boats, knowing when the tide is high can also make loading and unloading cargo easier. Checking the time for the high tide before you embark on a coastal walk may prevent you becoming stranded too!

Tide tables showing the high and low tides are published in newspapers and are available on the internet, but knowing the height of the tide at other times is often important too. For example, if you plan to walk out to an island that gets cut off by the sea, then you will need to know the times when the tide is low enough for the island to be accessible by foot, not just when the high tide occurs.

So if you know the times of the high and low tides at a particular location on a particular day, is it possible to develop a simple mathematical model to predict the height of the tide at other times during the day?

To illustrate how trigonometry and the modelling cycle can be used to help to answer this type of question, let's consider a particular example, namely:

> What was the height of the tide at different times of the day on 14 December 2009 at Milford Haven in South Wales?

The next step in the modelling cycle, after posing the question, is to collect relevant data and to make some assumptions so that the situation can be described mathematically.

A tide table for Milford Haven gave the information shown in Table 3.

Table 3 High and low tides in Milford Haven on 14 December 2009

Time	Type	Height (metres)
04:21	High	6.2
10:42	Low	1.7
16:45	High	6.2
23:06	Low	1.6

Source: Tide tables on the BBC Weather website at www.bbc.co.uk/weather/coast/tides

Over a day, the height of the tide rises and falls twice. The cyclical nature of these changes suggests that it may be possible to use a general sine function as a model. So a useful assumption to make is that the height of the tide, over the 24 hours of 14 December 2009, can be modelled by a function of the form $h = a \sin(b(t - c)) + d$, where t is the time since midnight in hours and h is the height of the tide in metres.

Now that the data have been collected and the assumptions have been made, the next step in the modelling cycle is to sort out the mathematics; that is, we need to decide on the values for a, b, c and d, and then use this model to make predictions. The values of a, b, c and d should be chosen to fit the data in the tide table, at least approximately, and you can do this by using what you have learned about how the features of the graph of a general sine function correspond to the values of the constants in the equation.

The constant a in the equation of a general sine function is the amplitude, which is half the distance between the minimum and maximum values. So you can choose an appropriate value for a by first choosing appropriate values for the minimum and maximum values. Each of the high tides in Table 3 has a height of 6.2 metres, so the maximum value should be chosen to be 6.2. However, the low tides have different values: 1.7 metres and 1.6 metres. So either of the values 1.7 or 1.6, or their average, could be chosen to be the minimum value. However, since the first low tide occurs close to the middle of the time period for which the model is intended to apply, it is best to choose the minimum value to be the height in metres of this low tide, which is 1.7. This gives the difference between the minimum and maximum values as $6.2 - 1.7 = 4.5$. So the amplitude a should be chosen to be $\frac{1}{2} \times 4.5 = 2.25$.

Since the amplitude is 2.25 and the minimum value is 1.7, the vertical displacement d must be $1.7 + 2.25 = 3.95$, as shown in Figure 43.

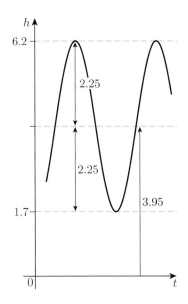

Figure 43 The vertical displacement chosen for the model

An appropriate value for the constant b can be chosen by first choosing an appropriate value for the period, the length along the horizontal axis that the graph takes to repeat itself. This is the same as the length between any two consecutive minimum values, or between any two consecutive maximum values. In this model the variable on the horizontal axis, t, represents time, so the period will be a time. The data in Table 3 show that the time between the two high tides is the same as the time between the two low tides – it is 12 hours and 24 minutes in each case – so the period should be chosen to be this time. Before this time is used to calculate the value of b, it has to be converted from hours and minutes to hours in decimal form. The time is $\left(12 + \frac{24}{60}\right)$ hours, which is 12.4 hours in decimal form. Hence

$$\frac{2\pi}{b} = 12.4, \quad \text{so} \quad b = \frac{2\pi}{12.4} = 0.507 \text{ (to 3 s.f.)}.$$

An appropriate value for the constant c, which is the horizontal displacement, can be chosen by first choosing an appropriate value for the time at which the first maximum value occurs. This should be chosen to be the time of the first high tide, which is 04:21, or 4.35 hours when converted to hours in decimal form. Figure 44 shows that, for any sinusoidal function (with the variable on the horizontal axis representing time), the horizontal displacement can be found by subtracting one quarter of the period from the time when the first maximum value occurs. In this case, the period is 12.4 hours, so one quarter of the period is $12.4/4 = 3.1$ hours. So the horizontal displacement c should be chosen to be

$$4.35 - 3.1 = 1.25.$$

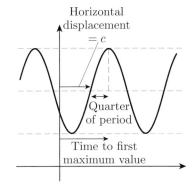

Figure 44 A maximum value occurs a quarter of a period after the horizontal displacement

Now that suitable values of a, b, c, and d have been determined, the equation of the model can be written down as

$$h = 2.25 \sin(0.507(t - 1.25)) + 3.95,$$

where t is the time since midnight in hours and h is the height of the tide in metres.

This equation can be used to predict the height of the tide at a particular time, or to predict the times at which the tide is a particular height. In the next activity, you are asked to use the model and then interpret your results. This interpretation is part of the fourth stage of the modelling cycle.

Graphplotter

Activity 28   *Predicting the height of the tide*

Use Graphplotter, ensuring that 'Trace' and 'Radians' are ticked on the Options page. Choose the function $y = a\sin(b(x - c)) + d$ from the drop-down list, and set a, b, c and d to 2.25, 0.507, 1.25 and 3.95, respectively. Set $x\min = 0$, $x\max = 24$, $y\min = 0$ and $y\max = 10$.

(a) Enter the value 4.35, which is the time in hours (in decimal form) of one of the high tides, into the x cursor box, and read off the corresponding y-coordinate of the curve. Check that it corresponds to the height of the high tide given in Table 3.

(b) Use the model to predict the times for which the tide is deeper than 4 metres. Give your answers in hours to one decimal place.

The other part of the fourth stage of the modelling cycle is to check the model against reality. Scientists at the United Kingdom Hydrographic Office (UKHO) have developed a computer model that accurately predicts the heights of the tide throughout the day. It takes into account the gravitational effects of the Sun and the Moon, and also uses data that have been collected by tide gauges at various locations on the coast.

The graph in Figure 45 shows the heights of the tide predicted by the UKHO for Milford Haven on 14 December 2009, with the sinusoidal model found in this subsection superimposed in red.

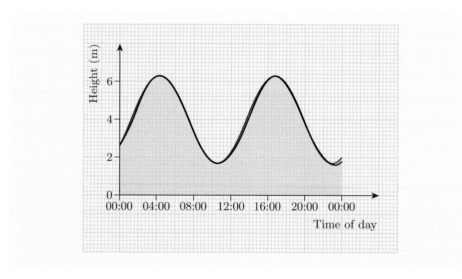

Figure 45   The heights of the tide at Milford Haven on 14 December 2009, with the sinusoidal model found in this subsection superimposed in red

You can see that the sinusoidal model is a close fit to the predictions made by the UKHO, so it is a good model for the height of the tide at Milford Haven on this particular day.

However, the sinusoidal model is not realistic over a longer period of time, such as a year. No single sinusoidal model for the heights of a tide can be realistic over a time period longer than a few days, because the heights of the high and low tides vary, as illustrated in Figure 46. Many other factors need to be taken into account in order to get a realistic long-term model, as you saw in the video for Unit 12.

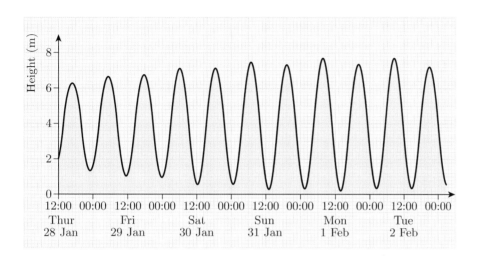

Figure 46   The variation in the height of a tide over several days

In fact, often the heights of the tide cannot be modelled by a sinusoidal function even over a single day. Figure 47 shows the heights of the tide at the entrance of the River Tees in the north-east of England on 11 December 2009. You can see that there is a difference of 0.6 metres between the two low tides, so a model based on a single sinusoidal function will not be accurate in this case.

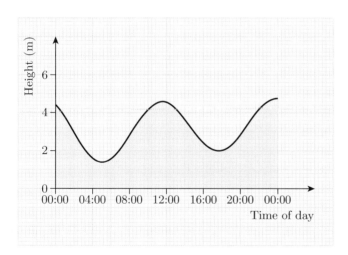

Figure 47   The heights of the tide at the entrance to the River Tees on 11 December 2009

In general, a sinusoidal function will provide a reasonably accurate model for the heights of a tide over a single day, provided that the heights of the two high tides are similar and the heights of the two low tides are also similar.

Your mathematical journey

This final unit of the module has touched briefly on some of the important aspects of your mathematical journey through MU123, highlighting just a few of the many ideas that you have studied. You have also developed some new skills in trigonometry and have seen how some of these can be used in modelling some real-life situations.

With the mathematical techniques that you have learned and the problem-solving skills that you have developed during MU123, you should now be well equipped to use mathematics for many different applications, both in your everyday life and in further studies.

We hope that the module has helped you to enjoy some of the beauty, power and fascination of mathematics, and convinced you to continue on your mathematical journey! If you would like to do this straightaway, then have a look at the links to popular mathematics books and other resources in the Resources section for Unit 14 on the module website. There are links to further modules that you can do in the 'What next?' section in the final week of the study planner.

Learning checklist

After studying this unit, you should be able to:

- understand how the probability of an event happening can be measured
- interpret newspaper articles on risk
- use a variety of ways for solving equations
- find the sine, cosine and tangent of angles measured in degrees and radians
- solve trigonometric equations for angles between $0°$ and $360°$
- use algebra to obtain and prove results
- describe the graph of $y = a\sin(b(x - c)) + d$ for different values of a, b, c and d
- understand the terms amplitude, period, horizontal displacement and vertical displacement
- appreciate the use of trigonometry in models.

Solutions and comments on Activities

Activity 1

The total number of babies is $377 + 367 = 744$. So the percentage of girls is

$$\frac{377}{744} = 0.506\ldots \approx 51\%.$$

This may not be an accurate estimate for the probability of having a girl in the country where the hospital is, as it is unlikely that the sample of births is representative of the whole country. A larger dataset of randomly chosen births throughout the country would give a better estimate.

Activity 2

The probability that the asteroid will collide with the Earth is

$$0.0004\% = \frac{0.0004}{100} = \frac{4}{1\,000\,000},$$

which is 4 in 1 million.

Activity 3

You need to know the probability (as a number) that a person in the general population who does not use a mobile phone will develop mouth cancer. You also need to know how many hours of mobile phone use per day caused the apparent increase in that risk. Other factors to consider are how many days the phone is used on, and perhaps the age and gender of the user.

Activity 4

(a) The risk of getting monkeypox for people who do not eat bananas is 1 in 20. So out of 1000 people who do not eat bananas, the approximate number that you would expect to get monkeypox is

$$1000 \times \frac{1}{20} = 50.$$

(b) The risk of getting monkeypox for people who eat bananas regularly is 1.25 in 20. So out of 1000 people who eat bananas regularly, the approximate number that you would expect to get monkeypox is

$$1000 \times \frac{1.25}{20} = 62.5 \approx 63.$$

(c) The answers to parts (a) and (b) tell you that for a group of 1000 people who eat bananas regularly, you would expect 50 people to get monkeypox anyway, and about 13 more to get monkeypox due to eating bananas. So, on average, eating bananas makes a difference to 13 people out of 1000.

Activity 5

(a) A superficial glance at the pair of graphs might lead you to think that the growth in the number of telephone lines, shown in the left-hand graph, is greater than the growth in the number of mobile phone subscribers, shown in the right-hand graph.

This impression is caused by the different vertical scales on the two graphs.

(b) Scaling up the 1997 picture by a scale factor of 15 to give the 2007 picture creates a misleading impression of the relative sizes of the two numbers of mobile phone subscribers depicted. This is because although the number of subscribers in 2007 is about 15 times the number in 1997, far more than 15 copies of the 1997 picture would fit inside the 2007 picture, giving the impression that the growth in the number of mobile phone subscribers is much greater than it actually is.

(In fact, from what you saw in Unit 8, the number of copies of the 1997 picture that would fit inside the 2007 picture is about $15^2 = 225$.)

Pictograms can be misleading if it is not clear whether the lengths, areas or volumes of the pictures are being compared.

Activity 6

(a) Your reflections are obviously personal, but things to watch out for are:

- clearly explained solutions rather than a string of calculations
- carefully constructed graphs, with clear titles and scales that are easy to read
- correct use of notation and vocabulary
- logically structured arguments
- appropriate rounding.

(b) You might like to write these points directly on the assignment as a reminder for when you start working on the questions, or as a check on any questions that you have already completed.

Activity 7

(a) The equation is

$$(x-3)(x+2) = 2.$$

You can solve it graphically by plotting the graphs of $y = (x-3)(x+2)$ and $y = 2$ on Graphplotter, and finding the x-coordinates of the crossing points.

You can plot the graph of $y = (x - 3)(x + 2)$ by choosing Custom function, and typing $(x-3)*(x+2)$ into the box. (Alternatively you can multiply out the brackets, which gives $y = x^2 - x - 6$, choose the equation $y = ax^2 + bx + c$, and set the values of a, b and c appropriately.)

The resulting graph is shown below.

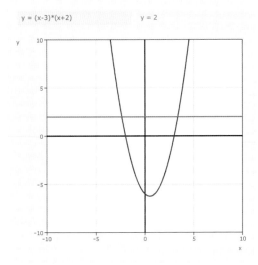

You can use the procedure described before the activity to find that the two solutions are $x = 3.37$ and $x = -2.37$ (both to 2 d.p.).

(b) The equation is
$$(x - 3)(x + 2) = 2.$$
It can be solved algebraically as follows.

Expand the brackets:
$$x^2 - 3x + 2x - 6 = 2.$$
Collect the terms all on one side:
$$x^2 - x - 8 = 0.$$
The expression on the LHS does not factorise easily, so we use the quadratic formula, which states that the solutions of the quadratic equation $ax^2 + bx + c = 0$ are given by
$$x = \frac{-b \pm \sqrt{b^2 - 4ac}}{2a}.$$
Here $a = 1$, $b = -1$ and $c = -8$, so
$$x = \frac{-(-1) \pm \sqrt{(-1)^2 - 4 \times 1 \times (-8)}}{2 \times 1}$$
$$= \frac{1 \pm \sqrt{33}}{2}.$$
Hence the solutions are
$$x = \frac{1 + \sqrt{33}}{2} \quad \text{and} \quad x = \frac{1 - \sqrt{33}}{2},$$
which are $x = 3.37$ and $x = -2.37$ (both to 2 d.p.).

These are the same values as found in part (a).

Activity 8

(a) The graphs of $y = 2x + 3$ and $y = x^2 - 2x + 1$ are shown below.

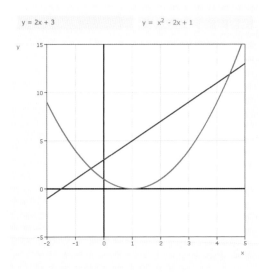

To find the coordinates of the crossing points, zoom in on each crossing point in turn, until both the x- and y-coordinates are displayed to at least three decimal places.

For the left-hand crossing point, you can find a point below the crossing point, and a point above the crossing point, that both have coordinates $(-0.45, 2.10)$ when rounded to two decimal places. So these are the coordinates of this crossing point.

Similarly, for the right-hand crossing point, you can find a point below the crossing point, and a point above the crossing point, that both have coordinates $(4.45, 11.90)$ when rounded to two decimal places. So these are the coordinates of this crossing point.

(b) The coordinates of a crossing point are values of x and y that satisfy both equations. That is, they form a solution of both equations simultaneously.

(So the solutions of the simultaneous equations are $x = -0.45$, $y = 2.10$ and $x = 4.45$, $y = 11.90$, to two decimal places.)

Activity 9

The equations are
$$y = x + 1, \tag{9}$$
$$y = x^2 + 2x - 5. \tag{10}$$
The right-hand sides are equal, which gives
$$x + 1 = x^2 + 2x - 5.$$
Simplify:
$$0 = x^2 + x - 6.$$
Factorise:
$$0 = (x + 3)(x - 2).$$

Hence $x = -3$ or $x = 2$. Substituting these values, in turn, into equation (9) gives $y = -2$ and $y = 3$, respectively. So the solutions are

$$x = -3, \ y = -2 \quad \text{and} \quad x = 2, \ y = 3.$$

(Check: Substituting $x = -3$, $y = -2$ into equation (10) gives

$$\text{RHS} = (-3)^2 + 2 \times (-3) - 5 = 9 - 6 - 5 = -2$$
$$= \text{LHS},$$

and substituting $x = 2$, $y = 3$ into the same equation gives

$$\text{RHS} = 2^2 + 2 \times 2 - 5 = 4 + 4 - 5 = 3 = \text{LHS}.)$$

Activity 10

Equations (a) and (b) are in a suitable form for cross-multiplying. (The right-hand side of equation (b) can be thought of as a fraction with denominator 1.)

(a) The equation is

$$\frac{x}{x+1} = \frac{2}{x+3}.$$

Assume that $x \neq -1$ and $x \neq -3$.

Cross-multiply:

$$x(x+3) = 2(x+1).$$

So $x^2 + 3x = 2x + 2$,

and hence $x^2 + x - 2 = 0$.

Factorise:

$$(x+2)(x-1) = 0.$$

So $x + 2 = 0$ or $x - 1 = 0$,

and hence $x = -2$ or $x = 1$.

These answers satisfy the initial assumptions $x \neq -1$ and $x \neq -3$, so the solutions are $x = -2$ and $x = 1$.

(b) The equation is $\dfrac{x}{x+1} = 2$.

Assume that $x \neq -1$.

Cross-multiply:

$$x = 2(x+1)$$

$$x = 2x + 2$$

$$x = -2.$$

This answer satisfies the initial assumption, so the solution is $x = -2$.

(You can cross-multiply in the equation here because the right-hand side can be thought of as the fraction 2/1. However, because the equation is fairly simple, cross-multiplying isn't really any quicker than just multiplying both sides by the denominator $x + 1$.)

(c) The equation is $\dfrac{x}{x+1} = \dfrac{2}{x} + 3$.

Assume that $x \neq -1$ and $x \neq 0$.

Cross-multiplying cannot be used, so use the usual method of multiplying both sides by an expression that is a multiple of all the denominators.

Multiply by $x(x+1)$:

$$x(x+1)\left(\frac{x}{x+1}\right) = x(x+1)\left(\frac{2}{x} + 3\right)$$

Simplify:

$$x^2 = 2(x+1) + 3x(x+1)$$

$$x^2 = 2x + 2 + 3x^2 + 3x$$

$$0 = 2x^2 + 5x + 2$$

Factorise:

$$0 = (2x+1)(x+2).$$

Hence $2x + 1 = 0$ or $x + 2 = 0$.

So $x = -\frac{1}{2}$ or $x = -2$.

These answers satisfy the initial assumptions, so the solutions are $x = -\frac{1}{2}$ and $x = -2$.

Activity 11

(a) The point R corresponds to the angle

$$180° + 25° = 205°.$$

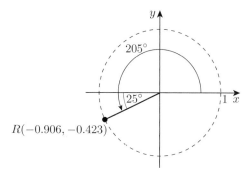

The point S corresponds to the angle

$$360° - 25° = 335°.$$

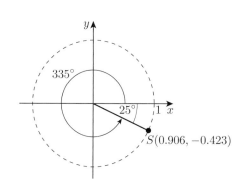

(b) The coordinates of R are

$(-0.906, -0.423)$.

The coordinates of S are

$(0.906, -0.423)$.

Both pairs of coordinates are given to three significant figures.

(c) The sine, cosine and tangent of the angle corresponding to R are

$\sin(205°) \approx -0.423, \quad \cos(205°) \approx -0.906$

and

$\tan(205°) = \dfrac{-0.422\,61\ldots}{-0.906\,30\ldots} \approx 0.466.$

Similarly, the sine, cosine and tangent of the angle corresponding to S are

$\sin(335°) \approx -0.423, \quad \cos(335°) \approx 0.906$

and

$\tan(335°) = \dfrac{-0.422\,61\ldots}{0.906\,30\ldots} \approx -0.466.$

All these values are given to three significant figures.

Activity 12

(a) The equation is

$\sin\theta = 0.2.$

The sine of θ is positive, so θ is a first- or second-quadrant angle.

One solution is

$\theta = \sin^{-1}(0.2) = 12°$ (to the nearest degree).

The other solution is

$\theta = 180° - 12° = 168°$ (to the nearest degree).

(Check: A calculator gives

$\sin 12° = 0.207\ldots \approx 0.2,$

$\sin 168° = 0.207\ldots \approx 0.2.$)

(b) The equation is

$\cos\theta = -0.6.$

The cosine of θ is negative, so θ is a second- or third-quadrant angle.

The related first-quadrant angle is

$\theta = \cos^{-1}(0.6) = 53°$ (to the nearest degree).

The solutions are

$\theta = 180° - 53° = 127°$ (to the nearest degree),

$\theta = 180° + 53° = 233°$ (to the nearest degree).

(Check: A calculator gives

$\cos 127° = -0.6018\ldots \approx -0.6,$

$\cos 233° = -0.6018\ldots \approx -0.6.$)

Activity 13

(a) The gradient of the line $y = mx + c$ is m.

So the gradient of the line $y = x + 3$ is 1, and the gradient of the line $y = x\sqrt{3} + 2$ is $\sqrt{3}$.

(b) Hence

$\tan\alpha = 1 \quad \text{and} \quad \tan\beta = \sqrt{3}.$

So, since α and β are acute angles,

$\alpha = \tan^{-1}(1) = 45°$

and

$\beta = \tan^{-1}(\sqrt{3}) = 60°.$

(c)

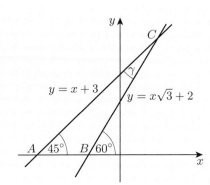

The angles on a straight line add up to $180°$. So in the diagram,

$\angle ABC = 180° - 60° = 120°.$

The angles in $\triangle ABC$ add up to $180°$. So

$\gamma = 180° - 120° - 45° = 15°.$

That is, the acute angle between the two lines is $15°$.

Activity 14

(a) A sketch of the line is shown below.

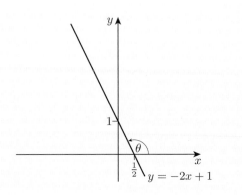

(b) The gradient of the line is -2, so

$$\tan \theta = -2.$$

The related acute (first-quadrant) angle is $\tan^{-1}(2) = 63°$ (to the nearest degree).

The angle θ is an obtuse (second-quadrant) angle, so $\theta = 180° - 63° = 117°$ (to the nearest degree).

That is, the angle of inclination is about $117°$.

Activity 15

(a) The equation is

$$\cos \theta = \frac{\sqrt{3}}{2}.$$

The cosine of θ is positive, so θ is a first- or fourth-quadrant angle.

One solution is

$$\theta = \cos^{-1}\left(\frac{\sqrt{3}}{2}\right) = \frac{\pi}{6}.$$

The other solution is

$$\theta = 2\pi - \frac{\pi}{6} = \frac{11\pi}{6}.$$

(b) The equation is

$$\tan \theta = -\sqrt{3}.$$

The tangent of θ is negative, so θ is a second- or fourth-quadrant angle.

The related first-quadrant angle is

$$\tan^{-1}(\sqrt{3}) = \frac{\pi}{3}.$$

The solutions are

$$\theta = \pi - \frac{\pi}{3} = \frac{2\pi}{3},$$

$$\theta = 2\pi - \frac{\pi}{3} = \frac{5\pi}{3}.$$

(c) The equation is

$$\cos \theta = 0.4.$$

The cosine of θ is positive, so θ is a first- or fourth-quadrant angle.

One solution is

$$\theta = \cos^{-1}(0.4) = 1.1592\ldots = 1.16 \text{ (to 3 s.f.).}$$

The other solution is

$$\theta = 2\pi - 1.1592\ldots = 5.1239\ldots = 5.12 \text{ (to 3 s.f.).}$$

(You can check these solutions on your calculator.)

Activity 16

(a) The equation is

$$\cos \theta = 0.7.$$

A suitable sketch graph is as follows.

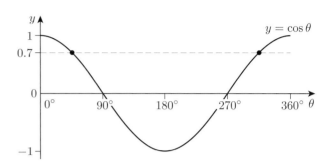

One solution is

$$\theta = \cos^{-1}(0.7) = 46° \text{ (to the nearest degree).}$$

The other solution is as far below $360°$ as the first solution is above $0°$, so it is

$$\theta = 360° - 46° = 314° \text{ (to the nearest degree).}$$

(b) The equation is

$$\tan \theta = 1.$$

A suitable sketch graph is as follows.

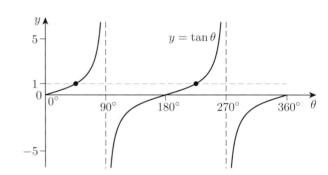

One solution is

$$\theta = \tan^{-1}(1) = 45°.$$

The other solution is as far above $180°$ as the first solution is above $0°$, so it is

$$\theta = 180° + 45° = 225°.$$

(You can check these solutions on your calculator.)

Activity 17

(a) An expression for the total number of animals is $c + r$. Also, chickens have 2 feet and rabbits have 4 feet, so an expression for the total number of feet is $2c + 4r$.

So c and r satisfy the simultaneous equations

$$c + r = 50,$$

$$2c + 4r = 122.$$

Rearranging the first equation gives $r = 50 - c$, and substituting this into the second equation gives

$$2c + 4(50 - c) = 122$$
$$2c + 200 - 4c = 122$$
$$200 - 2c = 122$$
$$2c = 78.$$

Hence $c = 39$ and $r = 50 - 39 = 11$.

So there are 39 chickens and 11 rabbits.

(You might have solved the simultaneous equations by elimination rather than substitution.)

(b) The original solution to the problem as quoted in *Sacred mathematics* is as follows.

> If rabbits were chickens then the total number of feet would be 100, so we know the extra 22 feet are all from rabbits, which implies 11 rabbits and 39 chickens.

Activity 18

(a) There is no single answer because cats and dogs both have four feet, so equations involving numbers of feet do not distinguish between them. You might like to consider what happens if you write down the simultaneous equations for this problem. (Hint: See Unit 7, Activity 25.)

(b)–(d) No specific comments are provided for these question parts: be creative and remember that you can compare your answers with the numbers of animals that you started with.

Activity 19

(a) The area of the large square is $(a + b)^2$.

(b) The area of triangle WEH is $\frac{1}{2}ab$.

(c) The triangles XFE, YGF and ZHG also each have an area of $\frac{1}{2}ab$. So the total area of the four triangles is $2ab$. The area of the small square can be found by subtracting the areas of the triangles from the area of the large square. So the area of the small square is

$$(a + b)^2 - 2ab = a^2 + 2ab + b^2 - 2ab = a^2 + b^2.$$

(d) The area of the small square is also c^2. So

$$a^2 + b^2 = c^2.$$

Activity 20

(a) For example, consider $\frac{1}{3}$ and $\frac{2}{3}$. Squaring the larger and adding the smaller gives

$$\left(\tfrac{2}{3}\right)^2 + \tfrac{1}{3} = \tfrac{4}{9} + \tfrac{1}{3} = \tfrac{7}{9}.$$

Squaring the smaller and adding the larger gives

$$\left(\tfrac{1}{3}\right)^2 + \tfrac{2}{3} = \tfrac{1}{9} + \tfrac{2}{3} = \tfrac{7}{9}.$$

So the two answers are the same. This applies to whichever numbers you try (even if one is positive

and one is negative – for example, 3 and -2).

So the conjecture is that the two sums are always the same.

(b) Since the numbers add up to 1, the smaller number is $1 - x$. So the first sum is

$$x^2 + (1 - x) = x^2 - x + 1$$

and the second sum is

$$(1 - x)^2 + x = x^2 - 2x + 1 + x = x^2 - x + 1.$$

The two sums are equal, so this proves the conjecture.

Activity 21

(a) AB is the side of the square, so it is 2 units long; BC is half of the side of the square, so it is 1 unit long. Since $\triangle ABC$ is right-angled, the cosine ratio can be used. This gives

$$\cos \angle ABC = \frac{\text{adj}}{\text{hyp}} = \frac{1}{2}.$$

So

$$\angle ABC = \cos^{-1}\left(\tfrac{1}{2}\right) = 60°.$$

Alternatively, $\triangle ABC$ is one half of an equilateral triangle, so $\angle ABC = 60°$.

(b) Since the paper has been folded over, α is half of $\angle ABC$. From part (a), $\angle ABC = 60°$, so

$$\alpha = 30°.$$

Also, as mentioned in the question, there are two layers of paper between the edges DB and EB, and an angle of a square is $90°$, so

$$2(\alpha + \beta) = 90°.$$

Hence

$$\alpha + \beta = 45°,$$

and therefore

$$\beta = 45° - 30° = 15°.$$

The triangle that contains α and γ is right-angled. So

$$\gamma = 90° - 30° = 60°.$$

Similarly, the triangle that contains β and δ is right-angled. So

$$\delta = 90° - 15° = 75°.$$

(c) The diagram at the top of the next page shows the folded square after step 3. An angle has been marked as θ. You can see that, if you were to unfold the paper again, then the three angles at E would be angles on a straight line. So

$$\theta = 180° - 2 \times 60° = 60°.$$

Hence, when the top right corner of the square is folded down in step 4, the angle θ lies exactly on top of the angle marked as $60°$, and so the folded-down corner lies exactly on the edge of the paper shape.

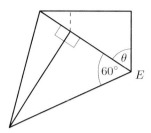

(d) The three angles of the final triangle are $\alpha + \beta$, γ and δ, as shown below.

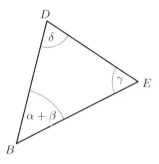

The sizes of these angles are as follows:

$$\alpha + \beta = 15° + 30° = 45°,$$
$$\gamma = 60°,$$
$$\delta = 75°.$$

(Check: $45° + 60° + 75° = 180°$.)

Activity 22

(a) The angles in an equilateral triangle are all $60°$.

(b) One way to fold the square into an equilateral triangle is as follows. First fold the top left corner to the centre line, as in step 2 of Activity 21. Then fold the top right corner to the centre line, as shown in the diagram below. Each side of $\triangle ABC$ was originally a side of the square, so this triangle is equilateral. If the paper is now folded back along a horizontal line through B, and finally folded along the lines AB and BC, then the square is folded into an equilateral triangle.

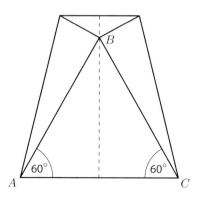

(There are other solutions.)

Activity 23

(a) In the diagram, $h = OG + ON$. The distance OG is 32 metres, as before, and the distance ON can be found by using the right-angled triangle OPN, as before. This gives

$$\cos\phi = \frac{\text{adj}}{\text{hyp}} = \frac{ON}{30},$$

so

$$ON = 30\cos\phi.$$

Hence

$$h = OG + ON = 32 + 30\cos\phi.$$

(b) Since $\theta = \pi - \phi$, it follows from the related angles diagram that the two angles θ and ϕ have the same cosine values, except possibly for the signs. Since ϕ and θ are first- and second-quadrant angles, respectively, it follows from the CAST diagram that their cosines are positive and negative, respectively. Hence $\cos\theta = -\cos\phi$.

(c) The equation $\cos\theta = -\cos\phi$ is equivalent to $\cos\phi = -\cos\theta$. Using this equation to substitute in the equation found in part (a) gives

$$h = 32 + 30(-\cos\theta) = 32 - 30\cos\theta.$$

This is the formula that was found for acute angles θ.

Activity 24

(a) The correct values for the constants in the first equation are $a = -30$, $b = 0.314$, $c = 0$ and $d = 32$, since these values give the graph of the equation $y = -30\cos(0.314(x - 0)) + 32$, which is equivalent to $y = 32 - 30\cos(0.314x)$. The correct values for the constants in the second equation are $m = 0$ and $c = 20$.

Suitable values for the minimum and maximum values on the y-axis are 0 and 65, respectively (since the height in metres of a gondola is always between these numbers).

The graph obtained is shown below.

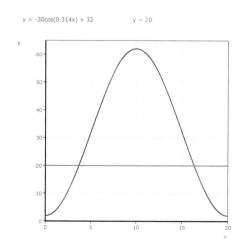

(b) The line and the curve cross when $x = 4$ and $x = 16$ (both to the nearest whole number). So the best views become visible approximately 4 minutes after the gondola was at its lowest point, and cease to be visible approximately 16 minutes after the gondola was at its lowest point.

Activity 25

(a) Changing the value of a stretches or compresses the graph in the y-direction. The maximum value reached by y is the magnitude of a (for example, if $a = 2$, then the maximum value is 2, and if $a = -2$, then the maximum value is also 2). The minimum value reached by y is the negative of the magnitude of a.

If you change the value of a to its negative, then the graph is reflected in the x-axis. So in the oscillation that starts when $x = 0$, the value of y first decreases to the minimum value and then increases to the maximum value, instead of the other way round.

(b) You should have found that if b is a positive integer, then the number of complete oscillations in the interval from 0 to 2π is b. This result also holds if b is fractional: for example, if $b = 2.5$, then there are two and a half oscillations in the interval from 0 to 2π.

If b is negative, then the number of oscillations in the interval from 0 to 2π is the magnitude of b.

If you change the value of b to its negative, then the graph is reflected in the y-axis. So, as in part (a), in the oscillation that starts when $x = 0$, the value of y first decreases to the minimum value and then increases to the maximum value, instead of the other way round.

(c) If you start with $c = 0$ and change the value of c, then the graph moves along the x-axis by c units. For example, if $c = 2$, then the graph is the same shape as the graph of $y = \sin x$, but moved a distance of 2 to the right. Similarly, if $c = -2$, then the graph is the same shape as the graph of $y = \sin x$, but moved a distance of 2 to the left.

So, in general, the graph of of $y = \sin(x - c)$ seems to be the same shape as the graph of $y = \sin x$, but moved to the right by distance c (the move is to the left if c is negative).

(d) As d changes, the graph moves up or down the y-axis. For example, if $d = 1$, then the graph is the same shape as the graph of $y = \sin x$, but moved 1 unit up the y-axis.

(e) The graph of the general cosine function changes in the same way as the graph of the general sine function when the values of the constants a, b, c and d are changed. This is not surprising, since the sine and cosine functions have the same basic shape. In fact, you can obtain the graph of $y = \cos x$ by shifting the graph of $y = \sin x$ by $\dfrac{\pi}{2}$ radians to the left, that is, by drawing the graph of $y = \sin\left(x + \dfrac{\pi}{2}\right)$.

Activity 26

Each of the equations is of the form
$$y = a\sin(b(x - c)) + d$$
or
$$y = a\cos(b(x - c)) + d.$$

(a) Here $b = 4$, so the period is $2\pi/4 = \pi/2$.

(b) Here $b = 5$, so the period is $2\pi/5$.

(c) Here $b = \frac{1}{2}$, so the period is $2\pi/0.5 = 4\pi$.

(d) Here $b = -1$, so the period is $2\pi/1 = 2\pi$.

(You might like to check these answers by plotting the graphs on Graphplotter.)

Activity 27

(a) The equation is $y = \sin 3x$. Here $a = 1$, $b = 3$, $c = 0$ and $d = 0$. So

  amplitude $= 1$,
  period $= 2\pi/3 \approx 2.09$,
  horizontal displacement $= 0$,
  vertical displacement $= 0$,
  minimum value $= -1$,
  maximum value $= 1$.

There are three complete oscillations in an interval of 2π. The graph is shown below.

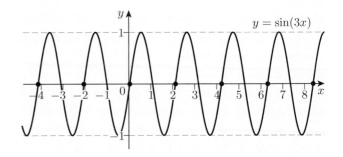

(b) The equation is $y = \sin(x + 2)$. Here $a = 1$, $b = 1$, $c = -2$ and $d = 0$. So

amplitude $= 1$,
period $= 2\pi/1 = 2\pi \approx 6.28$,
horizontal displacement $= -2$,
vertical displacement $= 0$,
minimum value $= -1$,
maximum value $= 1$.

The graph is obtained by shifting the graph of $y = \sin x$ by 2 to the left, as shown below.

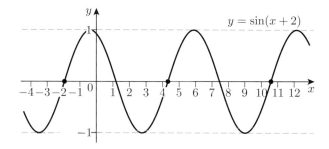

(c) The equation is $y = 2\sin(x - 1.5) - 1$. Here $a = 2$, $b = 1$, $c = 1.5$ and $d = -1$. So

amplitude $= 2$,
period $= 2\pi/1 = 2\pi \approx 6.28$,
horizontal displacement $= 1.5$,
vertical displacement $= -1$,
minimum value $= -1 - 2 = -3$,
maximum value $= -1 + 2 = 1$.

The graph is shown below.

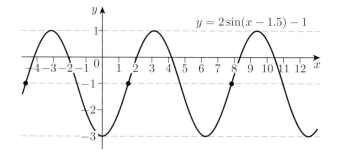

Activity 28

(a) The y-coordinate corresponding to the x-coordinate 4.35 is 6.2, and this agrees with the height of the high tide, which is 6.2 metres.

(b) If you add the line $y = 4$ to the graph (by using 'Two graphs'), then you can read off the x-coordinates of the crossing points, as illustrated below.

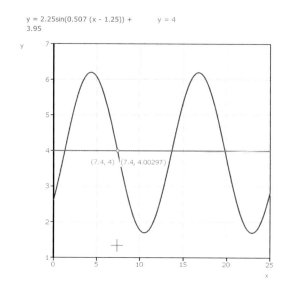

According to the model, the tide is 4 metres or higher between approximately 1.3 hours and 7.4 hours, and again between 13.7 hours and 19.8 hours.

(In practice, answers in hours and minutes may be needed. To obtain such answers, you should first find them in hours to more decimal places than given above, and then convert them to hours and minutes.)

Acknowledgements

Grateful acknowledgement is made to the following sources for permission to reproduce material in this book.

Unit 11

Figure 2: publisher unknown; Figure 6: © James Naughton; Text extract on page 17: © www.bbc.co.uk; Text extract on page 27: Trinity Mirror plc; Figure 20: Photograph of James Randi from www.wikipedia.org.

Unit 12

Figure 9: © Google Inc.; Figure 10: © Marco Ghitti, Flickr Photo Sharing; Figure 12: © Leo Reynolds, Flickr Photo Sharing; Figure 14: © David Corby, http://en.wikipedia.org/wiki/Hang_gliding; Figure 15: © Boris Panasyuk, Dreamstime; Cartoon on page 79: © ScienceCartoonsPlus.com; Figure 54: © Chrissy Pesch, Flickr Photo Sharing; Figure 56: © Visulogik, www.flickr.com/photos/55671677/@N00/111419737.

Unit 13

Figure 11: © Lee Turner, Flickr Photo Sharing; Figure 13: © Lisa McDonald; Figure 14: © Martin Fox, martinfox@elvis2k.co.uk; Figure 16: © Brendon Johnson; Figure 17: © Cathy Britcliffe, iStockphoto; Figure 18: © Tolga Musato, Flickr Photo Sharing; Cartoon on page 140: Reproduced with permission from 'The Physics Teacher' (1976), American Association of Physics Teachers; Figure 24: St. Andrews University; Figure 26: © Google Inc.; Figure 25: © Bettmann/Corbis; Figure 29: © James Benet, iStockphoto.

Unit 14

Figure 1: Image courtesy of Tony Rothman; Figure 2: © Ed Bock, iStockphoto; Table 1: © ITU 2009 all rights reserved; Figure 21: Image courtesy of Tony Rothman; Figure 25: Adapted from http://home.comcast.net/~tessellations/ (marjorice@sbcglobal.net); Figure 26: © http://commons.wikimedia.org/wiki/File:Truncated_octahedra_b.png. This file is licensed under the Creative Commons Attribution ShareAlike 2.0, http://creativecommons.org/licenses/by/2.0/deed.en; Figure 27: © Charlie Fong, www.wikipedia.org. This file is licensed under the Creative Commons Attribution ShareAlike 2.0, http://creativecommons.org/licenses/by/2.0/deed.en; Figure 28: © Domokos, www.wikipedia.org. This file is licensed under the Creative Commons Attribution ShareAlike 2.0, http://creativecommons.org/licenses/by/2.0/deed.en; Figure 31: Courtesy The Institute for Figuring, www.theiff.org; Figure 32(a): © Jens Petersen, Wikimedia. This file is licenced under the Creative Commons Attribution ShareAlike 2.0, http://creativecommons.org/licenses/by/2.0/deed.en; Figure 32(b): Courtesy The Institute for Figuring, www.theiff.org; Figure 33: © Genista, Flickr.com. This file is licensed under the Creative Commons Attribution ShareAlike 2.0, http://creativecommons.org/licenses/by/2.0/deed.en; Figure 35: © Tim Ellis, Flickr Photo Sharing. This file is licensed under the Creative Commons Attribution ShareAlike 2.0, http://creativecommons.org/licenses/by/2.0/deed.en; Figure 42: Rudi Tapper, iStockphoto; Figures 45, 46 and 47: © www.bbc.co.uk.

INDEX